The Visitor's Guide
to
EAST ANGLIA

INDEX TO 1:50 000 MAPS OF GREAT BRITAIN

Reproduced from the Ordnance Survey map with the permission of the Controller of Her Majesty's Stationery Office, Crown copyright reserved.

Shading indicates maps used in this guide.

THE VISITOR'S GUIDE TO
EAST ANGLIA

CLIVE TULLY

MPC

HUNTER
PUBLISHING INC

Published by:
Moorland Publishing Co Ltd,
Moor Farm Road West,
Ashbourne,
Derbyshire DE6 1HD
England

1st edition 1984
Revised & enlarged 2nd edition
1990

British Library Cataloguing in
Publication Data:
Tully, Clive
    The visitor's guide to East
    Anglia.
    1. East Anglia - Visitor's guides
    I. Title
    914.26'04858

ISBN 0 86190 356 0 (paperback)
ISBN 0 86190 355 2 (hardback)

Published in the USA by:
Hunter Publishing Inc,
300 Raritan Center Parkway,
CN 94, Edison, NJ 08818
ISBN 1 55650 237 0 (USA)

Colour and black & white
origination by:
Scantrans, Singapore

Printed in the UK by:
Richard Clay Ltd, Bungay, Suffolk

Cover photograph: *Cavendish,
Suffolk* (Clive Tully).

Illustrations have been supplied as
follows: East Anglia Tourist Board
Collection: pp 70, 154; S. J. Earl:
p66; The National Trust: p 123;
F. Moore: p86 (top); MPC Picture
Collection: pp 35 (top), 38 (bottom),
39 (both), 42, 43 (both), 54 (both),
90 (both), 91, 94, 95 (bottom), 99,
106, 107, 110, 111, 115, 126, 142
(both), 143 (both), 163, 167, 170
(both), 175 (both); J. P. Walker: p 95
(top).

All other illustrations are from the
author.

About the Author
Clive Tully was born in London,
spent his early years in Essex, and
after two years in Switzerland,
came to Norfolk, where he has
lived ever since. He is a freelance
journalist, contributing outdoor
leisure and travel features to
national newspapers and maga-
zines, and a leading authority on
equipment and clothing for
walking and lightweight camping.
He can also be heard on 'Sound
Advice' audio travel cassettes,
whose first release was, appropri-
ately, 'A taste of East Anglia'.
    A Fellow of the Royal Geo-
graphical Society, Clive is a keen
walker, backpacker, cycle tourer
and traveller, and whilst one or
more of these activities regularly
takes him to far-flung places all
over the world, he still finds time
to enjoy countryside closer to
home.
    Clive Tully lives near Norwich
with his family.

CONTENTS

Key to Symbols Used in Text Margin and on Maps

 Recommended walk

 Parkland

 Archaeological site

 Nature reserve/Animal interest

 Birdlife

 Garden

 Golf facilities

 Church/Ecclesiastical site

 Building of interest

 Castle/Fortification

 Museum/Art gallery

 Beautiful view/Scenery, Natural phenomenon

 Other place of interest

 Windmill

 Interesting railway

Key to Maps

▬▬▬	Main road	●	Town/Village
═══	Motorway	◯	Lake/Reservoir
══	Dual Carriageway	⊥⊥⊥⊥⊥	Canals
〜	River	— · —	County Boundary
▮	Town/City	- - - - -	Peddars Way
		— · — · —	Norfolk Coast Path

ACKNOWLEDGEMENTS

A s with many such books, *The Visitor's Guide to East Anglia* is the result of the bringing together and distillation of a tremendous amount of information from diverse sources, too numerous to mention here. Suffice it to say that I am indebted to the East Anglia Tourist Board for their help, which extended to the use of a desk at Toppesfield Hall on a couple of occasions to enable me to sift through their files! I should also like to thank Epson (UK) Ltd for their very practical support in the form of a battery operated PX16 portable computer, which continues to enable an exceptionally busy writer to keep working even whilst travelling about on all forms of public transport.

Clive Tully, FRGS

1

EAST ANGLIA
AN INTRODUCTION

The charm of East Anglia lies largely in the fact that, over the centuries, it has kept itself at a distance from the rest of Britain, without becoming totally isolated. The only notable change produced by the Industrial Revolution was the coming of the railway. So, while the character of many other parts of Britain changed radically during the nineteenth century, East Anglia has preserved much of its landscape, architecture and tradition.

Certainly its people have always been formidable. Queen Boudica (Boadicea) and her Iceni kept the Roman invaders at bay for some time before being defeated, and Hereward the Wake held out against the Norman invasion from his base in the Fens for five years! Five hundred years later, it took a professional army of twelve thousand to put down the rebellion of Robert Kett and his followers.

The East Anglians have had their share of oppression. The Danish raids up to the time of the Conquest were particularly savage and brutal. King Edmund tried to make peace with the Danes by giving himself up, in the hope that the slaughter would cease. Instead, the Danes tortured and murdered him. A close look at a map will reveal many place names with Danish influences, such as 'toft', 'thorpe' and 'thwaite'. It was King Alfred of Wessex who allowed the Danes to settle in East Anglia.

Of all the famous East Anglians throughout the ages, the most notable has to be the son of a Norfolk rector who became a sailor, despite the fact that he suffered from sea sickness, and England's greatest hero — Horatio Nelson. Born in North Norfolk in 1758, he

8

was educated in North Walsham and Norwich, and in 1771 he joined HMS *Raisonable*. Seven years later, he was semi-retired, living on half pay in Burnham Thorpe with his wife, Fanny. He spent the next five years farming thirty acres of glebe land, and visiting his various relatives throughout the county.

He was appointed captain of HMS *Agamemnon* on the outbreak of war in 1793, and a large proportion of his crew were Norfolk men. The next twelve years saw Nelson making his mark as England's greatest sailor, inflicting crushing defeats on Napoleon at the Battle of the Nile, the Battle of Copenhagen, and, despite losing his life, at the Battle of Trafalgar in 1805.

The region's name is derived from the land of the East Angles. Similarly, Norfolk and Suffolk originated from 'North Folk' and 'South Folk', while Essex comes from 'East Saxons'. Today East Anglia is generally regarded as encompassing the four counties of Norfolk, Suffolk, Cambridgeshire — which since the boundary changes of 1974 includes Huntingdonshire and the Soke of Peterborough — and Essex.

Many parts of East Anglia abound in natural beauty, and local authorities administer their respective regions, on the whole with sympathy for the area, but not forgetting the economic considerations of industry. The Norfolk Broads have recently been awarded the long awaited and much deserved status of National Park, and with increased funding from the Government this unique area of national and international importance should begin its recovery from poor water quality and insensitive development which have threatened it for so long. The Broads Authority, which administers the Broads, rivers and immediate surrounding areas, successfully balances the conflicting interests in Broadland.

Since the last war, massive changes have taken place in the countryside of East Anglia. That which isn't already under bricks and mortar is now cultivated, either for agriculture or forestry. Most of the old 'unimproved' grasslands, heaths and marshes have fallen to the plough, and hundreds of miles of hedgerow have been ripped out to enlarge fields for modern arable farming. Lamentable though the situation is, it is especially important that there still exist some havens for wildlife in the form of nature reserves.

Nature conservation has a special home in East Anglia. It was in Norfolk that the first of the County Naturalists Trusts was formed, with the purchase of Cley marshes in 1926. The reserves in East

Anglia offer some of the most varied wildlife habitats in Britain, and the richness of the flora and fauna is beyond compare. The wetland regions of the Broads and the Fens are host to several internationally important wildlife reserves, and the coastal regions have some fine salt-marshes and mud-flats. The heaths of Breckland, and the Suffolk coastal heaths also have wildlife havens, most of which are easily accessible.

Areas of Outstanding Natural Beauty are designated by the Countryside Commission, and are areas of land recognised to be sufficiently important in terms of landscape heritage to warrant a degree of protection and careful enhancement. There are three such areas in East Anglia: the North Norfolk Coast, the Suffolk Heritage Coast and Dedham Vale, and these are included in the chapters on North Norfolk, the Suffolk Coast, and Constable Country. Nevertheless, it must be said that wildlife habitats continue to disappear at the hands of farming and other land uses. The stone curlew, a bird found mainly in the chalky areas of East Anglia and in southern England, has suffered such a drastic decline in the last few years that its future as a breeding bird in this country now hangs in the balance.

The coastal regions in particular have much to offer. In the past the shifting sand and shingle, and the saltmarshes, made agriculture impractical. Today we have the technology to reclaim those areas, and indeed with forecasts of rising sea levels resulting from the continuing 'greenhouse effect', further sea defence work will need to be done if the shape of East Anglia's coastline is not to be drastically altered. If it is not, the consequences will be nothing new. Coastal towns have been claimed by the sea in the past, and even today it continues to nibble away at places like Overstrand on the North Norfolk coast.

As it is, the balance often seems fragile. It only takes a combination of spring and high tides with high winds, and the resultant surges can be devastating. The most destructive in recent times was in January 1953, when over 300sq miles of East Anglia was inundated by the sea, and a similar number of people lost their lives.

The East Anglian link with the Dutch lies not only in the similarity of landscapes. In medieval times, the backbone of industry in the area was the wool and cloth-weaving trade. Many Dutch and Flemish weavers settled here when sheep farming was at its height, and created a wool industry which became world famous. As a result, many buildings in East Anglia have a pronounced Dutch influence.

But mechanisation had its effects then as now. The weaving trade started to decline as long ago as the sixteenth century. When the first power looms were invented — devices relying on fast-running water to provide the power — the textile industry moved north to the Pennines, and when coal became the fuel for industry in the nineteenth century, the textile factories were already well placed to utilise it.

In the seventeenth century, more Dutch settlers had arrived to master-mind the incredible feat of engineering which led to the draining of the Fens. The Dutch, of course, are renowned masters of land reclamation — the greater part of their own country lies below sea level!

Of all the things which might be described as characteristic of East Anglia, the windmill has to be at the top of the list. Wind power, readily available on open land, has been used both for corn milling, and drainage in the low-lying parts of Fenland and Broadland. Windmills were actually an Arab invention, the idea brought over in the twelfth century by returning Crusaders. None, however, have survived from that period. The earliest still in existence is Bourn Mill, in Cambridgeshire, which dates from 1636. With help from the Broads Authority, The Norfolk Windmills Trust has embarked on a programme of restoration of many of the Broadland windpumps.

Churches in East Anglia give a fascinating insight into the past, and the people who built them. Visitors to the tiny village in Norfolk which gave its name to worsted cloth may wonder where the connection is until they see the size of the church. Many villages and towns in East Anglia celebrated their prosperity from wool in this way (building and decorating their churches undoubtedly eased their consciences), and a visit to such places can be most interesting.

Whilst looking at churches, it will also become apparent that the area is somewhat limited in its choice of building materials. The chalk band which runs across the south of England from the Berkshire Downs to north-west Norfolk is rich in flint. The early settlers were quick to find it, although their use was confined more to making tools and weapons. One of their mines can still be seen at Grimes Graves, near Weeting in Norfolk. The vast majority of churches too were built of flint, the poorer parishes making their towers round in order not to use so much! The first buildings to use flint merely had the stones embedded in mortar. Later the flints were split, so that a wall with a (relatively) flat face could be made and the different shades of colour could be used to produce patterns. The practice of knapping flints still continues in Brandon, as it has done for centuries.

The very rich, of course, imported their materials from afar, with stone brought down from the north, or, in the case of Norwich Cathedral, shipped from France. For this reason, most of the large buildings were erected on or near rivers with access to the sea. In parts of west Norfolk, there are also buildings made from a dark brown stone called carr-stone, but its use is not very widespread. In Suffolk in particular, there are many towns and villages with Tudor wood-framed buildings, the more elaborate having carved woodwork, and pargetting (moulded plasterwork) for the infill.

Look at any of the small groups of old cottages in an East Anglian village, and the chances are you'll find a pond nearby. It would have been made as a result of villagers excavating material to make the clay lump walls for their timber-framed cottages. And there are many fine examples of thatched roofs, demonstrating a craft which has survived the centuries. Norfolk reed is undeniably the best thatching material available, outlasting a wheat straw roof by a good thirty years. Harvested in the Broadland fens, it is still sent far and wide, to re-thatch buildings all over the country.

Mention will often be made of the fact that towns and villages were once ports for sea or river trade. Coastal erosion and longshore drift have closed all but the very best placed sea and estuary ports. Of the smaller ports, whose existence depended on river trade, the vast majority fell into disuse as the draughts of boats became larger, and the introduction of railways in the last century was the final nail in their coffin.

There are many interesting examples of remains from the past. Colcheste : is England's oldest recorded town, and although parts are in urgent need of restoration, many of the old walls and buildings are intact. There is a wealth of Norman architecture, mainly in churches, but also in a few castles and other buildings, not generally so well preserved. Norwich Cathedral is a fine example, as is the castle, although both have had additions over the ages.

Norfolk and Cambridgeshire have three cathedral cities between them: Norwich, Ely and Peterborough. These cities, along with the old towns of Cambridge, Bury St Edmunds, Colchester, Ipswich and King's Lynn, have seen expansion and change over the years. Fortunately, the worthwhile parts have all been preserved, and in some cases enhanced by careful management.

Undoubtedly the easiest way to see East Anglia is by car, if you are not to miss those areas not so well served by public transport. Travel to the region by car from other parts of the country can be frustrating, simply because the main roads are overloaded with heavy goods vehicles travelling to and from the East Coast ports. There are plans to 'improve' these roads over the next ten years, widening the main routes into dual carriageways. It will undoubtedly bring benefits to commerce, but one cannot help but wonder about the cost to the East Anglian character — the ersatz culture of the motorway, and the consequential spread of blandly uniform urban sprawl which always follows major road improvements has done nothing worthwhile for other areas of the country similarly transformed.

But a holiday here without a car need not be confined to a small area. Both British Rail and the Eastern Counties Omnibus Company operate schemes which offer unlimited travel in their particular regions, either for single days, or for a week, thus opening up the major towns at a very moderate cost. A cycling holiday in East Anglia need not be energetic. With flat, or at the very most, gently rolling countryside, it is ideal for a slow rambling tour, and the more isolated attractions of the region may be reached. Cycles, of course, may be taken in the guard's vans of many trains, a very useful way of extending the holiday.

To walkers, there is much to offer in East Anglia. There may not be any lofty peaks or desolate moors, but one can escape the crowds, and see some beautiful countryside. Thetford Forest has a multitude of forest tracks, while those who prefer the 'big skies' which have been the inspiration to so many painters have miles of marshes and heaths on the North Norfolk Coast and the Suffolk Heritage Coast, offering truly exceptional walking. Whichever way you choose, East Anglia must be explored gently — it is too good to be rushed!

Where walks have been suggested, particularly those not in towns or cities, the routes will become immediately apparent if you use the descriptions in conjunction with the appropriate Ordnance Survey 1:50,000 Landranger map. A compass is rarely necessary in East Anglia, although more dedicated walkers using the less well-trodden paths may find one useful for plotting the direction across a field where the farmer has neglected to restore the footpath after sowing his crop.

An explanation may be necessary of how such a large area has been described. The main body of this book looks at East Anglia in sections, some of which are reasonably topographical: The Broads, Breckland and the Fens. Others are perhaps a little more loosely based, taking an area of particular interest such as the North Norfolk Coast, or the Suffolk Heritage Coast, and extending it somewhat. Constable Country, a much used title, has the River Stour as a rough centre line, and is extended on either side without any geographical demarcation; the decision to include some towns in Constable Country instead of, say, Inland Suffolk, is purely arbitrary. Each chapter takes either a round trip, or progresses in one direction, as befits the shape and character of the land. The chapter on the Broads is different in that each of the five navigable rivers is followed, for the benefit of those who wish to cruise on the Broads, presently the best

Bales of straw after the corn harvest, a common sight in East Anglia

way of touring this charming but ecologically fragile area. While the Fenland rivers also offer some peaceful cruising, they are not so popular as the Broads, and Fenland is described in a more conventional manner.

Less detail is given around the edges of the area, particularly the southern reaches of Essex. There are other guides which deal with the outskirts of London, and although addresses are included of attractions as far south as Southend and Waltham Abbey in the Useful Information section there is no place for them in the guide. These extremities are not strictly East Anglia, and certainly anything now encompassed by the M25 orbital motorway has to be regarded as Greater London!

Finally, with an area so vast, it is inevitable that some will find fault with the formula, thinking that too much detail is given to some aspects and not enough to others. To enjoy the beauty of the countryside the visitor needs not a guide, but only a sensitive and understanding nature. Towns and cities however, are definitely appreciated all the more for some advice and guidance, especially by those who do not have much time to spare. Those who ask questions beginning with 'what? where? how? why?' or 'when?', have chosen the book to help them to appreciate East Anglia, and to enjoy their visit to the full.

2
NORWICH AND BEYOND

Every major road leading into the city has a sign saying: 'Welcome to Norwich — a fine city', and this greeting is absolutely right! This beautiful and ancient city has not been stifled by heavy industry, modern development having been controlled in sensitive areas to help preserve its unique character.

We know that the Romans had a settlement at nearby Caistor St Edmund, known as *Venta Icenorum*, as long ago as AD70. The city itself has existed for the best part of 1,000 years, situated amidst fertile agricultural land with the River Yare providing excellent communication with the sea.

In many places the old walls of the city can still be seen. A loop in the River Wensum formed a natural defence in which the city first developed, and a flint wall completed the barrier which guaranteed its security. Evidence of earlier building is not merely apparent, it positively shouts at the visitor! The Normans built the castle and the cathedral; both are still in good repair and are significant landmarks, despite attempts to obliterate the skyline with office blocks. Norwich used to be known as the city of public houses and churches, with 'a public house for every day of the year, and a church for every Sunday'. There was one or the other on virtually every street corner. 'Progress' has seen the demise of many of the smaller parish churches, and similarly many of the old public houses have been swallowed up by new developments. From well over three hundred pubs in Norwich in Victorian times, there are now just over sixty. The authorities try to ensure that churches which are closed through lack of support are taken over and converted to other uses sympathetic with the architectural heritage of the buildings. One of the more

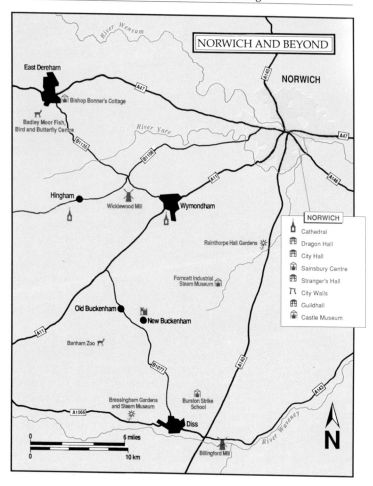

ambitious projects was the conversion of St James' Church in Barrack Street into the home of the Norwich Puppet Theatre.

The Old Cattle Market, in recent years a car park, is to be redeveloped in an imaginative scheme which will produce a covered shopping mall with underground car parking and a central landscaped park. Because of its position in the area of the castle's south bailey, it will become the site of the largest and most important urban archaeological excavation in Northern Europe before building commences. It is hoped that the excavations will not only reveal Norman remains, but parts of the earlier Anglo-Saxon town which stood on the same site.

The only way to fully appreciate Norwich is to walk around. While the most interesting places in the city centre are not scattered far and wide, the one-way traffic system can prove trying for the motorist. Like many other cities, Norwich suffers from chronic traffic congestion, so it is much more convenient to leave a car in one of the many car parks; double yellow lines and traffic wardens abound elsewhere!

The catalogue of places worth visiting in Norwich is almost endless, and a visit to the information centre in the old Guildhall is well worthwhile. Only the main places of interest are described here, with others listed in the box and Useful Information section.

The Castle. The present stone keep, with later additions, was not the first structure to be built on this site. Just after the invasion the Normans built a wooden castle on a mound, surrounded by a moat and other earthworks. Later, in the early part of the twelfth century, the wooden fort was replaced by the square stone keep. But if the present clean outline of the keep looks too good to be true, blame the Victorian restorers who refaced the walls with Bath stone in the 1830s. Critics maintain their efforts gave the ancient building a bogus look, although it has undoubtedly kept the building in a much better state of repair, and probably prevented it from collapsing.

For much of its life, until the end of the last century, Norwich Castle served as the county gaol. Its military importance disappeared when the city wall was built at the beginning of the fourteenth century, and even before it never really played any part in the defence of the city. It did fall into the hands of the French for a while during Henry III's reign, along with several other English castles, and was returned to English occupation when King Louis was defeated at Lincoln. Now it is a museum, with archaeological and natural history exhibits and an art gallery notable for its world famous collection of landscape paintings by Crome, Cotman, Ladbroke and Stannard — members of the Norwich School — who took their inspiration from the Dutch School of Cuyp, Ruisdael and Hobbema, and adapted the style to their own surroundings. The rotunda, housing a shop and refreshments area, is also used for the performance of plays and concerts.

A visit to the dungeons gives some idea of the misery of the poor unfortunates incarcerated there, for they house a collection of instruments of torture, along with the death-masks of some of the criminals who were hanged at Norwich Castle. A walk around the battlements is essential. The castle commands a fine view in all directions, looking out over what was once the second most important city in England.

Despite the ravages of the Great Storm of October 1987, in which the tree cover around the castle mound was somewhat thinned, the castle gardens, occupying the old moat around the mound, make a pleasant spot to while away a sunny hour or so. You may be lucky to see something going on at the Whiffler Theatre, a tiny open air theatre paid for by the Eastern Evening News. Whifflers were the men who cleared the way for processions on guild days in Norwich. The office was abolished in 1832, but the name lives on in 'Whiffler's City', a column in the Eastern Evening News.

The Market Place. The view towards the tower of the City Hall from the castle mound includes the brightly coloured patchwork of stalls comprising Norwich market. With a trading history spanning several hundred years, Norwich market today is one of the largest permanent markets in the country. Running along the bottom edge of the market is Gentleman's Walk, a street whose name recalls the days of the eighteenth-century dandies. The Walk is now a pedestrian precinct, and during the summer months is often a favourite place for a variety of street entertainments, from Morris dancing to jazz bands!

St Peter Mancroft. Not far from the market stands one of the largest and most impressive parish churches in England. With a fine peal of bells, St Peter Mancroft is noteworthy as the resting place of Sir Thomas Browne, the physician whose *Urn Burial* and *Religio Medici* are acknowledged prose masterpieces. A statue of Sir Thomas in pensive mood can be found on neighbouring Hay Hill. This paved pedestrian area is generally the scene of lively activities during the summer. Troupes of dancers and musicians, usually visiting Norwich to appear at the Theatre Royal and other venues in the area, quite often give outdoor performances here.

The Guildhall. This fine flint building, to the right of the market as one faces the City Hall, is almost 600 years old. Until 1938 it was the seat of local government, more recently home to the city's magistrates' courts, and now Norwich's Tourist Information Centre.

In 1908 this beautiful building was almost demolished, but was saved by the mayor's casting vote. Built using forced labour at the beginning of the fifteenth century, part of it was used as a prison, and played its part as 'Death Row' to such prisoners as Thomas Bilney, the Tudor heretic, and Robert Kett, the famous rebel. While not all of the inside of the Guildhall is open to visitors, it is interesting to note that the Spanish Admiral's sword, taken by Lord Nelson after the Battle of Cape St Vincent and presented to the city, is kept here.

The City Hall. The present City Hall, at the back of the market, is an impressive building opened by King George VI in 1938. Norwich has a great banking tradition (Barclays Bank was founded by the Gurney family), and the brick and stone City Hall occupies the former site of Norwich's first bank. The family is commemorated in nearby Chapel Field Gardens in an horological curiosity called the Gurney Clock, reputedly the most complex mechanical clock in existence. The bronze doors of the City Hall's main entrance, flanked by lions, depict in bas-relief scenes from the city's history and some of its industries.

London Street, leading off from the bottom of Guildhall Hill, was one of the first streets in the country to be turned into a pedestrian precinct.

The Cathedral. The Cathedral See of East Anglia was not always at Norwich. It was first at Dunwich, on the Suffolk coast, and was moved later both to North Elmham and to Thetford, before finally coming to the protection of Norwich. Bishop Herbert de Losinga started building the cathedral in 1096, using stone brought by boat from Normandy, up the river to Pull's Ferry, and then along a specially dug canal to the site. Despite being virtually finished twenty-five years later when de Losinga died, the cathedral was not actually consecrated until 1278. Since then, this magnificent building has been subjected to fires, riots and extensive damage caused by natural phenomena. During World War II it was a target for Hitler's Baedeker raids. The cathedral has, with careful restoration and maintenance, retained the same dignified grandeur of its earlier days.

The Cathedral Close sets the cathedral apart from the bustle of the city. Once a monastic precinct, it is now an attractive collection of medieval houses, cars being admitted only by permit. The King Edward VI School is in the Close; Horatio Nelson was its most famous pupil. Near the cathedral is a quiet spot with the grave of

Norwich's much-altered Norman castle, now a museum and art gallery

Nurse Edith Cavell, shot by the Germans in 1915 for helping allied prisoners to escape. Her memory is also perpetuated by a statue in Tombland, in front of the Maid's Head Hotel.

Tombland. The two main points of access to the Cathedral Close are the Erpingham and Ethelbert Gates, at either end of Tombland. A cobbled area with mature trees, and surrounded by an attractive mixture of old buildings, Tombland was, in medieval times, the original site of Norwich market. It was this, and the neighbouring monks' influence over it, that led to a riot in 1272. Some of the monastery buildings were destroyed, and the townsfolk were ordered to build the Ethelbert Gate as a penance.

Opposite the Erpingham Gate is a rather drunken looking fifteenth-century timbered building, the house of Augustine Steward, deputy mayor at the time of Kett's rebellion, until recently the Tourist Information Centre for Norwich. To the left of the house is the narrow Tombland Alley, leading into Princes Street, a cobbled street winding towards St Andrew's.

St Andrew's. At the bottom of Princes Street, on the right, stands the former nave of a Dominican friary. Norwich Corporation bought

Norwich's cathedral spire, seen here from the cloisters, is a dominant feature →

the building at the Reformation, and St Andrew's Hall has been used as a public hall ever since. The chancel of the old church was made into a separate, but connected, hall called Blackfriars, and this combination has seen events such as the knighting of Sir Thomas Browne by Charles II, civic receptions for royalty and other dignitaries, trade shows and rock musical concerts.

Elm Hill. Up Princes Street is a small crossroads, the junction with St Andrews being visible further on. Right here is Elm Hill. Sadly, the tree from which the street derives its name is no longer here. Not long ago, the elm at the top of this charming cobbled street contracted Dutch elm disease, and although it has since been replaced with a young and more hardy plane tree, Elm Hill will never be quite the same again.

The street contains a variety of buildings, from Tudor to Georgian, well worth a visit at night. It is beautifully lit, capturing the atmosphere of early Victorian street lamps with its award-winning lighting scheme.

The River Walk. Elm Hill emerges just below Tombland at the other end, opposite the Maid's Head Hotel, reputedly the oldest inn in the country — Queen Elizabeth I is said to have stayed here and it was the starting-off point for the first regular stage-coach service between Norwich and London. A left turn and short walk to Fye Bridge, and then a right turn brings one to the right-hand bank of the Wensum along the quayside. The riverside footpath follows the loop in the Wensum, the spire of the cathedral being always on the right.

Cow Tower was built in 1378 as a boom tower, controlling the flow of river traffic at the point where the city wall ended. It is the oldest surviving brick building in Norwich, and whilst all you may find living inside are a few pigeons, it is reputedly haunted by Old Blunderhazard, a ghostly rider who gallops past on Christmas Eve.

Further along is Bishop's Bridge, the only surviving medieval bridge in Norwich, and alongside it is the Lollards' Pit where heretics were burnt. In 1549, during the rebellion, the bridge's strategic value was evidenced by the bitter fighting which took place when Kett and his men stormed the city from their camp on Mousehold. Down river is Pull's Ferry, a fifteenth-century water-gate built on the spot where the canal for transporting stone for de Losinga's cathedral joined the river. To view Pull's Ferry from the other bank, one must either cross the river at Bishop's Bridge or Foundry Bridge, a short distance further on. Norwich Yacht Station lies on the opposite bank at this point, with the dome of Thorpe Station nearby.

Mousehold Heath. A break can be taken from the walk along the river by strolling up on Mousehold, where 190 acres of rolling, wooded heathland exist on the edge of the city, but still within the confines of the city ring road. Across the river at Bishop's Bridge, follow Bishop Bridge Road up to the roundabout (roughly opposite Cow Tower), and take Gurney Road up the hill. Alternatively, one can drive up, parking about half a mile up Gurney Road next to the restaurant. St James' Hill provides a classic viewpoint of the city, best taken on or below Britannia Road, just opposite Britannia Barracks. The heath itself has a web of paths running through it, allowing some healthy exercise in pleasant surroundings.

BEYOND NORWICH

East Dereham. Birthplace of George Borrow, Dereham has strong links with history through one of its more infamous sons, Bishop Bonner. Bonner, the rector of St Nicholas' Church in the 1530s, lived in a thatched cottage nearby (now a museum with displays of local domestic and agricultural exhibits). Bonner became Bishop of London in 1540, but lost the post after the separation from Rome. Reinstated during the reign of Mary Tudor, he earned the name 'Bloody Bonner' for his part in sending so many Protestants to be burned at the stake. He died in prison during the reign of Elizabeth I, unrepentant, and still loyal to the Church of Rome.

In the churchyard is St Withburga's Well. Withburga, daughter of the Anglo-Saxon King Anna, founded a convent at Dereham; (her sister, Etheldreda, founded one at Ely). When she died, she was buried in the churchyard, and miracles are said to have occurred at her shrine. Just over 300 years later, the Abbot of Ely and his followers removed her remains, and laid them next to those of her likewise-sainted sister in Ely. The spring which erupted from her desecrated grave is now known as St Withburga's Well.

Hingham. A lazy village of many fine Georgian and Queen Anne houses, and a church whose size is quite out of proportion to the village, indicating the local wealth in times past. In the early seventeenth century, many Hingham weavers emigrated to America for the freedom of their consciences, among them one Samuel Lincoln. Hingham, Massachusetts, was founded and one of Samuel's descendants became president, a connection commemorated by a bust of Abraham Lincoln in the church.

Fifteenth-century Pull's Ferry in the grips of winter

Wymondham. In recent years this market town has expanded considerably, with housing estates and light industry. Nevertheless, the town centre retains much of its charm, notably the octagonal wooden market cross, built in 1617. Its abbey cannot fail to attract. Its twin towers, once a landmark for wartime bomber pilots, are a legacy of the division between the monasteries and the common people.

In the thirteenth century, the monks of the Benedictine priory constantly quarrelled with the townsfolk, to such an extent that the Pope was called to arbitrate. He ordered the church to be segregated, the people having the nave, north aisle and north-west tower, the monks the rest. The monks walled off their portion, and, after the people built their own tower at the west end of the church in 1445, they added two other towers, at each end of their choir. With the Dissolution came the destruction of the priory, and while the majority of the monks' end of the church was pulled down, the pretty octagonal tower at the east end (once in the middle) was left. What remains is a pleasant hotch-potch of building: the Norman nave, fifteenth-century towers, and various scattered fragmentary remains of the priory.

Bishop Bonner's thatched cottage with decorative plasterwork, typical of East Anglia

Kett's Rebellion. Since both Wymondham and Norwich have central roles in this important piece of Norfolk history, it is worth examining the exciting but tragic saga. In the sixteenth century the landowners were upsetting the commoners by fencing off common land and putting it to their own use. There were many uprisings all over the country, most of them quelled very quickly, but Kett's rebellion took a full-scale army to suppress it.

In July 1549, a crowd of people tore down some fences which the local squire had erected illegally on common land near Wymondham. Robert Kett, a landowner himself, confronted the mob, and turned a sympathetic ear to their grievances. Kett and his brother William determined to put the matter right, believing that as they were on the side of the law, justice would prevail. He marched on Norwich, his followers gathering in numbers as he went, until by the time he made camp on Mousehold Heath, outside the city, his army numbered twenty thousand. The depth of feeling must have been very great, and Kett's leadership quite extraordinary, since everyone knew that they could be hanged for what they were doing.

Most of Norfolk was under Kett's control when a messenger from the king arrived offering a free pardon if they all surrendered. Kett sent him away with a flea in his ear, an action which caused the Mayor of Norwich to change his attitude to the rebels, and he closed the city to them. Incensed at this, Kett's men stormed the city, and overran it. Nevertheless, there was virtually no looting, and once the fighting was over, there was no further violence. The Marquis of Northampton moved into the city with 1,500 soldiers, but the rebels quickly ousted them, killing Lord Sheffield near the cathedral.

The Earl of Warwick arrived with an army of 12,000 men, including German mercenaries, and after recapturing the city, prepared to attack the rebel encampment on Mousehold. Kett uncharacteristically took some bad advice, and moved his men from the relative safety of Mousehold down to lower ground nearer the city. Warwick attacked on 27 August, and the rebel defences were devastated. Those who held their ground were slaughtered in their tracks. The rest were hounded across the county and the hangings went on for days, and in such numbers that a halt had to be called when the labouring community was in danger of being wiped out.

The Kett brothers were both captured; Robert was hanged from the walls of Norwich Castle, his brother from one of the towers of Wymondham Abbey. A plaque on Norwich Castle commemorates

Main Places of Interest In and South of Norwich

Norwich Castle Museum
Norman keep containing exhibits of local and natural history. Art gallery displaying many examples of the Norwich School of painting.

Norwich Cathedral
Norman cathedral and cloisters, some other remains of the monastery. Visitors centre and coffee room.

Stranger's Hall
Charing Cross. Medieval house containing exhibits of domestic life through the years.

Sainsbury Centre
University of East Anglia, about 2 miles from the city centre. Norman Foster's award-winning space age building housing Robert Sainsbury's art collection and regular displays of national exhibitions.

The City Walls
Most of the fourteenth-century walls have disappeared over the years, but in some places there are substantial remains. Quite a long stretch runs along Chapel Field, the Black Tower on Carrow Hill and Cow Tower being the best examples.

Bressingham Gardens
4 miles west of Diss on A1066.

6 acres of beds containing hardy perennials, heathers and conifers. Steam Museum containing over fifty steam engines of various types. Railway rides through the gardens.

Banham Zoo and Monkey Sanctuary
6 miles north-west of Diss on B1113.
20 acres of wildlife including a collection of rare primates.

Rainthorpe Hall Gardens
Tasburgh, 8 miles south of Norwich.
Large gardens of Elizabethan manor house, including an unusual collection of bamboos.

Forncett Industrial Steam Museum
Forncett St Mary, 10 miles south-west of Norwich.
Unusual collection of industrial steam engines, including one which used to open Tower Bridge.

Billingford Mill
1 mile east of Scole on A143. The last corn mill to work in Norfolk, it lost a couple of sails during the great storm of October 1987. Now fully restored, it has a five-storey red-brick tower, and a white boat-shaped cap.

the courageous struggle of the members of the Norfolk Rebellion.

Old and New Buckenham. These two villages about four miles south-east of Attleborough are in striking contrast to one another. New Buckenham was the first recorded example of town planning, the place carefully laid out around the market place, where the Market House of the 1600s still survives with its wooden whipping post. The place came into being when the 'new' castle was built nearby, in the twelfth century, replacing the one at Old Buckenham.

The village of Old Buckenham sprawls around a vast green dotted with ponds, its cottages straggling round the edges and a thatched church at one end of the green. The remains of its castle are just under a mile to the north-east. Old Buckenham is a picturesque reminder of village life from times past.

About two miles to the south is **Banham**, with a zoo which includes an extensive collection of rare primates.

Diss. This old market town in the Waveney Valley has seen much modern expansion, but the older parts of the town grouped around the Market Place repay some gentle exploration. The original town was built around a six-acre lake called the Mere, its southern edge bordered by a large village green. The Market Place and Mere Street contain an interesting architectural mixture of Tudor, Georgian and Victorian buildings, and in the Market Place is a museum with exhibits of local interest.

St Mary's Church has a fine knapped-flint chancel; one of its past rectors, John Skelton, a Poet Laureate, gave school lessons to the young Henry VIII.

Not far from Diss is **Bressingham**, where Alan Bloom's massive collection of hardy perennials and alpine plants grow in six acres of parkland setting, and a day's visit may be completed by seeing another of Mr Bloom's loves — steam engines. He has a fine collection of both engines and rolling stock, some being run up and down a short length of track. Children can enjoy rides on a miniature railway.

Burston, just three miles north-east of Diss, was the scene of the longest running strike in British history — twenty-five years. At the turn of the century, the labouring class in Norfolk still suffered from exploitation by farmers, many of whom took children out of school to work in the fields whenever they wanted. It was against this backdrop that Kitty and Tom Higdon arrived in Burston as headmistress and assistant teacher. They were committed to the ideals of

Christian socialism, and instilling a sense of fairness and justice in their pupils. This did not endear them to the Norfolk Education Committee, who had terminated their previous post in Wood Dalling. The Higdons' campaigns there to improve the lot of the school children, and their support of fledgeling labour movements caused considerable friction with the establishment.

The conditions of the working class were no different here, and very soon the Higdons were complaining about the unhygienic state of the school. Tom Higdon was elected to the Parish Council, and with sufficient supporters seeking the remaing seats, succeeded in ousting the farmers from their positions of power.

But the farmers, and the rector of Burston, who had suffered the ignominy of polling the least votes in the Parish Council elections, still formed the managing body of the village school, and it was their trumped-up charge which led to the Higdons' dismissal in early 1914.

On 1 April, the first day of their dismissal, sixty-six out of seventy-two children went on strike, and marched around Burston with banners proclaiming 'Justice' and 'We want our teachers back'. From that day on, the Higdons took school lessons on the village green. The authorities struck back by summonsing several of the parents and fining them. But the strike attracted national attention, and the authorities realised they weren't getting anywhere when fines were paid from collections. Leading Trades Union, labour and women's suffrage personalities came to Burston, and within three years, sufficient funds had been raised to build their own schoolhouse beside the village green. The opening in 1917 attracted a gathering of a thousand people.

The Strike School carried on in parallel with the council school all through the twenties and thirties, and in the later years there was even a friendly rivalry between the two, especially when it came to sports. The school closed shortly after Tom Higdon died in 1939. An exhibition inside the building recounts the twenty-five year strike, and it remains a symbol of freedom of speech and of free choice in education.

A map of the Candlestick (East Anglian name for a circular walk) is available at the Strike School, so that visitors may retrace the steps of the striking schoolchildren on their procession around Burston.

3
NORTH NORFOLK

Without any doubt, the most memorable part of a visit to North Norfolk is the beautiful coastline, stretching from Hunstanton in the west, round to Mundesley in the east. Virtually all of this has been designated an Area of Outstanding Natural Beauty by the Countryside Commission, with much of the coastal marshlands given over to nature reserves. The stretch from Holme to Cley is a perfect example of how hundreds of years of silt deposits can completely alter the character and fortunes of coastal towns and villages. What were once important ports now stand beside muddy creeks, a mile or so away from the sea which once came up to their doorsteps. Some are still accessible to small craft, while Wells-next-the-Sea has made a determined effort to remain open to larger sea-going vessels.

Further round the coast, the sea has taken its toll in the form of erosion. The cliffs from Sheringham to Mundesley have taken a great deal of battering, with substantial tracts of land, including houses, falling into the sea. Drastic action has been taken in many places, with huge sea defences stretching along the beach at the foot of the cliff. There are places where one can walk along the tops of the cliffs, (from Sheringham to West Runton, for example) but in general, the cliffs are not very safe, and must not be climbed.

Erosion of a different kind has affected parts of North Norfolk. In some areas, salt marshes and sand dunes have been damaged by indiscriminate trampling feet. As most of the North Norfolk Coast forms reserves for varying types of wildlife, it is very important to keep to footpaths and not to throw litter.

Cromer. One of the least spoilt of Norfolk's seaside resorts,

Cromer, the self-styled 'gem of the Norfolk coast', is known nationally for its crabs. It has long traditions as a fishing town, and its inhabitants are justly proud of their lifeboat, and of Henry Blogg, its most famous coxswain. Blogg commanded the Cromer lifeboat from 1909 to 1947, winning the RNLI gold medal three times, as well as many other honours. A bust of him can be found in North Lodge Park.

Cromer has long been a fashionable resort to visit, and it undoubtedly enjoyed its heyday with the coming of the railway. Jane Austen's novel *Emma* has one of her characters mentioning it as 'the best of all the sea-bathing places', and at the beginning of this century, Cromer gained national popularity as the 'Poppyland' of *Daily Telegraph* columnist Clement Scott. Even today, the summer fields in Norfolk can be a marvellous blaze of red, and the name has stuck, although Cromer's reputation as the place to be seen ended with the onset of World War I.

The church tower of St Peter and St Paul, once used as a lighthouse, rises majestically above the town. At 160ft, it is the tallest church tower in Norfolk, and visitors who climb to the top enjoy a breathtaking view. There are also two museums worth visiting. The Lifeboat Museum has models, pictures, photographs and a Tyne class lifeboat *Ruby & Arthur Read*, while Cromer Museum is housed in a late Victorian fisherman's cottage in Tucker Street and has displays on local history, geology and archaeology.

Two miles south-west of Cromer on the B1436 is the National Trust property of Felbrigg Hall, one of the finest seventeenth-century country houses in Norfolk. It has original eighteenth-century furniture, and outside are a walled garden, a park and a lakeside walk. Five miles south on the A140 is the Alby Lace Museum and Study Centre, a museum entirely devoted to lace with daily demonstrations of bobbin lacemaking.

Sheringham. Three miles west of Cromer, Sheringham is really two villages rolled into one. Down by the sea stands the old fishing village, now a pleasant resort. Upper Sheringham is up on the hill, and although its history goes back to Iron Age times, it is now the residential part of the town. Sheringham Park can be found here. Its gardens contain many unusual plants and are surrounded by rhododendron woods, and there are spectacular views of the park and the coastline.

The North Norfolk Railway is privately owned; its three miles of

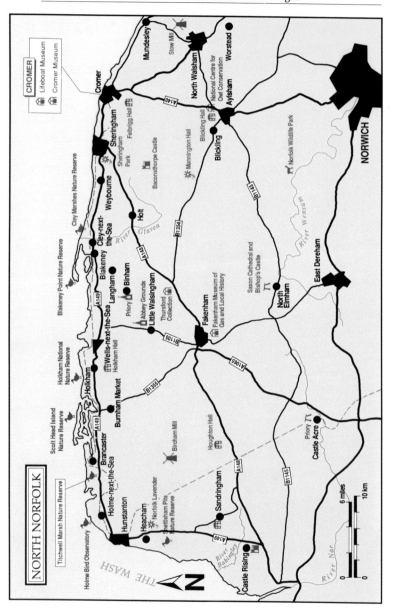

Nostalgia at the North Norfolk Railway's Weybourne Station with its steam locomotives

The fishermen's day off —their boats stranded high up Weybourne beach

track run from Sheringham to Weybourne, with a two-mile extension to Holt recently opened. Its charm lies in the fact that the service is run with steam engines and coaches from the early part of this century. The former Midland and Great Northern railway station at Sheringham also houses a static display of old steam engines and other vintage railway paraphernalia.

Sheringham is surrounded by attractive heath and woodland which provides some fine walking and pleasant views down onto the town.

Weybourne. This small resort has winding medieval streets and an uncluttered atmosphere. Situated at the point where the cliffs begin to rise from the marshland coast, Weybourne Hope was a deep-water anchorage and had some strategic importance — hence the saying: 'He who would old England win, must at Weybourne Hope begin'. It was used as an embarkation point for troops off to France in World War I, and during the last war, drones were launched from the cliffs for target practice by anti-aircraft guns on Stiffkey marshes.

The cliff path between Weybourne and Sheringham is particularly attractive, especially when the gorse bushes are in flower, providing a fine sight of vivid yellow splashes.

Holt. Four miles inland, this charming little town comprises mainly eighteenth- and nineteenth-century buildings in what is now designated a conservation area. Although there are not many clues to suggest it, Holt existed as a town before the Norman invasion, but it was destroyed by fire in 1708. Many of the cottages in its side streets make good use of Norfolk flint, while some of the grander buildings are in more traditional Georgian or Victorian styles. The colour-washed buildings around the market place make a very picturesque scene, and to visit something a little unusual, take a short walk down the High Street to the Pineapple Obelisk. Although it is not known how or when this strange column reached Holt, we do know that it was a gatepost from nearby Melton Constable Park. The mileages inscribed on the column are wrong for Holt!

Holt is also the home of Gresham's school, a public school founded in 1555 by Sir John Gresham, then Lord Mayor of London. In the grounds of the Kelling Park Hotel are aviaries with wildfowl and exotic birds, a water garden and a children's play area.

Three miles to the south-east, Baconsthorpe Castle is a large fortified Manor House, built mainly in the fifteenth century, and a mile south is Holt Lowes, an area consisting of ninety-eight acres of conifer woodland and 113 acres of heathland, where a nature trail can be followed. Glavenside Gardens, a mile west of Holt, occupies four acres of grounds on the River Glaven. There are rock and water gardens, a rose garden and a kitchen garden irrigated by water which is raised by a turn of the century hydraulic ram.

Cley-next-the-Sea. Other parts of the Norfolk coast suffer badly from erosion; here silt has built up over the years, and now Cley is actually more than a mile from the sea. There are some very attractive buildings here, including the eighteenth-century Custom House on the old quayside. Cley is now more widely known as the home of the very first nature reserve in Britain. Cley Marshes, acquired by the Norfolk Naturalists' Trust in 1926 and established as a bird sanctu- ary, now include Salthouse marshes as one of its later extensions. The area is the home of many species of birds, and others are frequent visitors. Displays on the history and conservation of the area can be found at Cley visitor centre, which has magnificent views of the reserve. Permits for the reserve are also available here.

Blakeney. On the other side of the Glaven estuary from Cley, Blakeney, like Cley and Wiveton, was also once an important medieval port. In fact, during the thirteenth century, Blakeney was ranked fourth in England's 'top ten' ports providing ships to carry the king and his entourage over to Sluys in Flanders, and in the sixteenth century the port sent no less than three ships to fight the Spanish Armada. Gradual silting up over the centuries, increased by land drainage and reclamation schemes, saw the decline of Blakeney as a port. Today, the village and its small quay lie beside a creek over a mile from the sea, with leisure boats taking the place of merchant vessels.

Blakeney Quay is now frequented more by pleasure craft and small fishing vessels, as only boats with a shallow draught can gain access here. The whole estuary is sheltered from the sea by a four mile long sand-and-shingle bank called Blakeney Point, built up over the years by the powerful action of the sea. The area, in the care of the National Trust, is a reserve for wildlife, well known as a tern colony, and a stopover for migrating birds. It is possible to walk out to Blakeney Point from Cley, although not advisable for the faint of heart, as the round trip is about ten miles of rough walking.

A four-mile walk starts from the car park next to Blakeney Quay, following the path out along the sea embankment and heading

Blakeney Quay, now popular with leisure boats

Blakeney Guildhall, with its Gothic-style arches

towards Blakeney Point. On the right, the marshland grazed by cows is all reclaimed from the sea. To the left are salt marshes and small tidal creeks. To walk to the end, you actually have to start from Cley, although summer tourists tend to take advantage of the boat trips from Blakeney and Morston Quays.

Follow the path around to Blakeney Eye, where it turns inland along the bank of the river Glaven. Here, you might make out the indistinct ruins of a thirteenth-century chapel in the fields, and on the other side of the channel, Cley windmill. Turn left onto the A149 (not

The Wells lifeboatmen, demonstrating their skills

Unusual brick-work on cottages in Clubb Lane, Wells-next-the-sea

as desperate as it sounds), and then as you come into Cley (pronounced Cly), turn right onto the Wiveton road. Almost immediately after, take a left and right onto Church Lane, down to the fourteenth-century St Margaret's Church. The church and green were once the centre of the village, but after a fire in the seventeenth century, new houses were built around the then harbour to the north.

Cross over the Green from the churchyard, and take the road towards Wiveton, over a stone bridge which crosses the Glaven. Follow the B1156, past the medieval St Mary's Church, and the

Bluebell Inn, heading back to Blakeney. The village's flint and brick cottages give it a charm which summer holidaymakers seek out. Before returning to your car, do stop for a look at the fifteenth-century vaulted undercroft of the former Guildhall.

Langham. A small village about two miles south of Morston, where the Victorian writer Captain Marryat is buried in the church-yard. The local public house proudly sports a much more recent claim to fame. Behind the bar hangs the Union Jack flown on South Georgia by naturalist film-makers Cindy Buxton and Annie Price during the Argentine occupation.

Stiffkey. A pretty little village, built mainly from flint and brick, popular building materials in this area. The sixteenth-century Stiffkey Hall, with its odd circular external towers now partly in ruins, was built by Sir Nicholas Bacon, keeper of the Privy Seal under Queen Elizabeth I. Stiffkey is particularly noted for its cockles, known locally as 'Stewky Blues'. And it was the infamous rector of Stiffkey whose involvement with prostitutes led to a national scandal in the 1930s.

Wells-next-the-Sea. Of all the old ports along the North Norfolk coast, Wells-next-the-Sea is the only one to have been able to sustain its existence as a trading town, despite the gradual silting which has left the quay beside a creek, a mile away from the sea. The harbour channel was straightened out in the nineteenth century, when the Earl of Leicester commissioned the embankment which cut off the winding creeks which characterise the salt marshes. It also enabled him to reclaim the land behind it, draining it sufficiently to be turned over to agriculture. As in centuries past, the port of Wells is used mainly for the export of locally produced grain. The area where the old harbour was, away from the town, is now a camping and recreation site.

The Wells and Walsingham Light Railway provides a scenic journey along the world's longest $10^{1}/_{4}$in narrow gauge steam rail-way. The train is pulled by a unique Garratt locomotive, built specially for the line in 1986.

Start this seven-mile walk from the quay, and head east, follow-ing the road past the Customs House and the ancient Golden Fleece pub. Carry straight on down the minor road where the main road turns off to the right, and then past the fishermen's huts, fork left onto the track which goes along the sea bank. In 1953, and again more recently, the sea broke through here, flooding all the low-lying ground to the right. Continue along the embankment and over a small creek onto Warham Greens. It can be a bit muddy along here, so stick to the path. During the summer months the marshes are tinged a delightful shade of violet when the sea lavender is in bloom.

Turn right down Cocklestrand Drove and cross over the main road, following the lane up the hill into Warham All Saints. Turn right at the crossroads, past the church, and then left at the B1105 Wells to Walsingham road. Take the next right, and carry straight on up Gallow Hill. Turn right at the junction and follow the lane north back to Wells.

Four miles east of Wells-next-the-Sea, off the A419, is Cockthorpe Hall Toy Museum, a sixteenth-century house housing over 2,500 antique and vintage toys.

Holkham. Holkham Hall is a magnificent Palladian stately home, set in beautiful timbered parkland. The Norfolk home of the Earls of Leicester, it was built between 1734 and 1759 by William Kent. In the early days, the estate was something of a wasteland, but under the hand of Thomas William Coke, who utilised some of the ideas put forward by 'Turnip' Townsend, it eventually became an agricultural success. A six-acre walled garden designed in the 1780s by Samual Wyatt contains original glasshouses, wall-trained fruit trees and ornamental flower beds with many unusual species.

A unique collection of cars, fire engines, tractors, farming and gardening implements can be seen, housed in nineteenth-century buildings adjacent to the hall. The mile-long Holkham Hall Lake, accessible only to organised groups with permits from the estate office, is home to moorhens, coots, grebes, cormorants and swans.

Holkham Bay is without doubt one of the best beaches in Norfolk, and a great family favourite, with its broad expanse of flat sand and shallow waters making it a safe bathing spot. Even on hot summer days, when the beach is extremely popular, its size ensures that it rarely seems crowded. Naturist bathing is allowed at the western end.

The row of Corsican pines behind the bay was planted in 1860 to stabilise the sand dunes so that the marshes inland could be reclaimed. Much of the area is a National Nature Reserve. It consists of extensive mudflats, sand and saltmarsh as well as the pine-fringed dunes, and can be reached by footpaths from Holkham, Wells and Overy Staithe.

Binham. Four miles south-west of Blakeney, Binham is an attrac-

Half-timbered buildings and ancient lock-up, Walsingham

tive little village with a medieval cross on a small green. The Benedictine priory at Binham dates back to the late eleventh century. Only the nave of the priory church remains, with part of the west front, the rest having been destroyed at the Dissolution.

Walsingham. Little and Great Walsingham lie about five miles south of Wells, the larger of the two villages being Little Walsingham. There have been pilgrimages to Our Lady of Walsingham for hundreds of years, the consequence of a vision of the Virgin Mary by

Burnham Overy Mill on a picturesque site overlooking the River Burn

The ruins of Creake Priory near Burnham Market

the wife of a Norman knight in 1061. An Augustinian priory was built around a hundred years later, and throughout the Middle Ages was the most popular place of pilgrimage in Britain.

The present shrine was built quite recently, in the 1930s, although the one it replaced, which was destroyed at the Dissolution, is reputed to have been identical to the house in Nazareth where the Archangel Gabriel appeared to the Virgin Mary. Pilgrims came from all over Europe, casting off their shoes at the last of the many shrines on the way to Walsingham, completing their journey barefoot. One such shrine at Houghton St Giles has been restored, and is known as the 'Slipper Chapel'.

Also of interest at Walsingham is the Shirehall Museum, a Georgian courtroom with original fittings. There are displays on the pilgrimage and the history of Walsingham.

Between Brancaster and Holkham there are no less than six villages prefixed with the name Burnham. The most important of them is **Burnham Market**, the local market town, about seven miles west of Wells. It has a broad green surrounded by Georgian houses and cottages, and a particularly interesting church, with its gallery of sculptures around the tower battlements. **Burnham Overy**, to the east of Burnham Market, has a fine windmill and watermill over the River Burn, both owned by the National Trust. **Burnham Overy Staithe** is a charming little village to the north, built after its parent town, as the sea receded from the original port. Even now, the harbour lies on a muddy creek, a long way from the sea.

To the south lies **Burnham Thorpe**, particularly worthy of mention as it was the birthplace of England's greatest seafarer, Horatio Nelson. The parsonage where he was born, the home of his father the Reverend Edmund Nelson, no longer exists, although its site is marked with a plaque beside the road. The thirteenth-century church contains several mementoes of this great seaman. The cross and lectern are both made from timbers taken from HMS *Victory*, and flags from that ship hang in the nave. Edmund Nelson lies in the chancel, with a bust of his famous son above. The names of all the local public houses, The Nelson, The Victory, The Hero, The Trafalgar, remind one of this famous Norfolkman.

Brancaster. Brancaster was an old Roman port, known then as *Branodunum*. It was the most northerly in a chain of forts along the east coast to the English Channel. Nothing remains of this settlement. Brancaster Staithe is a small harbour, great plains of saltmarshes separating it from the sea. Beyond is **Scolt Head Island**, a nature reserve, which like the foreshore opposite is owned by the National Trust. The island consists of shingle and sand dunes with salt marshes. It is a haven for wildfowl and waders, which can be seen by following the nature trail. It can be visited by boat from either Brancaster or Burnham Overy Staithes.

Also near Brancaster is Titchwell Marsh. The reed beds, marshes and sandy shores, with their wide range of waders and winter wildfowl, are accessible via a sea-wall footpath, and there is a visitor centre which is open during the summer months.

Holme-next-the-Sea. There may well have been a small port here a long time ago. This is the point where the ancient track of the Peddars Way ends. The other end of the path is in Breckland some fifty miles away, but if the line were continued it would reach the Roman fortress town of Colchester. Similarly, it is thought that perhaps the line of the Peddars Way extended northwards across the Wash into Lincolnshire. In those days, when much of Fenland was under water, a short sea trip from Holme would have cut weeks off a trip from Colchester or Norwich to somewhere like York.

Holme also marks the dividing line between two very different coastlines. The Wash coast just around the corner is flat, bleak and muddy, and although it does have points of interest, is not so pretty as the salt-marshes, creeks and sand dunes of the coast from Holme to Cley and Salthouse.

This part of the coastline is an Area of Outstanding Natural Beauty, with a string of nature reserves internationally famous in the birdwatching world, visited each year by a large variety of wildfowl and waders. The salt marshes around Holme are colonised by such plants as thrift and sea lavender, and in July and August, are a wonderful blaze of colour. Even if nature spotting isn't your strong point, the peace and solitude of the area will almost certainly appeal, and this six-mile walk provides the best impression. From the A149 at Holme, take the turning signposted 'Beach Road', and start from the car park at the end.

The first part of the walk follows the Norfolk Coast Path and is well signposted. A wide sandy track leads out into the dunes where a signpost announces that you are entering the Holme Nature Reserve, and 'Norfolk Heritage Coast' arrows can also be seen. Sand dunes are formed by wind action on dry sand. It collects around small objects, and gradually builds up. The yellowy-green long

Broad Water, Holme Bird Observatory

spiky grass is marram grass, whose extensive root systems hold the dunes together, and stops them from shifting.

A boardwalk goes past a lagoon called Lavender Marsh, and further on past Gore Point, or at least, what used to be Gore Point. There was a spit of sand and shingle here, but the tides have done their work, and carried it away.

To the right is the sanctuary area of the nature reserve, described as dune scrub and dune slack. Scrub is fairly obvious, thorny bushes such as sea buckthorn. Slack is the wet parts of the dune area — fresh water rather than sea. Beyond is the farmland which has actually been reclaimed from salt marshes by draining.

The route passes some concrete World War II defences, nestling in amongst dunes which are much older and more stabilised, where crushed sea-shells in the sand have encouraged the growth of such plants as bird's foot trefoil, normally found on chalk grassland.

Just past the trees, Corsican pines planted to stabilise the dunes, is the entrance of the Holme Bird Observatory, run by the Norfolk Ornithologists Association. Non-members can walk straight in and buy a permit from the warden to use the hides. The stretch of water overlooked by one of the hides is called Broad Water, and was once a drainage channel for the old saltmarshes. The boardwalk then turns inland along Thornham Bank, an embankment built in 1860 to help with drainage of the land behind. The marshes behind the bank are freshwater. On the other side, they are obviously salt marshes.

When the boardwalk stops continue straight along the top of the bank, and where it turns left, with another one joining the bend in the middle, take the footpath going straight ahead, keeping to the left of the drainage channel and leaving the Norfolk Coast Path. Cross the channel over a small footbridge into the next field, and then continue to follow the path as it veers away to the right. Further on the path widens out into a track, with orchards on either side and farm buildings beyond.

The track emerges on the main road. Cross straight over, but as you ascend the hill, do stop and take a look behind you. The views of the coast are magnificent, and on a clear day you can see twenty miles or so across the Wash into Lincolnshire, in a panorama stretching from Boston to Skegness.

Turn right at the trig pillar, and shortly after, as the road bends to the left, take the broad track going right, intermittently dotted with hedgerows and trees on either side. It opens out for a while, then turn right down the track which passes to the right of a deciduous wood, before arriving at the main road once more.

The bottom of Eastgate Road bends sharp left passing the church, curious in that the tower is built at one corner of the nave rather than squarely at the end. Continue along Kirkgate Street, and when you come to the T junction, turn right. This leads onto the Beach Road and back to the car park.

Hunstanton. This is a seaside resort which has sprung up in the last hundred years, largely as a result of the arrival of the railway. The summer generally sees the place crowded with holidaymakers who come to explore the pleasures of the funfair and gift shops. It is also possible to walk underwater here! The Sea Life Centre provides visitors with the opportunity to come face to face with a variety of sea creatures beneath the waves, as they walk along the 'Ocean Tunnel'.

Nearby Hunstanton cliffs tower 60ft above the beach in a magnificent triple-banded array of colour, made from layers of carrstone, red and white chalk. On a clear day 'Boston Stump', the tower of Boston parish church can be seen, twenty miles due west on the other side of the Wash. Hunstanton has the distinction of being the only resort on the east coast where the sun can be watched setting over the sea.

Old Hunstanton, to the north, and virtually at the mouth of the Wash, has a fine sandy beach and an excellent golf course. Inland there is some superb walking country. Two miles away are the chalk downs of Ringstead. Unusually for Norfolk, or at least for the popular conception of a flat county, these rolling downs are at the end of a chalk ridge which runs north-east across the country from Wiltshire.

About three miles to the south of Hunstanton, at **Heacham**, is Caley Mill, the home of Norfolk Lavender. This is the largest commercial producer of lavender in the country, and in July or August, when the plants are being harvested, a tour of the mill will show how the lavender is dried and distilled. The myriad varieties of lavender plant can be seen in the grounds of the mill, a marvellous blaze of lilac colour.

A four-mile walk follows some lovely green lanes, including part of the Peddars Way, one of the few ancient monuments on which people are encouraged to walk! Start at **Fring**, about four miles south-east of Heacham, taking the road signposted for Sherbourne. Go straight past the turning for Sedgeford and the unsignposted right-hand turning that follows. As you come up the hill, where the road bends around to the right, take a left turn onto the Peddars Way.

This section leads onto a gentle rise, giving some expansive views. Go straight over the minor road, and approaching a wood some distance to the right, ignore a track going off to the right. About 50yd further on is one going off to the left, lined with trees. Go down this one.

Continue straight over two roads (both of which head for Bircham), and turn left onto the path which crosses yours a quarter of a mile later. The way back to Fring continues straight on here, along a mixture of path and wide track. When you eventually reach the road, turn left to return to the village.

Sandringham. Sandringham House, traditionally the gathering place for the Royal Family in the New Year, was originally bought by Queen Victoria as a twenty-first birthday gift for Edward, the then Prince of Wales. Her intention was that he should spend his off-duty time 'away from town... to enjoy the benefits of a healthy, country life.' It is still used as a holiday home by the Royal Family.

The house and gardens are open to the public during the summer except when any member of the Royal Family is in residence. Outside, there is free access to the rest of the estate which is very beautiful — its heath and forestland has been described as a 'piece of Scotland south of the Tweed'. The church, standing nearby amidst the beautiful parkland, is really quite old, but it has been restored and added to so much by its royal neighbours, that it looks mainly Victorian. Visitors may attend services provided there is space once parishioners are seated.

Start this four-mile walk from the car park for Sandringham House and Country Park, opposite the war memorial, and turn left onto the road. The roads around the Sandringham estate are characterised by wide grassy verges, always immaculately kept. Follow the red carr-stone wall along to the impressive wrought-iron Norfolk Gates. They were made in Norwich for the 1862 Great Exhibition, and were presented to the Prince and Princess of Wales the following year as a wedding gift.

Continue past the Norfolk Gates along the wall to a small wooden gate with the very stately title of East Entrance, and opposite, the wrought iron gates bearing the initials EA (for Edward and Alexandra) leading to the flower gardens. Continue along the road around to the Jubilee Gates, another fine entrance, marked with the mono-

Sweet-smelling Caley Mill, Heacham, a good place to visit to see lavender production

grams of King George V and Mary to commemorate their Silver Jubilee in 1935. Carry on down the road for a short distance, past the sign for West Newton, and then turn right down a small lane, which affords some excellent views across the park.

Through the trees can be glimpsed York Cottage, birthplace of George VI. Past the school, turn right at the 'T' junction. Go downhill and past the Sandringham Club (no pubs in estate villages, just clubs!). **West Newton** church opposite has a fine lych gate with pillars of carved oak. Further down the road is a turning leading to a flax factory. King George V and Queen Mary had visited an exhibition of Irish linen, and were asked if they would like to grow some flax at Sandringham. The first crop was sown in 1931, and the resulting flax sent to Northern Ireland to be processed into linen. But the local industry grew enough to warrant building a factory to handle all the produce.

Continue along the road and then fork right, following a pine-fringed road to the crossroads at Lynn Lodges. Cross over, and then shortly after, fork right onto a wide grassy track. Further uphill it

Castle Acre — with its impressive ruined priory and village sign, typical of East Anglia

crosses a wide vista. Turn right here, rejoining the road at Scotch Belt which takes you straight on back to the car park.

Castle Rising. The great Norman keep of Castle Rising once used to stand sentinel over a busy port. Even after the sea receded, the town of Castle Rising retained its importance into the seventeenth century as a parliamentary borough on a par with the rest of the county. The earthworks on which the castle stands are of Roman origin, and the keep, built around 1150, is largely intact.

Trinity Hospital was founded in 1614 by Henry Howard, the Earl of Northampton. The red brick almshouses were set up to provide homes for 'twelve poor women, single, 56 at least, and no haunters of alehouses'. The place still functions, and the present inmates can

Places of Interest in North Norfolk

Glandford Shell Museum
3 miles south of Blakeney on the B1156.
Sir Alfred Jodrell's collection of shells from all over the world, including jewels, pottery, and relics from Pompeii.

The Thursford Collection
Laurel Farm, Thursford, 6 miles north-east of Fakenham off the A148.
Steam locomotives, traction engines, and mechanical organs, with live concerts on the Wurlitzer cinema organ, every week from Easter to mid-June, and daily thereafter to the end of September.

Bircham Mill
Great Bircham, 8 miles south-east of Hunstanton on the B1153.
One of the best surviving corn mills in Norfolk.

Felbrigg Hall (National Trust)
3 miles south-west of Cromer, between the A140 and A148.
Seventeenth-century house with fine interiors, standing in mature parkland. Orangery with camellias, walled garden, and woodland walk.

Blickling Hall
(National Trust)
2 miles north-west of Aylsham Jacobean red brick mansion with long gallery containing fine plasterwork ceiling. Beautiful gardens.

Norfolk Wildlife Park
Great Witchingham, 12 miles north-west of Norwich off the A1067.
Philip Wayre's famous collection of European animals and birds is probably the largest of its kind in the world. Many endangered species have been bred successfully here.

Houghton Hall
10 miles west of Fakenham, off the A148.
Built in the early eighteenth century for Sir Robert Walpole, the first Prime Minister of England. The original village of Houghton was pulled down at Walpole's behest, to improve the view from the hall. As well as the finely furnished staterooms, there is a collection of some 20,000 model soldiers and other militaria.

Fakenham Museum of Gas and Local History
One of the more unusual tourist attractions, Fakenham's gas works, opened in 1846, is the only surviving example of its type in England. The 1888 gas holder and gas engine have been restored to working order (albeit on compressed air), and the system is demonstrated from time to time.

be seen going to church wearing their traditional red cloaks with the Howard badge, and pointed steeple hats.

Castle Acre. This is a popular overnight halt for walkers on the Peddars Way. The village takes its name from a Norman castle, built in the eleventh century, and of which the Bailey Gate is the only prominent surviving feature. Nearby is a Cluniac priory, in ruins after the ravages of the Dissolution, but impressive nonetheless. Founded in the eleventh century, its remains include the church and decorated west front, sixteenth-century gate-house, monastic buildings and the prior's lodging.

Start this five-and-a-half mile walk from the village green, and head south past the church. The lane takes you past the priory on your right, and over a bridged ford. Fork right in South Acre, past the church, and then turn left onto a sandy track just past the farm. Continue to the crossroads in the track after passing through Fingerhill Plantation, and turn right. Continue straight on for about a mile, and turn right down the hill just before you come to the West Acre road.

Cross the road at the bottom, continuing along a footpath, and then turning right across a narrow hedged lane. The path crosses a short section of heath before coming to a road and the ford near Mill House. Cross over, taking the path over two footbridges, and then along the edge of a wood. The path then comes out onto the delightful pastures along the River Nar. After just over a mile, the path comes up to a 'T' junction. Turn right here, and follow the lane uphill back into Castle Acre.

North Elmham. About seven miles north of East Dereham on the B1110, North Elmham is a small village with an important past. The ruined Anglo-Saxon cathedral shows that North Elmham was once the seat of the Bishopric of East Anglia (after it was moved from Dunwich, and before being transferred to Thetford and Norwich). The ruins are intermingled with the remains of the Bishop's Palace, and the surrounding earthworks suggest that the place was heavily defended.

Blickling. Two miles north-west of the market town of Aylsham is Blickling, a small village known widely for its magnificent Jacobean red brick hall with Dutch gables and brick chimneys. The hall stands on the site of an earlier building, which was the family home of Anne Boleyn. The view from the road with the main gate in the foreground, and the driveway to the house flanked by immacu-

Jacobean Blickling Hall near Aylsham

late lawns should lure the visitor into taking a closer look. Inside the house is a long gallery with a superb moulded plasterwork ceiling symbolising The Five Senses and Learning', and many other fine rooms containing period furniture and tapestries. The adjoining gardens are glorious, particularly on a sunny day, and should not be missed.

One of the outbuildings now houses the Hawk Trust's National Centre for Owl Conservation. The focal point of the centre is an interpretative exhibition about the conservation of the Barn Owl, whose numbers have plummeted by seventy per cent in the last fifty years. Despite being protected by law, owls and other birds of prey are still under extreme pressure, chiefly as a result of the destruction of habitats.

The centre, including its dramatic hologram of a flying owl, is also the headquarters of the owl conservation network, which aims, with the co-operation of farmers and landowners, to protect and expand the Barn Owl's few remaining strongholds in Britain.

Up the road from the main gate, past the Buckinghamshire Arms (a pleasant pub almost worth a separate visit!), is Blickling Park, which stretches out behind and beyond the hall. Pathways across the park allow very pleasant walking through cornfields, woods and open parkland, the mausoleum and lake being particularly interesting.

North Walsham. North Walsham, and the nearby village of Worstead (which gave its name to the woollen cloth still widely used today), were prosperous in weaving times. Worstead was the weaving centre, and the goods were sold in North Walsham, a town which has held a weekly market for the past 700 years. The Paston Grammar School, founded in 1606, and still flourishing, was attended by Nelson.

About a mile south of the town is a cross commemorating the Peasants' Revolt of 1381. Harsh laws concerning labourers led to a mob descending on Norwich and killing Sir Robert de Salle, the commander of the city. The Bishop of Norwich led a counter-attack, finally defeating the peasants on North Walsham Heath. Their leader, Geoffrey Lister, was dragged from the sanctuary of nearby North Walsham church, and granted absolution by the bishop before being drawn and quartered.

Not far from the coast, between the small resort of Mundesley and the North Sea gas terminal village of Bacton, is **Paston**. This tiny hamlet was once home to the powerful Paston family, who made their fortune from the wool trade, and later, farming. But the Pastons are best known for the Paston Letters, many of them written by Margaret Paston to her husband John, who spent much of his time practising as a lawyer in London. It was down to Margaret to dutifully manage the estates in his absence, which entailed collecting the rents, and defending the properties from incursions — both legal and violent! She reports all of these activities in her letters, interspersing them with snippets of local news and gossip, providing us with what is probably the most important commentary on fifteenth-century daily life in existence.

Worstead. The village of Worstead gave its name to the cloth it produced, which first gained popularity in the thirteenth century. When Edward III married Philippa of Hainault, the import of foreign material was banned, giving the home weaving industry a valuable fillip. As a result, Flemish weavers came over to this country, settling in East Anglia, and bringing their style of architecture and culture with them. Many of their old houses can still be seen in Worstead.

The Weavers Way. So called because of the region's past importance in the weaving industry. The Weavers Way started as a fifteen-mile walk linking Stalham, North Walsham and Blickling, largely following a disused railway track. The railway has been closed for over twenty years, and nature is predominant, making for a delightful ramble through woodland, pasture and arable land. More recently, extensions from Blickling to Cromer and Stalham to Great Yarmouth have been added, making fifty-six miles in all. Taken with the Peddars Way/Norfolk Coast Path, Norfolk now has a major long-distance route offering probably more scenic variety than any other path in the country.

The Weavers Way is well signposted along small country lanes and public footpaths, and car parks are available at various places along the walk. A leaflet covering the walk in more detail has been produced by Norfolk County Council, and is available from Tourist Information Centres.

4
THE BROADS

It is a rather sad fact that to a great many people the Broads are known only for the boating holidays which are available there. Broadland, which covers an area from Norwich to Great Yarmouth and from Stalham as far south as Beccles in Suffolk, has a curious mixture of natural and man-made landscape which is unique.

Scientific research has shown that the Broads are not natural lakes, but are the result of peat-digging over the course of around four hundred years, ending around 1300. Norfolk at that time can be likened in importance for fuel to one of today's major coalfields. Then, five to six hundred years ago, the extensive diggings began to flood, gradually turning into the reed-fringed lakes we know today. The surrounding fens are largely the result of constant reed cutting; Norfolk reed has been used for thatching for hundreds of years. Left to its own devices, the fenland surrounding the Broads would gradually turn into woodland over a period of about twenty-five years.

Linked together by the rivers Yare, Waveney, Bure, Thurne, Chet and Ant, along with artificial cuttings called dykes or fleets, the Broadland waterways meander across Norfolk until they disgorge into the mudflats of Breydon Water, and then into the sea at Great Yarmouth. In the days when the rivers were an important part of the transportation network, the workhorse cargo boats were wherries. Unlike the barges used on other waterways, the wherries were clinker built, usually put together on the river banks without any plans and nothing more than the builder's seasoned eye to ensure the hull was true. The wherries were often very fast, with a large black gaff mainsail on a mast, hinged and counterbalanced to pass under the numerous bridges spanning the rivers.

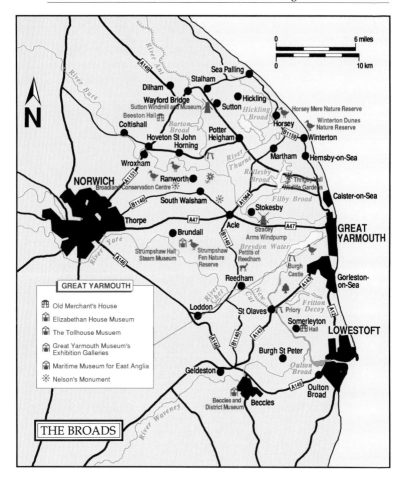

Typical cargoes were coal, timber, bricks, grain and beet. Changes in the types of cargo carried, and land-based transportation, spelled the end of the line for the sailing wherries. The last was built in 1912, and they continued working the rivers up until World War II, although by then most of those remaining had engines. Whilst there are several pleasure wherries in existence, built at the turn of the century when holidaying on the Broads first became popular, the *Albion* is the only trading wherry afloat, converted to carry passenger charters and seen regularly on the Broads rivers. Another trading wherry, the *Maud*, is currently undergoing restoration.

In all, something like 130 miles of Broadland is navigable by boats, and every summer sees vast numbers of sailing boats and cruisers travelling up and down the waterways. Conservationists may well give this overcrowding and misuse as one of the reasons why the Broads and their flora and fauna are threatened. While tourism and leisure pursuits can be blamed for erosion of the river banks and silting up of shallower stretches of water, caused by the

Swans are a common sight on Broadland waterways

wash from motor-boats, other factors have also been at work. More insidious is the change which has taken place in the waters themselves. Phosphate pollution from sewage and detergents has combined with nitrates from agricultural fertilisers, encouraging the growth of algae. This has effectively choked the growth of other water-borne plant life, so breaking the food chain for fish, insects and wildfowl. Of the forty-six Broads in the region, very few contain any plant life at all.

Agricultural drainage too has played its part. Much of the grazing marshland of the Broads has been turned over from the uneconomic grazing of cattle to arable farming. The dykes which criss-cross the marshes support a myriad of wildlife, of which some species are now facing extinction in the face of twentieth-century spoliation. As the wetlands are drained, so they become 'arable prairies', incapable of providing a hospitable wildlife habitat.

Fortunately, the outstanding wildlife and natural beauty of the Broads is being preserved, although naturalists may well argue that what exists is not enough. The Broads area is now England's newest National Park, and the Broads Authority is instituting a number of long-term plans to improve the water quality, including mud pumping and the introduction of vast numbers of water fleas, whose appetite for algae is prodigious.

The Norfolk Naturalists Trust has nature reserves at several broads, including some which have been designated Sites of Special Scientific Interest (SSSI). At Ranworth, the Trust owns a reserve covering the broad and much of the surrounding fens, while at Hickling there is a reserve of international importance, and for visitors, the $2^1/_2$ hour Water Trail is highly recommended.

Having taken a brief look at the origins of the Broads and their importance as part of our natural heritage, each of the main rivers of Broadland will be considered. This section follows the rivers in a manner largely benefiting the boat traveller. While the majority of the places can be reached by other forms of transport with relative ease, it is a boat which affords the most comprehensive look at this beautiful area.

The Bure

Wroxham. If Wroxham is regarded as the capital of the Broads, then the Bure is its motorway. The majority of boating holidays start from here, and the banks of the river are lined with boatyards crowded with Broads cruisers. It was here that the concept of boating holidays started just over a hundred years ago. Since then the twin villages of Wroxham and Hoveton St John, generally known together as Wroxham, have grown into a thriving tourist centre.

Easily reached from Norwich, Wroxham is only about seven miles away by road or rail. By boat it is somewhat further, as one must follow the Bure all the way to Great Yarmouth and then back along the Yare to Norwich. Both Wroxham and Hoveton have fourteenth-century churches well worth visiting, and no visit to Wroxham would be complete without a visit to Roys: 'the largest village store in the world'.

A recent visitor attraction is the Bure Valley Railway which runs on a 9-mile stretch of the old Great Eastern Railway route from Wroxham to Aylsham. The 15in-gauge line has both steam and diesel locomotives.

Three miles north-east of Wroxham on the A1151 is **Beeston St Lawrence**, where the Georgian country house Beeston Hall can be visited. Its interior is in the classical style, there is an art gallery and wine cellars, and a woodland walk in the grounds.

Coltishall. To the west of Wroxham the river is navigable only as far as Coltishall, winding upstream through woodland, first to Belaugh, where the Church of St Peter stands at the top of a steep wooded bank, rising from the river. A mile and a half further on is Coltishall, popular with anglers and also well known for its nearby RAF station. Made famous during the Battle of Britain by the presence of Douglas Bader, the base was for many years the home of the Battle of Britain Flight of Spitfires, Hurricanes and a Lancaster, before it relocated to RAF Coningsby in Lincolnshire.

Salhouse. To the east of Wroxham, just past Wroxham Broad, is Salhouse Broad and the village of Salhouse, about a half a mile away down a pleasant footpath. The twelfth-century Church of All Saints has a somewhat curious lop-sided appearance, the legacy of unfinished subsequent work.

Horning. Further down river, a dyke leads off to Hoveton Little Broad, where cruising is allowed only in the summer months. While Horning has become quite a boating centre, it is not as commercialised as Wroxham, and its charming main street of thatched houses runs for about a mile parallel to the river. There are plenty of moorings at the various public houses and hotels along the river — one historic public house is at Horning Ferry.

It is said that this point in the river has seen various means of crossing for the last thousand years. Certainly the old chain ferry, which no longer exists, operated for many years.

Across the river from here, and reached by car from Woodbastwick, is a boardwalk nature trail leading along the river bank to Cockshoot Dyke, and along that to Cockshoot Broad. This is one of the Broads Authority's major successes, and a demonstration that nature has the power to recover once the conditions are right. The broad, about eight or nine acres, had silted up so much that it was filled with phosphate-enriched mud to within two or three inches of the surface.

The authority dammed off the broad so it could not be further enriched, and then they pumped out about 4ft of mud, roughly equivalent to forty-four Olympic-sized swimming pools full. Within two to three months, seeds which had lain dormant for thirty to forty years started to germinate. They also transplanted water plants from other broads and marsh dykes to help kick-start the process. The result is that Cockshoot Broad is clear, and once more supports plant life. Nevertheless, it is an artificial state in as much as it must remain dammed off from the river until the water quality there has been

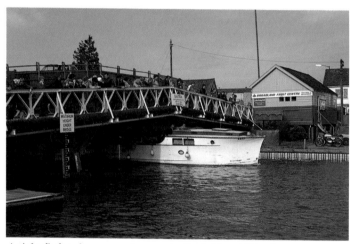

A tight fit for pleasure cruisers under the bridge at Wroxham

improved. There is a bird hide for public use overlooking the broad.

Ranworth. No trip to Broadland, whether by land or water, should omit a visit to Ranworth. The view from the tower of St Helen's Church is magnificent. The church also has one of the finest and best preserved painted rood screens in the country.

Visitors interested in wildlife and conservation will enjoy the Broadland Conservation Centre, organised by the Norfolk Naturalists Trust. The centre is reached by following the nature trail, through the woods and marshes, to the unique thatched building floating on pontoons at the edge of Ranworth Broad. The building houses an excellent display illustrating the diversity of interests in the Broads, and one may also sit in the upper gallery overlooking the broad,

A pleasant way to enjoy the Norfolk Broads — a pleasure wherry on the River Bure

which is closed to boats, and observe many different species of waterfowl through the binoculars and telescopes provided. The nearest mooring for boats is at the staithe on Malthouse Broad.

St Benet's Abbey. Not far along the river, which has now changed from its tree-lined banks to open fens, past the mouth of the River Ant, stands the strange and unmistakable ruin of St Benet's Abbey. In the ninth century the site was on the shore of the estuary to the North Sea. The first abbey was destroyed by the Danes in AD870 and was later rebuilt by King Canute. When the Normans invaded, the Benedictine monastery held out in a state of siege for four months, until it fell to them through the treachery of one of the lay-brothers. When it was all over, the Normans made him abbot of St Benet's for life, and then promptly strung him up on a gibbet as a reward for his treachery.

The abbey continued until the Dissolution of the Monasteries in the reign of Henry VIII, when much of the building was dismantled. A windmill was built into the remaining walls of the gatehouse some 200 years ago, the ruins of which form the rather confused structure seen today. The abbot of St Benet's became Bishop of Norwich at the

Dissolution, and his successor, who holds both titles to this day, holds an open-air service at the ruins once a year, on the first Sunday in August.

South Walsham. Leading off from the river opposite the abbey is Fleet Dyke, which opens out into South Walsham Broad. The Inner Broad, at the western end, is private, and although sailing is permitted, fishing, swimming and mooring are not. The Fairhaven Garden Trust, beside the broad, can be visited in summer. The woodland and water gardens contain rare shrubs and plants, and home-made teas are available. By road, South Walsham is but a stone's throw from Ranworth, and the Church of St Mary contains a fifteenth-century rood screen. There is, in fact, another church, St Lawrence's, in the same churchyard, but the latter fell into disrepair after it was damaged by fire some 150 years ago.

Acle. Continuing down the Bure, about a mile and a half past the mouth of the River Thurne is a short dyke leading to Upton village. The town of Acle lies on the main road between Norwich and Yarmouth, with moorings for boats about a mile away at Acle Bridge. The old bridge, no longer standing, was the scene of many grisly executions in former times; the hapless criminals were hanged from the parapet and left to rot. No wonder the old bridge had a reputation for being haunted!

There are some interesting places to explore around Acle. Three miles north-east of the town, at Burgh St Margaret, is **Fleggburgh Bygone Village**, a forty-acre site on which a reconstruction of a Norfolk village has been built. Cottages are set around a village green and there is a non-alcoholic pub, as well as a working steam exhibit and Burgh Hall Glass Works.

Just down river is the pretty village of **Stokesby**, and from here the Bure follows a course east towards Great Yarmouth, with the Yare and Breydon Water coming down to meet it just before the sea. The land around here is very flat and marshy, with windmills dotted about, giving the landscape the Dutch' look favoured so much by artists of the Norwich School. In the days when these windpumps were actually used to drain the marshes, cows would be put out to graze in the summer, and in the winter the marshes would be left to visiting wildfowl. Inadequate drainage meant the marshes would probably flood to a depth of several inches over a wide area.

Just after World War II, the old windpumps were replaced by electric pumps which kept the water level rather more stable, if a little lower than before. More efficient drainage enabled farmers to increase the profitable use of their land, although to the detriment of the unique landscape of grazing marshlands. This particular stretch of land, known as Halvergate marshes, represents the largest single remaining piece of this type of landscape in the country.

It was this that presented a big problem for Broadland during the run up to the 1981 Wildlife and Countryside Act. Section 41 had an arrangement which encouraged farmers to seek management agreements with authorities wanting to protect the landscape. But whilst fifteen to twenty thousand acres of traditional Broads grazing marsh landscape, mostly in the Halvergate area, were under serious threat of being drained and ploughed up for cereal production, the Broads Authority simply could not afford to pay to protect it. The threat was exacerbated by the drainage schemes being put on stream at public expense by Ministry of Agriculture support grants. The autonomous Internal Drainage Boards could set up these schemes on the basis that production was the call of the day — despite the fact that having paid for this extra production, the public would simply see the grain succumb to the Common Agricultural Policy, finding its way onto an EEC 'mountain'.

The result was a change in EEC directives, allowing the Ministry of Agriculture for the first time to make payments for conservation purposes. The Broads Grazing Marsh Conservation Scheme, with fifty per cent funding from the Countryside Commission, thus broke the mould.

Nearly ninety per cent of the farmers approached took up the offer of £50 per acre per year to continue with traditional grazing, rather than going for profit with cereal. So the Grazing Marsh Scheme became the catalyst which provided the model for Environmentally Sensitive Areas, and the entire Broads area was designated an ESA.

A Wetlands walk on Halvergate Marshes.

Halvergate marshes represent the largest block of grazing marshland in the country, and their serene character of fields of cows, dykes and old windpumps has been the inspiration to many painters. It is flat country, close to the sea, so any cold breezes will tend to bite if you don't wrap up on a cold day.

This walk of approximately seven miles starts in Halvergate, or just outside the village, where the road from the Stracey Arms makes a sharp bend. Follow the track eastwards, past Manor Farm, and on

Stracey Arms windpump near Halvergate

A silent electric boat enables the visitor to get closer to the wildlife of the Broads

into South Walsham marshes. Keep to the edge of Fleet Dyke until the point at which the railway line crosses the mouth of the dyke which opens out into Breydon Water. Follow the edge of Breydon around to Berney Arms, where there is a windmill open to the public (see page 76).

Just before that is the Berney Arms pub (see page 76), a great favourite with the cruising public and one of the few pubs in East Anglia which doesn't have a road to make the deliveries easier. Don't drink too much — unless you hitch a ride on a boat going to Yarmouth or Reedham, the only way back to civilisation is on foot! From the mill, the railway halt half a mile away can be seen. Follow this line, over the railway, across the lazy expanses of fields and dykes, to Fleet Dyke, where a track leads back towards Halvergate.

Alternatively, if you want to add an extra mile or so to the walk, instead of crossing the track between the railway halt and Fleet Dyke, turn left and follow it to Wickhampton, and then along the road back to Halvergate.

Many of the old windpumps have been restored, at least structurally, and are open to the public. The Stracey Arms Windpump, on the A47 opposite the turn-off for Halvergate, is a well-preserved example. Palmers Hollow Post Mill, the very last hollow-post plunger-pump can be found at Upton Dyke.

Great Yarmouth. The river Bure joins the Yare at the eastern tip of Breydon Water, where it flows southwards to the sea, with the sand bank on which Great Yarmouth stands on its eastern bank. The title 'Great' became official in 1272, when Henry III granted the town its charter. Whilst it is now more widely known as a base for the North Sea oil industry, Great Yarmouth was for many hundreds of years the hub of the herring industry, where the fish was salted and exported all over Europe. The forty-day-long Great Yarmouth Herring Fair was first held in 1270, and continued annually well into the eighteenth century. The growth of the holiday industry has seen many changes in the town. Some of the more commercialised aspects do not enhance the town, but anyone willing to explore it will find much of interest. There are at least five museums which are worth visiting, and on the central seafront is Great Yarmouth's butterfly farm, housing hundreds of butterflies from all over the world. They fly about tropical gardens under glass, and tropical plants and birds can also be seen.

THE ANT

The River Ant flows lazily from the North Norfolk coast, joining the Bure at St Benet's Abbey. While it is not navigable very far up river, it does flow through some very beautiful parts of Broadland, some of which are accessible only by boat.

Barton Broad. Past Ludham and Irstead Shoals, Barton Broad forms part of the channel of its parent river, unlike most broads which are connected to theirs by a dyke. The broad itself, one of the largest of the Norfolk Broads, is owned by the Norfolk Naturalists Trust, and several rare species of bird can be found on the nature reserve. Limekiln Dyke leads off from the western side of the broad, ending up at Neatishead.

Sutton. Up river, past the tiny village of Barton Turf (the church has an exceptional fifteenth-century rood screen), lies Sutton Broad, to the east of the river. Just outside the village stands the tallest tower

Places to Visit in Great Yarmouth

Old Merchant's House
(English Heritage)
South Quay
Seventeenth-century house with
interesting panelled rooms and
ornate plaster ceilings.

Norfolk Pillar
South Denes
144ft-high monumental column
to commemorate Nelson, built in
1819, twenty-four years before
its counterpart in London.
Designed by the Norfolk-born
architect William Wilkins (who
also designed the National
Gallery in London), the statue at
the top is not of Nelson, but
Britannia.

Elizabethan House Museum
(National Trust)
South Quay
Sixteenth-century house
furnished as seventeenth-century
merchant's house. A meeting
was supposedly held in this
house in 1648 in which the
execution of Charles I was
planned.

Tollhouse Museum
Tollhouse Street
One of the oldest municipal
houses in England; this medieval
building, once the town's
courthouse and gaol, now
houses local history exhibits.

windmill in the country, last used in the 1940s, and in the process of
renovation. The current restoration was set back as a result of the
Great Storm of October 1987; however the owner hopes soon to have
a full set of sails, and the mill working in the not too distant future.
An adjacent building houses an extensive Broads Museum, with
exhibitions of domestic, farm and trade tools as well as local bygones.

Stalham. A pleasant little market town, ideally situated for
holidaymakers who want to explore Barton and Hickling Broads,
and quite close to the seaside towns of Happisburgh and Sea Palling.
For the walking enthusiast, Stalham is a good starting point for the
Weavers Way footpath. Continue up the Ant to Wayford Bridge;
holiday cruisers may not go beyond this point, although smaller
vessels can continue a short distance further.

A Riverside Walk. With shops nearby and ample moorings,
Ludham Bridge is a useful stop for river cruisers. This five-mile
circular walk can start from here, or for land-based travellers, from
the crossroads at Ludham church which is where this description
begins. Take the road signposted for Catfield and Stalham. Outside
the village at a bungalow on the right called 'Eversley', take the

Great Yarmouth

St Benet's Abbey, Ludham, with a windmill tower rising incongruously above the ruins

bridleway signposted to the left.

The path crosses wide, open fields, and goes over a minor road. Turn right onto a hedge-lined green lane. Further on the track makes a sharp turn to the left, with small embankments on either side dotted with occasional trees.

At another line of hedges the track makes a right-hand turn, with an attractive row of oak trees to the left, interspersed with the hedge. The path comes out onto a minor road opposite a white house. Turn left here, heading for the old windmill in the distance.

Turn right at the mill house into the grounds of How Hill. The impressive thatched house with pargetting around the windows is not as old as it looks, but was built at the end of the last century. The house and grounds were used by Norfolk Education Committee for residential field studies courses up until 1983. Now, the 365-acre estate is run by the Broads Authority as an environmental education centre.

Go through the car park, and pick up the track into the woods, clearly signposted as the public footpath to the river bank, where you turn left. Toad Hole Cottage, a marshman's cottage, is worth a visit. Once the home of an eel-catcher, it was restored to give a wonderful feel for Victorian country living.

Past the trees there is a magnificent view to the left of How Hill, and on the opposite bank of the river, Turf Fen windpump. The path leaves the bank for a moment, passing through some fairly typical Broadland Fenscape, with ditches, reed beds, and patches of alder carr. The path arrives at a junction where a footbridge crosses a ditch. Do not go over this — follow the path around to the right, which brings you back to the river bank.

Follow the river round to the main road at Ludham Bridge, and turn left towards the village. Just past The Dog public house, turn right (signposted for Hall Common) and then first left, following a track across fields. Another one comes in from the right, but keep to this one as it bends around to the left, heading for the main road. Turn right here, and follow the road back to the church.

THE THURNE

Another tributary of the Bure, the Thurne flows in a south-westerly direction from Horsey, not far from the coast, across flat, open countryside. With no tree-lined banks to shelter the waterways from the breezes blowing in from the sea, the river and accompanying broads are, needless to say, great favourites with sailing enthusiasts.

The point where the river joins the Bure is called Thurne Mouth, and just upstream from here is the village of Thurne, with a windpump standing on each side of the river.

Potter Heigham. With a headroom of only 7ft, the old bridge at Potter Heigham has been the downfall of many a holiday sailor. When in doubt, wait for low-tide! Traffic lights control the flow of single-file traffic over the bridge, further crowded by summer throngs gathered along the parapet watching the boats and their ungainly attempts to pass underneath. One mile north lies the village itself which, as the name suggests, was the site of a Roman pottery. The church is interesting, with its thatched nave, and round tower supporting an octagonal belfry.

Martham. An attractive village, with Georgian houses and cottages grouped around The Green. The broad itself is actually closer to the head of the river at West Somerton. Access for boats to the largest of the Broads, Hickling Broad, and Horsey Mere, is up Candle Dyke, roughly halfway along the Thurne between Potter Heigham and Martham. Past Heigham Sound the channel divides into two, Hickling Broad at the head of one, and Horsey Mere up the other.

Hickling. The broad and much of the surrounding area forms a National Nature Reserve owned jointly by the Nature Conservancy Council and the Norfolk Naturalists' Trust. Boats are allowed only along the marked channels, and access ashore is forbidden without a permit. The best way to see the reserve is by taking the Water Trail, a $2^1/_2$ hour guided tour arranged by the Norfolk Naturalists Trust. Visitors are taken by boat to see a variety of Broadland features: reed and sedge beds, marshes and woodlands, and birds such as the marsh harrier and the bittern can be seen from the hides and observation hut.

Horsey. Horsey Mere is about a mile up Meadow Dyke from Heigham Sound, and at the eastern end stands the four-storey Horsey Windpump. Owned by the National Trust, this most impressive landmark affords some fine views across the marshes.

THE WAVENEY

The Waveney is the most southerly of the main Broads rivers, and much of its course forms the boundary between Norfolk and Suffolk. The limit of navigation is Geldeston Lock, west of Beccles, and the river discharges into the sea at two points: at Lowestoft via Oulton Broad, and at Great Yarmouth via Breydon Water. The New Cut between St Olaves and Reedham provides a short cut between the Yare and the Waveney.

Beccles. In the days when the wherries plied their way up and down the rivers transporting goods from the sea ports or from one town to another, Beccles was a thriving port. Now the traffic all goes by road, evidenced by the fact that there are main roads leading directly to Yarmouth, Lowestoft, Norwich, Thetford and Ipswich. Despite the heavy traffic, this attractive old market town is still a good place to visit. The church has a separate tower, 92ft high, with some superb views out over the surrounding marshes. The church's main claim to fame is that Nelson's parents were married there. Beccles and District Museum on Newgate has a nineteenth-century printing press, farm implements and other local history exhibits.

Burgh St Peter. Travellers on the Waveney cannot fail to notice the striking church out in the marshes on a bend in the river, looking like a pile of children's building blocks placed one on top of the other. Overlooking Oulton Broad, the church, with its sixteenth-century tower, has an even older thatched nave which is unusually narrow.

Oulton Broad. Connected to the Waveney by Oulton Dyke, this is like an overgrown boating pond. Next door to the seaside resort of Lowestoft, Oulton Broad attracts vast numbers of sailing vessels and motor boats, and is also the scene of powerboat racing. Like its neighbour, it has suffered at the hands of commercialisation.

Somerleyton. The Waveney passes close by this attractive Victorian estate village, with red brick cottages grouped around the green. Somerleyton Hall dates back to Jacobean times, although extensively rebuilt in 1846 by Sir Samuel Peto, who had made his fortune out of the railways. The mansion has some lavishly furnished state rooms, and the gardens include a maze.

St Olaves. A popular place for mooring, St Olaves has the remains of a thirteenth-century priory, notable for its early fourteenth-century undercroft, a very early brick construction. Just down the road lies Fritton Lake, also known as Fritton Decoy, harking back to its

Thurne Dyke windpump

A typical Broadland scene on the River Thurne

wildfowling days. Now it is a country park, with lakeside gardens, woodland walks and a picnic area, together with opportunities for boating and fishing on the three-mile-long lake.

Burgh Castle. In Roman times the waterways of Broadland were far more extensive than they are today; what is now flat marshland was then under the sea. The fort of *Gariannonum* was built on the banks of the vast estuary, with the town of Caister on the opposite bank. Now all that remains of this huge river is Breydon Water. The ruins of the castle stand at the southern end, where the rivers Waveney and Yare come together.

The view out across the marshes is quite impressive, with Berney Arms Mill and Halvergate marshes on the opposite bank. While the mudflats of Breydon Water present a challenge to the inexperienced pleasure-boat sailor, they are the home of many species of waterfowl and seabirds.

THE YARE

The river which gave Great Yarmouth its name, the Yare, rises in Norwich, with only two broads: Rockland and Surlingham, in its vicinity. The largest of the Broadland rivers, the Yare supports a healthy traffic in sea-going cargo ships sailing between Yarmouth and Norwich. But there is plenty of room for all, with care.

Berney Arms. Just upstream from the point where the Yare flows into Breydon Water, Berney Arms is the first safe place for pleasure boats to moor after running the tidal gauntlet of Breydon. The Berney Arms is probably one of the least accessible public houses by land, with no roads, only a half mile walk across the fields from the railway halt. While boating holidaymakers may enjoy the exclusivity of the Berney Arms, it is something of a pity that the tallest of the Broadland drainage mills shares the same isolation. The Berney Arms Mill has been restored to complete working order, and houses an exhibition on windmills.

Reedham. Traditionally the seat of the East Anglian martyr King Edmund, who was killed by the Danes in 870 for refusing to renounce Christianity, but now more well known for its chain-ferry (which operates every day between 8am and 10pm), Reedham provides the only crossing over the Yare between Norwich and Yarmouth. Driven by a diesel engine, the ferry clanks across the river, pulling itself along the chains.

Just up-river from Reedham is the mouth of the River Chet.

Places of Interest on the Broads

Beeston Hall
Beeston St Lawrence, near
Wroxham
Flint-faced Georgian country house
with classical interiors.

Broadland Conservation Centre
Ranworth
Exhibition about Broadland and its
ecology. Bird watching gallery with
binoculars and telescopes.

Stracey Arms Windpump
3 miles south-east of Acle on A47
Fully restored drainage pump
containing exhibition of photographs depicting the history of
Broadland windpumps.

St Benet's Abbey
near Ludham
Ruins of monastery established
1,000 years ago by King Canute.
Remains of windmill built into
gatehouse.

**Norfolk Wildfowl Conservation
Centre**
Dilham, 5 miles south-east of North
Walsham
17 acres of lakes, streams and
marshes with around 120 species
of ducks, geese and swans.

Boardman's Mill
How Hill, near Ludham
Open-framed timber trestle
windpump in grounds of How Hill
residential education centre.

Toad Hole Cottage
How Hill, near Ludham
Marshman's cottage, once the
home of an eel catcher.

Horsey Windpump
(National Trust)
Horsey, near Winterton
Four storeys high, with good views
across the marshes.

Thurne Dyke Windpump
Thurne
Fully restored windpump with small
exhibition of photographs of
Broadland windpumps.

Wherry Albion
Ludham
The last trading wherry. Visits only
by prior arrangement.

Somerleyton Hall
5 miles north-west of Lowestoft
Jacobean house, completely rebuilt
in the last century in Anglo-Italian
style, with splendidly furnished
panelled rooms. Gardens, including
maze.

St Olaves Priory
(English Heritage)
near Beccles
Early fourteenth-century undercroft
with brick-vaulted ceiling.

Burgh Castle
(English Heritage)
near Great Yarmouth
Ruins of Roman fort overlooking
the Waveney at its outfall into
Breydon Water.

Berney Arms Mill
(English Heritage)
near Reedham
The tallest marsh mill on the
Norfolk Broads. Exhibition on
Norfolk windmills.

Pettits of Reedham
Camp Hill, Reedham
Aviary of rare pheasants, ornamental birds and waterfowl. Feathercraft and taxidermy workshops.

Strumpshaw Hall Steam Museum
Strumpshaw
Collection of steam vehicles
including pumps, wagons, engines
and tractors.

Hardley Cross stands here, marking the boundary of jurisdiction between Norwich and Great Yarmouth.

THE CHET

As the Chet is navigable for only three-and-a-half miles to Loddon and Chedgrave, it makes more sense to explore it before continuing the journey up the Yare to Norwich.

Loddon. The Chet winds through wooded countryside and marshes, the bridge which forms the boundary between Loddon and Chedgrave being its navigable head. Once a port for the wherries carrying their cargoes from one Broadland town to another, Loddon is a pretty market town which has retained an 'olde worlde' atmosphere. The fifteenth-century church contains a painting of Sir James Hobart and his wife. Sir James, Attorney General to Henry VII, was responsible for the building of the church.

Back on the Yare is **Cantley**, two miles up river from the mouth of the Chet. It was here that the first sugar beet factory in the country was built in 1910. Since then, the factory has been substantially enlarged to cope with the increased modern-day demand for sugar. At **Langley** there are the remains of an old abbey, unfortunately not open to the public.

A good spot for fishing can be found at **Rockland Broad**, a small reed-fringed stretch of water, reached from the Yare by one of two dykes.

Surlingham. Surlingham Broad is the biggest of a group of small broads linked together by a series of waterways. The lesser broads are not open to navigation, and the whole swamp-like area forms a nature reserve owned by the Norfolk Naturalists Trust.

Thorpe. Just under two miles up river is Bramerton Wood's End, a secluded public house on the wooded bank of the Yare. There are plenty of moorings here, either alongside the common, a short distance downstream, or at the public house itself. Past the sailing clubs of Whitlingham is Thorpe, a suburb of Norwich. Thorpe village itself is on the Old River. In 1844 a new cut was dug from one corner of the loop in the river to the other. The New Cut improved the passage of commercial ships heading for Norwich, which previously had to negotiate two railway bridges.

5
THE SUFFOLK COAST

Rich in natural beauty and wildlife, and steeped in history, the
Suffolk coast, stretching from Lowestoft to Felixstowe, offers a
variety of landscapes from eroding cliffs to steep shingle beaches,
interspersed with the long, winding mudflat estuaries of the Rivers
Blyth, Alde, Ore and Deben. In the hinterland there are vast stretches
of heath and forest, all of them areas containing a number of
important nature reserves and Sites of Special Scientific Interest.
Dotted here and there are villages and towns of historical and
architectural interest. There are no amusement arcades except in
Lowestoft, in an area to be explored at a gentle pace, as befits its
character.

The Suffolk Heritage Coast

The unique and environmentally sensitive area of land stretching
from Kessingland to Felixstowe is designated a Heritage Coast, so
that the beauty of the landscape, and the abundance of wildlife can
be preserved for the enjoyment of all. New developments are carefully vetted to ensure they are not intrusive, and efforts are made to
remove existing eyesores.

Conflicts of interest arise when tourists arrive in the area during
the summer. They should follow the Country Code — perhaps a
shortened version from America: 'Leave nothing but footprints, take
nothing but photographs, kill nothing but time'. The Suffolk Heritage Coast Path is a forty-two-mile waymarked path offering walkers the best possible way of sampling the delights of the shingle
beaches, coastal marshes, woodlands and heaths. The windmill at

Thorpeness is an information centre on the Heritage Coast, and details of the coast path can also be obtained from Suffolk County Council.

Lowestoft. The most easterly town in Britain, this fishing port is also a popular holiday town, having rail links with Norwich and London. Only a stone's throw from the Broads, and at the northern tip of the Suffolk Heritage Coast, it is a good base for exploration. The beaches are sandy and safe for bathing, with the north beach at Corton designated a naturists' beach. The harbour is a bustling place, full of interest. In the summer months there are guided tours to give visitors a taste of the local fishing industry. There are also two museums with exhibitions related to the sea. The Lowestoft and East Suffolk Maritime Museum has models of fishing and commercial boats along with other maritime paraphernalia, while the Royal Naval Patrol Service Museum has model ships, uniforms and naval documents.

The next coastal village to the south of Lowestoft is Kessingland, the site of the Suffolk Wildlife and Country Park, and two miles south-west of the town are Carlton Marshes, grazing marsh and fenland with many varieties of wetland birds and plants.

Southwold. Visitors will delight in this uncommercialised seaside resort with its quaint old houses and sprawling open greens. In fact, the greens which give the town its charming character are the result of a great fire in 1659. Many of the houses destroyed were never replaced, resulting in the firebreaks which are now seven pleasant greens.

Thirteen years later saw the Battle of Sole Bay, one of Southwold's claims to fame. During the Anglo-Dutch wars, the British fleet of seventy-one ships lay at anchor off Southwold, with the allied French fleet. Many of the sailors were ashore, celebrating Whit Sunday, when the Dutch fleet was spotted approaching from the south. The French wasted no time in beating a hasty retreat, leaving the British to face the attack alone. The people of Southwold lined the cliff-tops to watch the carnage of the vicious and bloody battle being waged offshore. There were no real victors; thousands were killed and wounded, but only ten years later the tables were reversed. England had a Dutch king, and the two nations were fighting together, this time against the French! Southwold Museum has exhibits associated with the battle, along with displays on local history and the old Southwold railway.

One of the greens leads to Gun Hill, where six eighteen-pounder cannons stand on the cliff-top facing the sea. Presented to the town in 1745, they were cast in Elizabethan times and had changed hands in several battles before the Duke of Cumberland captured them at Culloden. They were buried for a while during World War I, after the Germans bombarded Southwold from the sea, claiming it to be a fortified position.

From any point in Southwold the white lighthouse can be seen ❋ looming above the roof-tops. Not far away is the Mecca for all local beer drinkers: Adnams brewery. Southwold Harbour stands on the River Blyth, about one mile south of the town, and just across the river lies the village of Walberswick. To reach it on foot is not too strenuous, just where the river joins Buss Creek (which effectively makes Southwold an island) there is a footbridge, or one can take the rowing-boat ferry across the river from the harbour. Motorists must take a longer route, about nine miles, via Blythburgh.

Walberswick. Rather detached as a village, Walberswick stands amidst marshes and heath, flanked by a broad shingle beach. It is a delightful place, and much favoured by local artists. Of the many pleasant walks in the area, one of four miles starts from the car park 🚶 opposite Southwold Harbour, following the river wall inland to the footbridge. Turn left onto the tarmac cycle track, and follow its path through gorse bushes until it curves to the left, as a bridlepath forks off to the right. The gorse gives way to heath, and after about three-quarters of a mile, the path comes to the B1387. Turn right here, and a couple of hundred yards down the road, take the bridleway on the left, keeping to the left of a small pine wood. The path crosses a minor road and heads for another clump of trees called Hoist Covert. Either follow the path along the wood, leading back to the road which leads into Walberswick, or take the footpath to the right just before the trees. This leads out into the marshes, heading for a windmill. Turn left here, following the path beside the dyke for half a mile, where it turns left onto a small road leading back to the village.

Blythburgh. There is much to suggest that Blythburgh was quite an important place in bygone times. Now a small village on the A12, it was once a thriving port. In the same way as many other river ports, it lost trade when its waterways could no longer cope with the increasing draughts of cargo ships. The 83ft church tower presents an imposing picture from across the marshes, even more so at night, when it is floodlit, and visible for miles. The White Hart Inn, once a

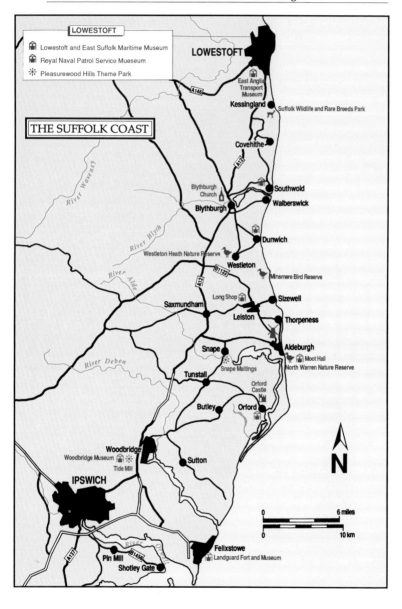

LOWESTOFT

- Lowestoft and East Suffolk Maritime Museum
- Royal Naval Patrol Service Mueseum
- Pleasurewood Hills Theme Park

THE SUFFOLK COAST

LOWESTOFT

East Anglia Transport Museum

Kessingland — Suffolk Wildlife and Rare Breeds Park

Covehithe

Blythburgh Church

Southwold
Walberswick

Blythburgh

River Waveney

River Blyth

Dunwich

Westleton Heath Nature Reserve

Westleton

Minsmere Bird Reserve

River Alde

Long Shop

Sizewell

Saxmundham

Leiston

Thorpeness

Snape

Aldeburgh

Moot Hall

Snape Maltings

North Warren Nature Reserve

River Deben

Tunstall

Orford Castle

Butley

Orford

N

Woodbridge

Woodbridge Museum
Tide Mill

Sutton

IPSWICH

| 0 | 6 miles |
| 0 | 10 km |

Pin Mill

Felixstowe
Landguard Fort and Museum

Shotley Gate

Thorpeness windmill, now an information centre

courthouse, with its Dutch gables and moulded ceilings, is also worth seeing.

Dunwich. Once a great city whose fortunes depended on the all-powerful sea, Dunwich has existed for hundreds of years, but floods and drifting shingle banks spelt the end for it as a port. The ever-encroaching sea nibbled away at the town in successive floods, the last medieval church disappearing into the sea at the beginning of this century.

In the seventh century, Dunwich was the centre of Christianity in East Anglia, when St Felix was installed as the first bishop. Even after the Danish invasion, when the cathedral was moved to North Elmham, Dunwich remained an important port.

By the fourteenth century the harbour was silting up and the cliffs were being eroded by the sea. One historian dates the beginning of the end as 1286, when a violent storm caused considerable damage. By 1342, four hundred houses had been lost. Two hundred years later, three-quarters of the town and the all-important harbour had slipped beneath the waves. Finally, a savage storm in 1739 swept away the majority of what had survived of the town, leaving just a few houses, and its last church. Over the years, the sea claimed that too, and the whole fascinating history is related in Dunwich museum. That last church to go over the cliffs fell in piecemeal, and a number of old photographs and paintings show it in various stages of decay.

As you face the sea, standing on top of the cliffs, it is hard to imagine that once there was half a mile of land in front, covered with hundreds of houses, and several churches! Now all that remains is a tiny cliff-top village, where legend has it that a careful ear will discern the church bell ringing from beneath the waves. Whilst the sea has scoured most of the old remains away, divers still manage to find relics to bring to the surface.

Dunwich Heath lies south of here, 214 acres of heathland next door to the Minsmere bird reserve. It was acquired by the National Trust in 1968 with a grant from food manufacturers H.J. Heinz & Co as their contribution to 'Enterprise Neptune', the Trust's campaign to save what remains of the country's unspoilt coastline.

A very pleasant walk starts from the cliff-top car park. Head inland, past the WC block, and then left down a track to Docwra's Ditch, the boundary with the RSPB reserve. Follow the path along this ditch to the end, where the path bears away to the right. Continue straight ahead where the path crosses a track, and shortly before it comes to a dead end, bear right, uphill towards a birch wood. The marked footpath takes you to the old quarry picnic area, and on to the warden's hut. Take the path signposted towards the beach, and follow the cliff-top path back to the car park from where you started.

Bird lovers should not fail to visit the **Minsmere Reserve**. Awarded the Council of Europe Diploma in 1980, it is the flagship reserve of the Royal Society for the Protection of Birds, and internationally recognised as a model for nature conservation. Public hides are open along the beach, with free access. Entry onto the reserve itself is by permit only.

Sizewell. Not a very significant place except for a rather imposing building which dominates the skyline for miles along the coast, and an unwelcome intrusion on what is supposed to be an Area of Outstanding Natural Beauty. This is one of Britain's first Magnox nuclear power stations. Its replacement, Britain's first pressurised water reactor, an even larger blot on the landscape and currently under construction, has been and remains the subject of much controversy.

Yet oddly, the beach here is attractive to bathers, as the hot water outfall from the power station provides one section of beach with slightly warmer water. Those who indulge in this pursuit are either unaware of (or perhaps not bothered about) the fact that to expel vast quantities of water, it first has to suck it up. Water is pumped in direct from the sea, and once it has cooled the turbines, is pumped back — shredded fishes and all!

Leiston. A small town north-west of Aldeburgh, Leiston became an industrial centre at the hands of the Garrett family in the nineteenth century. The town's engineering industry dates back to the Industrial Revolution, and the Long Shop, built in 1853, was a pioneer design for the manufacture and assembly of steam traction engines using production line techniques. The Long Shop is now a museum housing relics of the Richard Garrett Engineering Works, including steam engines, threshing machines, a trolley bus and two fire engines.

The carpentry of the roof of the church is a masterpiece of Victorian ingenuity, a product of the eccentric architect E.B. Lamb, who was also responsible for Eye town hall. North of the town are the flint and brick ruins of the fourteenth-century Leiston Abbey. Of the church, only the Lady Chapel remains as a complete building, a result of its usefulness for storing grain after the Dissolution.

Snape. The village of Snape lies to the north of the River Alde and, like Aldeburgh, had something of a tradition for smuggling. Just

The rowing-boat ferry across the River Blyth at Walberswick

The Suffolk coast is popular with anglers

Suffolk's many coastal paths are popular with both walkers and cyclists

outside the village is the site of a burial ship, similar to the one at Sutton Hoo.

To the south of the village, on the River Alde, is the nineteenth-century industrial complex, now a concert hall known as Snape Maltings. Opened in 1967 and famous the world over as the home of Benjamin Britten's Aldeburgh Festival, the hall suffered a setback in 1969 when it was completely gutted by fire on the first night of the festival. Completely restored within a year, the Maltings also house an art gallery and craft shop, as well as offering activity holidays which make full use of the surrounding countryside.

Thorpeness. Thorpeness was originally conceived as a sort of Edwardian fantasy holiday village in 1910 by the estate owner, Mr Glencairn Stuart Ogilvie. It was inspired by an accident, when the Hundred River flooded producing a lake. Ogilvy decided to keep it, building his holiday village around it. While many buildings have been erected since then, the originals remain a fascinating collection of houses. The curious 'House in the Clouds' standing a short distance away is in fact a water tower. The upper part conceals the tank, while the creosoted portion below provides living accommodation.

The nearby post mill originally ground corn at Aldringham, but was moved to its present position in the 1920's to pump water into the 'House in the Clouds'. It is open to visitors, and as well as housing exhibits about the mill itself, is also an information centre for the Suffolk Heritage Coast.

Aldeburgh. Just down the coast from Thorpeness, Aldeburgh was another ancient large town to suffer at the hands of the sea. The name is Old English for Old Borough, and there is certainly much evidence to show that the Romans knew the place well. The means of prosperity changed over the years, from fishing and shipbuilding to the not-so-official business of smuggling.

Inside the timber-framed Tudor Moot Hall (moot is Old English for meeting) by the beach is a small museum with original 'before and after' maps. One shows the hall in roughly its current position, the earlier shows it standing in the middle of the town! Just south of the town stands the most northerly Martello tower in Britain, one of a line of coastal towers built in Napoleonic times against a possible French invasion.

Aldeburgh has been the home of several famous people over the ages — more recently, of course, Benjamin Britten put the town on the international musical map by instituting the annual Aldeburgh Festival. It was while Britten was in America during the last war that he read an article by E.M. Forster about the Aldeburgh poet George Crabbe. It was a turning point in his life, and he decided that Suffolk, and Aldeburgh, would provide him with the inspiration for his music.

The first Aldeburgh Festival came about in 1948, founded by Britten, the singer Peter Pears, and Eric Crozier. They had toured Europe the previous year, performing *Albert Herring* and *The Rape of Lucretia*, two operas which London, Edinburgh and Manchester had refused to support. They concluded it was time they received a better airing at home, and so decided to set up a modest festival, initially held in Aldeburgh's Jubilee Hall and various churches in the area. The festival's popularity grew to the point where a permanent home for the festival was founded at Snape Maltings.

The poet George Crabbe, whose poem about the embittered fisherman Peter Grimes inspired Britten's opera of the same name, was born in Aldeburgh in 1754, and Elizabeth Garrett Anderson, the first woman Doctor of Medicine and founder of a hospital in London, also became the first woman mayor of an English Borough when she took up office in Aldeburgh in 1908.

A five-mile walk heads north from Aldeburgh. The two-mile stretch to Thorpeness along the shingle beach can be heavy going, so an alternative is to follow the path beside the road.

Pass the Meare, follow the road round to the left signposted to Aldringham, and turn left fifty yards further on, signposted as a public footpath to the B1122. The route continues past the golf club, and onto a small footpath around the edge of the course, with a wide stream and deciduous trees to the left. The footpath comes to a group of cottages and an old level crossing. Turn left onto a woodland track, part of the old Great Eastern Saxmundham to Aldeburgh railway line.

After a slight jump sideways, the path turns to the right into the RSPB's North Warren Reserve. Carry straight on where a path goes off to the right, and as it comes out of the woods onto a heath, the path widens into a pleasant grassy lane. Turn left onto the B1122 and follow the signs back to Aldeburgh.

The River Alde almost reaches the sea at Slaughden, just south of Aldeburgh. Silting up over the ages has built up a spit of land called Orford Ness. The Alde continues its course for another eight miles,

The Tudor timber-framed Moot Hall in Aldeburgh — now houses the local museum

Aldeburgh's annual carnival

The Martello tower in Aldeburgh, one of many built around the south and east of England to guard against possible invasion by Napoleon

and is then joined by the Butley River before discharging into the sea as the River Ore at Hollesley Bay. The marshes around here are particularly favoured by birdwatchers and naturalists.

Tunstall. Between Snape and Orford lies Tunstall Forest, which, with Rendlesham and Dunwich Forests, make up the fourteen square miles of the Aldewood Forest. It is similar to Breckland in that the land was heathland with little agricultural potential when the Forestry Commission planted Scots and Corsican Pines along with Douglas Firs in the 1920s. There are several picnic areas and way-marked footpaths.

Orford. A visit to the castle can hardly be missed by visitors stopping at Orford. The great keep stands sentinel over the town, affording a superb view over what was once a thriving medieval port before the shingle bank of Orford Ness cut off direct access to the sea. Orford was important because it guarded the coast where Flemish mercenaries were brought ashore by the Earl of Norfolk, whose castles far out-numbered royal castles in East Anglia. Built by Henry II in the late 1160s, the castle has two major claims to fame. It was the first to be built with a keep which is cylindrical inside and polygonal outside, reinforced by three projecting rectangular turrets. Secondly, it is the oldest castle for whose building there exists documentary evidence, in the form of the Pipe Rolls, the financial records of the King's exchequer.

Legend has it that a naked, wild man was caught in the nets by local fishermen, who took him to the castle. The merman would not speak, despite torture, and showed no sign of reverence when taken into the church. He was taken to the harbour where he was made to swim about, flanked by nets suspended from floating lines. The merman's captors underestimated his capabilities, and he dived beneath the nets, and made good his escape to sea.

Of the land opposite, only Havergate Island, an RSPB reserve, is accessible, to those who have a permit. It is interesting to note that the lagoon at the southern end of the island originally developed during the last war as a result of its use as an artillery range. One of the shells damaged the sluices controlling the water level: now it is a breeding ground for avocets. The spit beyond is owned by the Ministry of Defence. Orford Ness was used by Robert Watson-Watt for radar research during World War II.

Woodbridge. Standing near the head of the River Deben, Wood-bridge was once a thriving commercial port. Now it is a busy centre for sailing enthusiasts. The town traces its history back to Roman times, but it was not until the Middle Ages that it became a major port. A wealth of interesting buildings dating back to the fifteenth century include the Shire Hall, Friends' Meeting House, and St Mary's Church. On the river bank a tide mill stands alongside boatyards and a marina. A mill has stood here since the twelfth century, and the present one, probably built during the seventeenth century, continued working until 1956 when the shaft of the water-wheel broke. Careful restoration has returned the mill to working condition. The principle on which it works is the same as any other watermill, except here the driving force comes from a pond filled twice a day by the tide. Another mill can be found on Burkitt Road. Buttrums Mill is a fully restored six-storey tower mill which was originally built in 1835. Those interested in local history should visit Woodbridge Museum on Market Hill, which also houses an exhibition on the Sutton Hoo ship burial.

One of Woodbridge's more notable inhabitants was Edward FitzGerald, the poet who translated *The Rubaiyat of Omar Khayyam* into English.

Butley. Although now a private house, the twelfth-century gate-house to Butley Priory is a most interesting building. Built by Ranulf de Glanville, a crusader, the gatehouse is all that remains of a great priory, and is a superb example of East Anglian flint flushwork. Not far from Butley is Staverton Thicks, an ancient forest of stunted oaks with dense undergrowth. It is reputed to have been planted by Druids or monks who were permitted to take only one crop from the land.

Sutton Hoo. About three miles north-west of Butley is the village of Rendlesham, not very significant now save for the close proximity of a USAF base on the edge of the forest. It has been established that the first Scandinavian kings of East Anglia, of the Wuffinga Dynasty, set up their Great Hall here. Nothing remains to be seen, although their burial site at Sutton Hoo has produced some spectacular finds.

The hillside facing the Deben Estuary contains a number of burial mounds, some of which were found to have human remains. The biggest of all, excavated in 1939, contained an 89ft ship filled with priceless treasures, as befitting the burial of an important Saxon chieftain. He is thought to be Raedwald, the king of the East Angles, who died in AD625. Undisputedly the largest archaeological find in the country to date, the treasures, including a gold mounted harp, an

The keep of Orford Castle stands guard over the town

An unusual sight — a thatched church near Orford

Orford

Places to Visit on the Suffolk Coast

Lowestoft Maritime Museum
Whapload Road
Models of fishing and commercial boats and other items of maritime interest.

Royal Naval Patrol Service Museum
Sparrows Nest, Lowestoft
Model ships, uniforms and naval documents.

Suffolk Wildlife and Country Park
Kessingland, on the A12 south of Lowestoft
Collection of animals, birds and reptiles.

Southwold Museum
Exhibits depicting local history etc.

Walberswick Heritage Coast Centre
1½ miles south-west of South-wold.

Dunwich Museum
4 miles south-west of Southwold
Exhibits chronicling the gradual disappearance of the town.

Minsmere (RSPB)
near Dunwich

1,500 acres of marsh, heath and woodland, rich in birdlife. Free access to public hides along the beach.

Leiston Abbey
(English Heritage)
Remains of fourteenth-century abbey.

Thorpeness Windmill
Heritage Coast Centre
Working mill containing exhibits on the village and the Suffolk Coast.

Snape Maltings
Beside the River Alde, south of Snape on the B1069.
Concert hall, home of the Aldeburgh Festival.

Moot Hall
Aldeburgh
Fifteenth-century building used for council meetings, containing museum of local history.

Orford Castle
(English Heritage)
Unique castle built by Henry II.

Landguard Fort Museum
Off Carr Road, Felixstowe
Exhibits depicting history of the fort.

iron battle standard and numerous gold brooches and other jewellery, are now in the British Museum, although some replicas are on show in the Ipswich Museum. Excavation of the site by a team from Birmingham University continues, and during the summer season it is possible to join guided tours of the dig.

Felixstowe. At the tip of the peninsula, with the Rivers Stour and Orwell on one side, and the Deben on the other, this town is a bustling seaside resort and container port. On South Hill is the Q Tower, a Martello tower built as part of the coastal defences against possible French invasion. Visitors can look at an exhibition and enjoy refreshments here. Also of interest is the Landguard Fort Museum on View Point Road which has exhibitions depicting the history of the fort. Further north, between Felixstowe and Ipswich, are some excellent stretches of marsh and heath suitable for walking.

THE SHOTLEY PENINSULA

This is the tapered spit of land between the Rivers Orwell and Stour, and the parts bordering both estuaries are designated Areas of Outstanding Natural Beauty. On a peninsula there is usually a good view of the sea. On Shotley however, even if you stand at the tip, only the encircling arms of the Felixstowe and Tendring peninsulas to the north and south respectively will be seen, with sea-going ships setting off from the ports of Harwich and Felixstowe, and down-river from Ipswich.

Pin Mill is on the north coast of the peninsula about halfway along, and a dead end for cars. To reach it, turn off at Chelmondiston, and there is a panorama of the Orwell estuary. There are some marvellous walks to be enjoyed along the river bank in both directions, but the vicinity of Pin Mill is very popular in the summer months. The place is much frequented by yachtsmen, attracted by the old-world charm of the Butt and Oyster pub.

Shotley is steeped in naval tradition, the home of the former HMS *Ganges*, the Royal Navy's training school. This shore establishment gave its young recruits a stiff taste of discipline to fit them for their careers in the navy. Each boy would be required to climb the 150ft high mast from HMS *Cordelia*, and every year cadets at the passing out ceremony had to climb the rigging, the pride of place going to the 'button boy', who perched on the eleven inch diameter top of the mast.

Shotley Gate is an interesting spot to spend a few hours. Drive as far as the road allows, and come to the water front; HMS *Ganges* is on the left, and straight ahead all the comings and goings of ships across the estuary can be seen: yet with only a few minutes walk in either direction, you can be alone beside the river estuary in very beautiful surroundings. **Erwarton** is a small village not far from Shotley,

Woodbridge, a busy centre for sailing enthusiasts — the restored tide mill in the background

Woodbridge has many interesting buildings, such as the Shire Hall on Market Hill

overlooking the Stour estuary. The church here has a casket reputed to contain the heart of Anne Boleyn.

Moving inland along the Stour estuary, is **Holbrook**, and the 198ft-high clock tower of the Royal Hospital School. About two miles away to the north-west, on the other side of Alton Reservoir, is **Tattingstone**, which as well as its medieval church, has the Tattingstone Wonder. This is a group of three cottages with a mock tower at one end, and the whole affair looks like a church. It was built by a squire who said his neighbours used to wonder at nothing — this certainly gave them something to wonder at!

6

IPSWICH AND INLAND SUFFOLK

M any people tend to draw a comparison between Ipswich and Norwich as the major towns in their respective counties. Although both are founded on ancient communities, as a port Ipswich is more important than Norwich. Situated at the head of the Orwell Estuary, even as far back as the seventh century Ipswich was not merely a trading port, it was already the biggest in the country. Known then as *Gippeswic*, this Anglo-Saxon port survived many Viking raids, and by the beginning of the thirteenth century its status was confirmed with its first charter, awarded by King John. The basic street pattern of the town centre is still that of the medieval town, including a fine range of buildings dating from the fifteenth century onwards. Like Norwich, Ipswich was once surrounded by a wall, a legacy of which can be found in many of the street names, such as Westgate and Northgate.

In Georgian times the town suffered a commercial decline, but its prosperity was restored by the Industrial Revolution, evidenced by the large number of nineteenth-century houses. Today Ipswich is an industrial and commercial centre as well as an important port, despite the presence of the two major ports of Harwich and Felixstowe only ten miles away at the mouth of the Orwell.

A very good Town Trail Guide is available from the Tourist Information Centre. The following walk takes in the essential elements of the route, which is signposted at various points by black-and-white Town Trail signs.

The Cornhill was once the market place of the town, as well as the site where several 'heretics' were burned at the stake. The walk starts along Westgate Street, where the former West Gate once stood, part of the town's wall which was pulled down two hundred years ago. Although the wall existed in medieval times, there are no remains now. Turn left into Museum Street, where you can escape the bustle of one of the main shopping streets and enter the nineteenth-century charm of the town's business world. The building on the corner of Arcade Street was once the museum which gave the street its name — now it is a shop and dancing school.

The fifteenth-century St Mary Elms Church stands at the junction of Museum Street with Elm Street. Behind the church is a cottage standing in a row of old buildings, built over five hundred years ago and probably the oldest inhabited building in Ipswich. Continuing down Museum Street and past the junction of Princes Street, one faces an imposing space-age office building of international insurance brokers. This reflective glass-walled building with roof-top gardens, designed by Norman Foster, also responsible for Norwich's Sainsbury Centre, has been hailed internationally as a masterpiece of modern architecture. Turn left down Friars Street, along one side of the building, and right to follow the next side.

To the left, in contrast to its next-door neighbour, is the Unitarian Meeting House, built about 1700. Inside, four great wooden pillars, said to be from ships' masts, form part of the structure, while the carved pulpit is quite probably the work of Grinling Gibbons. It is likely that this building was one of the first purpose-built nonconformists chapels, the Toleration Act having been passed only ten years previously.

The footpath meets Franciscan Way; there a left turn brings one to St Nicholas Street, with its line of sixteenth- and seventeenth-century timber-framed shops. The official trail turns left here, but fifty yards away, on the corner where St Nicholas Street is joined by Silent Street, stands a magnificent group of Tudor houses with a carved corner post. Cardinal Wolsey is reputed to have been born in this area, and a plaque on one of the houses commemorates this.

Returning to St Nicholas Street and towards the town centre is another attractive line of old shops, two of which used to be the manse, or minister's house, of the Unitarian Meeting House on the other side. Cross the junction with Falcon Street and Friars Street, and continue along Queen Street. Ahead is the old Corn Exchange, a solid and elaborate Victorian building which has only outlived its

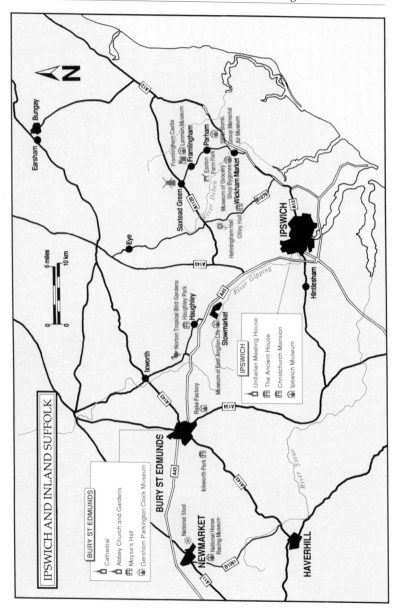

IPSWICH AND INLAND SUFFOLK

N

6 miles
10 km

Bungay

Earsham

A12

Eye

Framlingham Castle
Lanman Museum
Framlingham
Parham
Saxtead Green
Easton
Farm Park
A120
River Deben
Museum of Grocery
Shop Bygones
Wickham Market
Otley Hall
Helmingham Hall
B1079

390th Bomb
Group Memorial
Air Museum

IPSWICH

A12

A140

A14

River Gipping

Hintlesham

Norton Tropical Bird Gardens
Haughley Park
Haughley
Museum of East Anglian Life
Stowmarket

IPSWICH
Unitarian Meeting House
The Ancient House
Christchurch Mansion
Ipswich Museum

Ixworth

A143

Rake Factory

A134

BURY ST EDMUNDS

Ickworth Park

A45

A14

A1141

River Stour

HAVERHILL

BURY ST EDMUNDS
Cathedral
Abbey Church and Gardens
Moyse's Hall
Gershom Parkington Clock Museum

National Stud

NEWMARKET
National Horse
Racing Museum

B1061

A11

An archetypal English scene, Tudor houses in Silent Street, Ipswich

Christchurch Mansion, Ipswich

original function in the last ten years or so.

Take a right-hand turning here into the Buttermarket, where on the corner with St Stephens Lane stands the Ancient House. This remarkable building is over five hundred years old and the walls of its upper floors, with their bay windows, overhang the lower part. The interest of the building lies in the elaborate moulded plasterwork designs on its outer walls — it is probably the best surviving example of pargetting in Britain. The panels below the first-floor windows represent the continents of the known world at that time: Europe, Asia, Africa and America, along with the arms of Charles II (who, it is said, hid here after the Battle of Worcester) over the main doorway. The building is in use as a bookshop, and inside there are panelled rooms and ornamental ceilings.

The next stage of the Town Trail is up Dial Lane, so called because of the clock which once projected from nearby St Lawrence Church. Turn right through the churchyard, left into St Lawrence's Street, and right into Tavern Street. On the left is the Great White Horse Hotel, which despite its Georgian façade, is a timber-framed building dating back to the sixteenth century. Famous visitors have included Dickens (who wrote about it in Pickwick Papers), George II in 1736, Louis XVIII of France in 1807, and Lord Nelson in 1800. Opposite the hotel stands a group of buildings which appear to be Tudor, but are in fact reproductions, built in the 1930s when such imitations were in vogue. These are particularly good examples, and lend additional character to the street.

Turn left into Northgate Street and past another row of attractive old buildings to the Bethesda Church, above which peer the trees of Christchurch Park. Though not forming part of the official trail, Christchurch Mansion should be visited. Built on the site of the twelfth-century priory of the Holy Trinity, this Tudor country house is now a museum, its adjoining art gallery housing a fine collection of paintings by Constable and Gainsborough.

At the top of Northgate Street, turn left into Tower Ramparts, and left again into Tower Street. St Mary-le-Tower Church gives its name to the street, and it was in the churchyard in 1200 that the people of Ipswich were told that the town had been granted a royal charter. Coming to the junction with Tavern Street, take a final glance down Dial Lane and the Ancient House beyond. Turn right up Tavern Street and back to the Cornhill.

There are, of course, places not included in this walk around the town which are well worth visiting. Down St Nicholas Street and St Peter's Street towards the docks is College Street, on the left. Not far down here is Wolsey's Gate, the only surviving part of Cardinal Wolsey's College of Cardinals. The building was started in 1528 and would have been quite extensive. But Wolsey fell from grace, and the building was never completed. The brick gateway, with its barely discernible royal cipher, is all that remains.

Further along College Street, and into Key Street, is the Old Customs House, overlooking the huge Wet Dock. It was the construction of this in the nineteenth century that rescued Ipswich after two centuries of commercial decline — at the time it was the largest wet dock in Europe. Just to the north of Neptune Quay is Grimwade Street, and up here on the right are four sea captains' houses, sharing the longest carved bressumer beam in existence.

BEYOND IPSWICH
Wickham Market. About six miles north of Woodbridge, Wickham Market lies just off the A12, near the River Deben. In the High Street is the unusual Museum of Grocery Shop Bygones, a grocery shop museum with eighteenth-century fittings and old grocery curiosities including a collection of chocolate moulds. Not far away is Easton Farm Park. The attractions of the Victorian farmstead include a dairy and vintage farm machinery. At Letheringham, an early eighteenth-century watermill survives on the River Deben, still in working order and set in four acres of gardens.

Parham. This is a pleasant village three miles south-east of Framlingham, with a thatched vicarage and a sixteenth-century hall (now used as a farm) enclosed by a moat and jealously guarded by a family of ducks.

Framlingham. This interesting town, full of buildings with character, is best known for its castle, built in 1190 by the famous Bigod family, and one of the first castles not to include a keep. Instead it has thirteen separate towers linked by a curtain wall, a Saracen idea brought back by returning crusaders. While all but one of the buildings enclosed by the walls are now gone, the walls and towers of the castle are well preserved, and it is possible to take a spiral staircase up one of the towers and walk right around the top of the walls to enjoy magnificent views across the countryside. The red brick Tudor chimneys which adorn most of the towers are rather whimsical additions — the majority of them are dummies!

*Wickham Market
church*

In the seventeenth century it made a transition in use from castle and prison to a poor house and school, the consequence of the bequest of the castle to Cambridge's Pembroke College, on the condition that a poor house should be built within the castle walls.

It was at Framlingham in 1553 that Mary Tudor organised her army of supporters to march on Lady Jane Grey, and here, later, she proclaimed herself queen. Surprisingly, the castle is built of limestone in an area with no local supply. The stone was brought by sea from Northamptonshire, and up the River Ore to Framlingham. (It is worth noting that the vast majority of major medieval stone buildings in East Anglia were built for this very reason on a river or canal with access to the sea.)

Not far from Framlingham is **Brandeston**, where you can visit the Priory Vineyards winery. Here they produce fine English wines made from Muller-Thürgau and Schönburger grapes. Their emblem, a sort of linocut picture featuring a man hanging from a gibbet, is based on a little local history. In 1646 John Lowes, the vicar of Brandeston, was hanged at the age of 90 for witchcraft, sent to the gallows by Mathew Hopkin, the Witchfinder General.

Saxtead Green. Well known for its eighteenth-century post mill, so-called because it was built on a single pivot post and balanced by wheels running around a circular track, similar to the mill at Thorpeness. The mill has two pairs of stones, and a fantail which keeps the mill into the wind, and was working regularly until 1947.

Heveningham Hall. While many stately homes have undergone a great deal of change since their original conception, Heveningham Hall has stayed almost the same as it was when it was built in the latter part of the eighteenth century. The interiors were designed by James Wyatt, its furniture designed to match the mood of each room. The park and gardens were laid out by Capability Brown.

Bungay. A prosperous town in times past. The rather odd name

Framlingham Castle with its flint towers and red-brick decorative chimneys

is probably derived from *bongue*, a good ford, or *le bon eye*, a spit of land thrusting out into a river. Trading wherries used to sail through Geldeston Lock near Beccles (now the limit of navigation), up the Waveney as far as Bungay. Certainly it was an important crossing point for the Romans — Stane Street ran right through here to *Venta Icenorum*, the town just south of present day Norwich.

Bungay was another seat of the powerful Bigod family. Roger Bigod's son Hugh rebelled against Henry II in 1174, and was ordered to dismantle his newly constructed keep as a forfeit. But Hugh paid a fine instead, and Henry spared the castle. Even today there is evidence as to how close the demolition came before Hugh paid the ransom. Under one corner of the keep is a mine gallery, part of the demolition process, whereby the walls are undermined. Wooden props holding up the stonework would be set on fire at the appropriate time, causing the walls above to collapse. As it was, the defiance did not stop there. The children's rhyme had Sir Hugh singing:

> 'Now that I am in my castle of Bungay
> Upon the River Waveney
> I will ne care for the King of Cockney.'

What remains of the castle is nothing more than ruins, with just two towers and some walls left standing. As with many such buildings, when it fell into disuse the local inhabitants took the opportunity to remove stones — scarce in East Anglia — for more pressing building needs!

The lamp post at the centre of the market square sports a weather-vane depicting Black Shuck, East Anglia's resident phantom hound, which made an appearance here one dark storm-whipped Sunday in 1577, causing terrible chaos in the church. There have been regular sightings of Shuck throughout the region over the centuries, and indeed he provided Conan Doyle with the inspiration for his Sherlock Holmes classic *The Hound of the Baskervilles*.

Bungay has a long tradition as a printing town, an industry which began here at the end of the eighteenth century. The first edition of *Alice in Wonderland* was printed here.

Just across the river, in Norfolk, is **Earsham**, where the Otter Trust runs a unique and very successful programme of breeding otters and releasing them into the wild where the right conditions prevail.

Eye. The tall flush-work church tower was described by Pevsner as 'one of the wonders of Suffolk'. In the porch, you can find a red brick dole table, used to distribute charitable gifts of bread to the poor. The town oozes character from every corner — the fine half-timbered sixteenth-century guildhall, ancient houses and pubs, and crinkle crankle walls. These are brick walls, built in corrugations, thus obviating the need for reinforcing piers required every so often along straight walls. The result is just as sturdy, and much more attractive.

The railway between Stowmarket and Norwich, opened in 1849, and now part of the main line between Norwich and London, was originally planned to have gone through Eye. But the local squires refused to have it cutting through their land, and the line went to Diss instead.

Ixworth. Not to be confused with Ickworth! Ixworth Abbey near the edge of Breckland, has stood since the twelfth century. When Henry VIII married Anne Boleyn, he built the Palace of Nonsuch to impress her. In order to build it where he wanted, he had to move the Coddingtons, the existing owners, and gave them Ixworth Abbey in exchange, recently vacated as a result of his Dissolution. Financial constraints on successive families living here have resulted in some interesting modifications to the buildings, and it is these which give the place its charm. The fourteenth-century church contains the tomb of Richard Coddington.

Bury St Edmunds. The only cathedral town in Suffolk, Bury lies in the western reaches of the county, about fifteen miles south of Thetford. A monastery was set up here in the seventh century, when the place was an Anglo-Saxon settlement called *Beodricksworth*. The present name arose from the savage murder of the young East Anglian King Edmund at the hands of the Danes. Several years after his martyrdom his body was brought to St Edmundsbury, where the shrine, and the abbey which rose around it, became a place of pilgrimage, and several miracles are said to have taken place here. Very little remains of the original abbey today, although the lines of the walls amongst the ruins in the abbey gardens may be seen.

The best place to start an exploration of Bury is Angel Hill, bordered to the east by the abbey precincts and dominated on the opposite side by the Angel Hotel, an old coaching inn which gave its name to this open space and which was immortalised by Charles Dickens in *Pickwick Papers*. To the south is the Athenaeum, a splendid white Assembly House of the early eighteenth century. All in all,

The centre of Bury St Edmunds

Angel Hill is a most imposing 'square', marred only by the clutter of parked cars.

The abbey gardens can be reached from Angel Hill by going through the enormous Abbey Gate, which once led into the monastery courtyard. When it was built it was intended for defence. (An earlier gateway had been destroyed by the townsfolk during an uprising against the harsh rule of the abbey.) Through the gateway the River Lark is straight in front across the gardens. To the right lie the ruins of the abbey church. The site of the high altar was excavated to the original floor level by the Department of the Environment, and there is a plaque commemorating an important historical event.

The thirteenth-century English barons believed in certain principles of government, and had drawn up a charter which they wanted King John to ratify. On 20 November 1214, they met at the abbey church in secret and swore an oath to compel the king to sign, by force if necessary. They chose to meet here, at an important place of pilgrimage, and hoped that their assembly would go unnoticed. The king signed on 12 June of the following year, at Runnymede, and the Magna Carta has formed the basis of government of this country, and all others believing in the authority of freedom under law, ever since.

The west front is the largest surviving portion of the abbey church. The feudal oppression of the abbey over hundreds of years fired a deep-rooted hatred in the common folk, and the Dissolution in the sixteenth century brought about the destruction of most of the abbey buildings. Much was dismantled for building materials, evidence of which can be found in other parts of the town. The dwelling houses which were built into the surviving rubble of the west front are still inhabited.

Across the courtyard from the west front is the Norman tower. Built by Abbot Anselm in the twelfth century, the tower was originally the great gateway to the abbey church. Now it houses the bells of the Cathedral Church of St James, which stands adjacent. The church dates back to the sixteenth century, when it replaced the earlier one built on the same site by Abbot Anselm, becoming the

St Edmundsbury Cathedral

Cathedral Church of the Diocese of St Edmundsbury and Ipswich in 1914.

Looking south across this precinct, you can see the Chapel of the Charnel, an early fourteenth-century building with a crypt, and beyond it, St Mary's Church, a fifteenth-century building which is the burial place of Mary Tudor, sister of Henry VIII. It is particularly noted for its decorated 'Angel Roof' nave. The west end of the church opens out onto Crown Street, which runs south from Angel Hill. Facing the very end of this road, on its junction with Westgate Street, is the Theatre Royal, one of only three surviving Regency theatres in the country. It was built in 1819 by William Wilkins, architect of the National Gallery. With many of its Georgian features still intact, it is now in the care of the National Trust. The theatre is famous as being the scene of the world premiere of *Charley's Aunt*, in 1892.

The street layout in Bury owes its planning to Abbot Baldwin, who designed the grid system along the lines of Roman towns. Abbeygate Street, the central shopping street leading from Angel Hill, has an interesting variety of shop fronts. Right is the Buttermarket, with stalls on market days (Wednesdays and Saturdays), and ahead stands Moyse's Hall, a twelfth-century building made of flint and stone, and now the Borough Museum.

Moyse's Hall, probably the oldest Norman domestic building surviving in East Anglia, has had an interesting and varied history. Although its original purpose is somewhat uncertain, it is known that the hall served as an inn, a house of correction and a police station before being taken over as a museum in 1899. Across the Cornhill stands the Market Cross, an old building remodelled in the eighteenth century by Robert Adam, formerly the Town Hall, and now an art gallery.

Cupola House is just around the corner, down the Traverse which runs parallel with the Buttermarket. Built in 1693, this fine old inn is reputed to have entertained the author Daniel Defoe. Also in the Traverse is the Nutshell, one of the smallest public houses in England. Along the Traverse, the Corn Exchange is passed on the right. At the top of Abbeygate Street, Guildhall Street on the left contains the medieval Guildhall. A mid-thirteenth-century doorway graces the inner entrance arch of this meeting hall, although much of the rest of the building has been modernised over several centuries.

Further down Guildhall Street, turn left onto Churchgate Street (parallel with Abbeygate Street), and nearly halfway down on the

Places of Interest in Inland Suffolk

Ancient House
Ipswich
Building over 500 years old with elaborate moulded plasterwork designs on its outer walls.

Christchurch Mansion
Ipswich
A Tudor country house, built on the site of a twelfth-century priory. Now a museum, with an adjoining art gallery housing a fine collection of paintings by Constable and Gainsborough.

Haughley Park
4 miles north-west of Stowmarket just off the A45.
Jacobean manor house set in parklands.

Ickworth Park (National Trust)
Horringer, 3 miles south-west of Bury St Edmunds on A143.
Palladian house comprising rotunda and flanking curved wings.

Helmingham Hall Gardens
4 miles south of Debenham on B1077.
Moated gardens, rare roses, ornamental wildfowl and Highland cattle.

Framlingham Castle
(English Heritage)
7 miles west of Saxmundham on B1119.
Castle with twelfth-century curtain walls, once the seat of the Dukes of Norfolk.

Moyse's Hall
Bury St Edmunds
Twelfth-century building of flint and stone, now a museum.

National Horse Racing Museum
Newmarket.
Subscription rooms next door to the Jockey Club, housing collection of racing exhibits including the skeleton of Eclipse, one of the original Arab stallions from which all race horses are descended.

Museum of East Anglian Life
Stowmarket.
Exhibits relating to the rural life of the area.

left is the Unitarian Chapel. Built in Wren's style in 1711, the chapel contains its original three-decker pulpit. Walking down Churchgate to the bottom leads to Chequer Square, and left onto Angel Hill.

If you have time on your hands, a visit to the Gershom Parkington Clock Museum would seem an appropriate way to pass it. It is housed in a fine Queen Anne town house, owned by the National Trust, at the corner of Angel Hill. The museum is particularly noted for its collection of seventeenth-century German clocks, seventeenth- to twentieth-century English clocks and a collection of European watches dating as far back as 1550.

There are several places within a few miles of Bury St Edmunds which are worth visiting. At Great Barton is Craft at the Suffolk Barn, consisting of crafts in a traditional Suffolk barn with the additional attraction of a herb and wild flower garden. Gifford's Hall, at Hartest off the A134, is a small country park with ten acres of vines, a winery, rare breed sheep, wild flower meadows, an organic vegetable garden and a small apiary. And at Norton Tropical Bird Gardens, seven miles east of Bury on the A1088, exotic birds can be seen throughout the year.

Newmarket. Every approach to this town passes through the surrounding heaths, where lines of slim, graceful racehorses can be seen exercising. Its main industry is racing, originally started here by Charles II (James I, his grandfather, came before him, and built the King's House here, but he was more interested in hunting). Queen Victoria's son revived the royal involvement in racing when he was

Newmarket, a Mecca for all lovers of horse racing

Ickworth, one of the many houses now owned by the National Trust

Prince of Wales, the origin of the interest in horses and racing among some members of the present Royal Family. Charles II is remembered by the name of one of the courses here, the Rowley Mile. It was as a result of his many mistresses and illegitimate children that the king himself was christened with the name of one of his stallions: Old Rowley! One of Charles's more well-known companions was Nell Gwynne, whose house still stands at 5 Palace Street.

As the headquarters of horse racing, Newmarket is home to the Jockey Club, housed in an impressive building in the High Street. The fascinating story of horse racing is told next door in the National Horse Racing Museum, whose exhibits include the skeleton of Eclipse, one of the three Arab stallions which founded the pedigree of English thoroughbreds. Today the ancestry of around ninety per cent of all British racehorses can be traced back to Eclipse.

Newmarket is also home to the National Stud, set up here in 1963 on 500 acres of land leased from the Jockey Club. It was originally formed during World War I, when Lord Wavertree presented his large band of top-class bloodstock to the government. Today, the stud is not just one of the principle stallion stations in Britain, but a venue for training courses on stud farming. Perhaps its best-known sire was Derby winner Mill Reef.

Just outside the town, on the verge of the road, is the grave of a gypsy boy. The story goes that he was put in charge of a flock of sheep. The next day, the sheep were gone, and the boy lay dead. Though no one ever sees who does it, fresh flowers are placed on the grave each day. On Derby Day, the colours of the flowers are supposed to correspond to the colours of the winning jockey, although it must be said that the horticultural tipster is by no means infallible!

 Ickworth. Three miles south-west of Bury St Edmunds is Ickworth Park, some 1,700 acres of parkland and gardens surrounding an eccentric neo-classical house. The land had been in the possession of the Hervey family since 1485. The house dates back to 1794, when Frederick Hervey, the fourth Earl of Bristol and former Bishop of Derry, started the building to house his ever-increasing art collection. He took to travelling all over Europe, collecting all things artistic. The collection might have been considerably larger had it not been for Napoleon, whose troops confiscated everything he had collected on a trip to Italy in 1798. He died of gout in 1803, long before his brainchild was completed.

The house, basically a central rotunda with a domed roof flanked by two sweeping wings, with a total frontage of 625ft, remained untouched until 1821. Work recommenced and was finished in 1829. It has been owned by the National Trust since 1956. The present marquis lives in one wing, but the rest of the building is open to the public. The staterooms contain much late Regency and eighteenth-century French furniture, along with portraits by Gainsborough, Hogarth, Lawrence and Reynolds. There is also a collection of silver regarded as the finest in the country.

 A seven-mile walk around the Ickworth estate offers spectacular views of the house itself, and passes through beautiful woodland and countryside. Parts of 'The Grand Tour' are also suitable for the disabled. Cards detailing the route are available at any time from a special dispenser.

 Haughley Park. Just north of the A45 outside Stowmarket lies Haughley, its red-bricked Jacobean manor house housing a fine collection of seventeenth-century Dutch paintings. Outside there are beautiful gardens in attractive parkland.

Stowmarket. Stowmarket is a market town with a strong agricultural background, although it is now becoming to some extent industrialised. The Museum of East Anglian Life provides a most interesting visit. Exhibits relating to the rural life of the area are on display, including several ancient buildings rescued from demolition on their original sites and re-erected here. The Eastbridge Smock Drainage Windpump, a nineteenth-century windpump which was originally used to drain marshes at Minsmere, has been reconstructed and restored to working condition at the museum.

At Cotton, five miles north of Stowmarket off the B1113, the Mechanical Music Museum is worth a visit, with its displays of organs, street pianos, gramophones and Wurlitzer organ, while at Woolpit, six miles to the north-west of the town, is the Bygones Museum, depicting life in a Suffolk village. To the north-east, the Mickfield Fish and Water Garden Centre is also worth a visit, with its large displays of freshwater and marine coral fish.

Helmingham. Helmingham Hall is the home of the brewing Tollemache family, and although the house itself is not open to the public the very fine gardens are. The walled garden, in the Elizabe- than style, contains many rare roses and a variety of animals, including red and fallow deer and Highland cattle. The sixteenth-century house is surrounded by a moat, and the drawbridge is raised every night.

Hintlesham. The rood screen of the church here contains a number of fine examples of grotesque faces, including one figure pulling his mouth open in a rather rude gesture. Hintlesham Hall's Georgian façade masks an earlier Tudor wall.

7
BRECKLAND

Breckland owes its distinctive character to the last Ice Age, which deposited light sandy soils after the retreat of the glaciers. In neolithic times, this type of soil could be cultivated fairly easily with primitive ploughs, and did not require much draining or tree felling. There is evidence to show that Breckland was originally a large open forest, probably oak, which was cleared away by early settlers using flint-headed tools from nearby Grimes Graves. The technique of 'slash and burn' was widely used, and when the soil was unable to support crops any longer, the people just cleared another section of land. Grazing animals prevented the redevelopment of the forest, and sheep farming continued until relatively recently. Rabbits, introduced into the sparse heathlands, became a valuable source of food, although not without affecting the countryside. The many local place names which retain the name Warren are a reminder.

In 1922 the Forestry Commission planted the first 6,000 acres of trees. Now over 50,000 acres of Scots and Corsican pine stretch for miles where once there were sand dunes. Even in the last quarter-century changes have taken place. Since the myxomotosis epidemic of 1954-5, the decline in the rabbit population has produced an increase in vegetation. The pines have reproduced themselves naturally, to such an extent that conservationists have had to take action on affected nature reserves to prevent the heathland from being overtaken.

The strangest phenomena of Breckland are the meres, or lakes, the water levels of which rise and fall without any apparent relation to the recent rainfall: sometimes they even disappear. In fact, their levels are determined by the water table in the underlying chalk

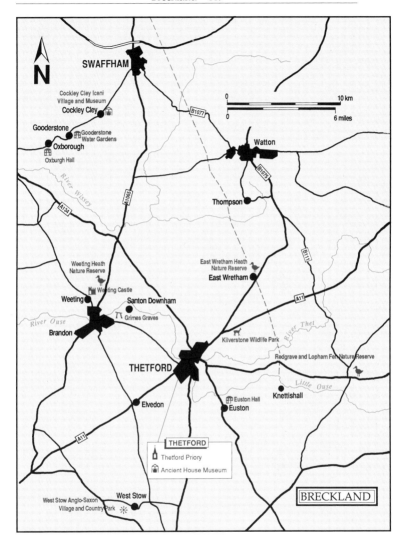

rather than run-off. Two such meres are Lang Mere and Ring Mere, in East Wretham Heath Nature Reserve.

Some of the least changed parts of natural Breckland are, unfortunately, the least accessible. Stanford Battle Area, owned by the

Ministry of Defence and covering about 100sq miles of land west of East Wretham, was taken over from private ownership in World War II and has been retained as a training ground, complete with its villages. The only civilians who can visit these villages are those who were born there, when they return to be buried!

The Peddars Way skirts the edge of the Battle Area for several miles, and along all approaches to the area are notices warning of the danger of unexploded shells and bombs on the other side of the fence. Consequently, the natural forests and wildlife of the Battle Area are best admired from the safe side of the fence!

Most of Thetford Forest can be explored along the various tracks and rides which intersect it, and the Forestry Commission have prepared a number of marked trails which can be followed from the information centre at Santon Downham. Elsewhere there are picnic areas, clearly signposted, which also provide a good base for short walks.

The forest is one of the last strongholds of the red squirrel in the south of England, and there are four species of deer, the most common being the roe. But whilst they exist in large numbers, they are difficult to see because they are rather timid and tend to keep in small family groups rather than larger herds. Fallow and red deer can also be seen, as can the tiny muntjac deer — not native to this country, but the descendants of escapees from Woburn Park in Bedfordshire at the end of the last century.

Swaffham. The market town of Swaffham was once known as 'the Montpelier of England'. In Regency times it was a fashionable place to live, and there are still many fine Georgian and Queen Anne buildings. There is a splendid fifteenth-century church, lavishly appointed and, according to local folklore, paid for by John Chapman, the Pedlar of Swaffham.

Apparently he had gone to London, where he met a stranger who described a dream in which he had discovered a treasure in a garden in the town of Swaffham. The description matched the pedlar's place, and so he returned home to find everything just as he had been told. He was so overjoyed at his good fortune that he paid for the rebuilding of the north aisle of the church.

The distinctive two-sided town sign, to be found in the market place and depicting the pedlar, is one of many village signs through-out East Anglia carved by Harry Carter, nephew of the famous discoverer of Tutankhamun's tomb. Carter was arts and technical crafts master at Hamonds Grammar School in Swaffham, and this first of many such carvings was erected in 1929.

Three miles south-west of Swaffham is **Cockley Cley**, where an Iceni encampment has been reconstructed on its original site.

Oxborough. Four miles down the road from Cockley Cley, Oxburgh Hall (the name of the house adopts the shorter spelling of the village) is probably one of the finest halls in Norfolk. It was built by Sir Edmund Bedingfield, whose family have lived here ever since. Dating back to 1482, this red brick fortified manor has one of the largest fifteenth-century gatehouses in existence, eighty feet high. Inside the gatehouse is a true tribute to the bricklayers art: a spiral staircase in bricks.

Oxburgh Hall is a transition between building styles. It is neither a heavily fortified baronial castle, nor like the undefended Tudor manor houses which followed not many years later. The result is quite spectacular, although the house has not passed through the centuries without its losses. In 1775, the Great Hall and Great Kitchen, which formed the south side of the building's quadrangle, were demolished, opening up the once enclosed courtyard to the moat.

The King's Chamber over the gateway was once used by Henry VII, and the Queen's Chamber above may have been slept in by Elizabeth I. It was most certainly slept in by Mary, Queen of Scots. Some of her imprisonment in England was spent here, and she whiled away the time with needlework. Over a hundred panels, depicting plants and animals, are sewn into the Oxburgh Hangings.

A four-and-a-half mile walk starts at Oxborough. Go up the road past the Bedingfield Arms public house, towards the phone box, then straight on where the road bends sharp left at the Post Office. Go through the large gate which appears on the right and follow the edge of the field behind the farm, with a hedge to the left. When it opens out on both sides, follow the line of young trees across the fields, continuing along the same line at a row of mature trees.

Keep this line of trees and hedge on the left and go on to a gate, coming out onto a road. Turn right and go over a small bridge. The road veers left just here, and takes you into Gooderstone. Take the lane running down beside the church (Clarkes Lane), and go over a bridge. Turn right at the junction, then shortly after take the track to the left, where there are a few pine trees.

Continue to the wood, and at a junction with another track, go

Sunset over Ring Mere

left. Go straight ahead at the metalled road towards Caldecote Farm. Take the track going left passing through an avenue of trees before coming out into the fields, where the track turns sharp right. Carry on to the road and then turn left. Go down to the crossroads and go straight over, back into Oxborough.

Grimes Graves. Probably the most important prehistoric site in East Anglia, Grimes Graves are not really graves at all! Now a patch of dimpled heath in the forest, the depressions left as a result of back-filling the shafts as they became exhausted gives the landscape a strange lunar quality. As a flint mine, the area was once the equivalent of our modern coalfields, and the effort to extract what was at the time the perfect tool-making stone must have been colossal. Three hundred and sixty-six mines were dug over an area of thirty-four acres, some merely shallow depressions where the flint was near to the surface, others dug quite deep. The more elaborate shafts were sunk through some forty feet of chalk before coming to the flint floorstone; from here the prehistoric miners scraped a myriad of tunnels radiating outwards, the first workings being dated about 2,900BC.

Moated Oxburgh Hall

Although it is possible to descend one of the shafts and see a number of tunnels disappearing into the gloom, one of the best representations of the original workings can be found in Norwich Castle Museum. Although average sized humans were much smaller than their twentieth-century counterparts, they clearly worked in appalling conditions, hewing flint in tiny cramped passages with antler picks, with perhaps animal fat candles for light, and woefully inadequate ventilation.

Brandon. Local flint abounds everywhere in this pretty Suffolk village. The flints were chiselled into their squared-off shape by flint-knappers, and the spare chippings were made into flints for lighters and flintlock rifles. Any residue was ground for sale to potteries, to be used for glazing. A reminder of this past craft is the Flintknappers Arms, where the work was carried out. Incredibly there is still a market for gun flints, from Africa and from muzzle-loading enthusiasts in America. The knapping continues in a yard nearby.

The forestry industry has expanded the place considerably, the Forestry Commission Produce Depot now enclosing several acres. Much of the timber is used to make pit-props and chipboard.

A mile south of Brandon on the B1106 are the grounds of Brandon Park House, situated in Thetford forest and offering forest walks, a picnic area and visitor centre.

Santon Downham. Although a settlement of long standing with a Norman church, the village of Santon Downham, tucked away in the forest, owes its continued existence to the Forestry Commission. In the church there is a record of the fact that the village was buried by sand in the Middle Ages, a sorry testimony to centuries of cultivation followed by over-grazing.

There are several walks which can be taken in the forest here, using the Forestry Information Centre as a starting point, such as this one to Grimes Graves. Take the road heading for Santon Warren, crossing a bridge over the Little Ouse. Continue along the road until just before the level crossing and take the forestry track to the left. It runs roughly parallel to the railway line, then through an underpass where it continues on the other side.

Follow the red painted posts which mark the Forestry Commission's twenty-five-mile West Stow to High Ash long-distance footpath. Turn right into the forest (still following the red posts), crossing over a long straight track just inside the forest. The track winds through the forest until it opens out into a vast clearing. The visitor centre and ticket office for Grimes Graves are ahead.

The return along the same route provides a walk of around three and a half miles, although a look at the Ordnance Survey map reveals several possibilities for planning longer circular routes.

Thetford. A settlement has existed on the site of Thetford for over a thousand years, and with its cathedral it was at one time the most important city in East Anglia, until the removal of the Bishop's throne to the city of Norwich. Indeed, the first authoritative survey of the land, the *Domesday Book*, suggests that Thetford was amongst the top six cities in England. Thetford Priory, founded by the Norman warrior John Bigod, dates back to the twelfth century, and although the remains from the ravages of the Dissolution of the Monasteries are now somewhat fragmentary, it is not a place which should be passed by.

Of the castle, probably first built in the eighth century, only the mound remains, surrounded by trees. Unlike other wooden castles in the region, this one never made the transition to a more lasting structure of stone. As it is, the motte is the highest in East Anglia, 80ft, with a circumference of 1,000ft. Although a fair view of the town and the surrounding forests may be enjoyed from it, the climb up its steep banks is definitely only for the energetic.

In the town are other monastic remains and some very fine houses dating from medieval to Georgian times. The timber-framed Ancient House Museum in White Hart Street houses a collection of natural history and archaeology exhibits depicting the history of the Breckland people, together with an interesting display of the locally knapped flints used for different types of old firearms. The place is also worth visiting for its beautifully carved beam ceilings.

The River Thet joins the Little Ouse at Thetford, which in 1700 became a port for ships coming from the sea past King's Lynn in an attempt to regain the wool trade which had gone to the east coast towns and villages with their easier accessibility. The move came too late, and with the advent of the railways in the mid-nineteenth century, it died out as a port. In the eighteenth century the town tried to promote itself as a spa town, with little success, although the attempt is still remembered in the name of Spring Walks, the paths laid out along the riverside.

Undoubtedly, Thetford's most famous son was the radical political writer Thomas Paine, the friend of humanity and enemy of kings. Born and educated in Thetford, Paine travelled to America in 1774 at the suggestion of Benjamin Franklin, where he edited the Pennsylvania Gazette. The American Revolution was much influenced by his advocacy of independence, and he was duly rewarded by the new republic, holding various offices.

Returning to England, he published his most famous work *The Rights of Man*, which favoured the revolution in France, a concept which did not endear him to the rulers of England, and indeed, he was forced to flee to France where his popularity was such that he was invited to stand for several public offices despite not being able to speak a word of French! But whilst supporting the French Revolution, he spoke out against the extent of the executions of the nobility and was sent to prison by Robespierre, where he wrote *The Age of Reason*. He spent his last years living in poverty in America.

Although he was considered a traitor by his own government, his philosophy rose above that, and the gilt statue standing in front of King's House (presented by the American Thomas Paine Society) commemorates him as a champion of human rights.

There are a number of interesting places to visit within a few miles radius of Thetford. A mile north-east is Kilverstone Wildlife

The replica Anglo-Saxon village at West Stow Country Park

Park, a lovely place for a family outing. The fifty acres of parkland houses a varied collection of animals, with a particular emphasis on Latin American species. There are also some attractive gardens and a pleasant walk along the River Thet.

East Wretham Heath Nature Reserve is a Norfolk Naturalists Trust reserve five miles north-east of the town. A nature trail crosses typical Breckland heath and woodland, and examples of the curious meres can be seen.

Six miles east, off the A1066, is Knettishall Heath, 350 acres of Breckland heath and woodland with walks and picnic areas. The western end of the heath also marks the beginning of the Peddars Way long distance footpath.

Elvedon. Maharajah Duleep Singh, the king of the Sikhs, bought the house at Elvedon in 1813 after being banished from India by Queen Victoria. His crime was his part in the Sikh wars, but the queen graciously allowed him to live out his exile in England. In the 1860s his vast wealth financed the transformation of the Georgian house into an amazing oriental palace, with copper dome and tons of Italian carved marble.

Stonebridge, a short road section of the Peddars Way

On the maharajah's death, the palace was bought by Lord Iveagh of the Guinness brewing family. Not far away, beside the A11, stands a column, 113ft and 148 steps high, with a breathtaking view of the forests from the top. This well-known landmark was built by Lord Iveagh as a war memorial to the men of his estate.

West Stow. At West Stow is a magnificent Tudor brick gate-house, part of what was once a large hall built by Sir John Crofts, Master of Horse to Mary Tudor. Half a mile north of the village is the King's Forest Information Centre, the start of a walk in the forest along the Forestry Commission's long distance footpath. The path actually runs for twenty-five miles between West Stow and High Ash, near Ickburgh. Much of the path runs along wide forest droves, and if the whole walk is too much for one day it is probably best to go from West Stow to Brandon on the first day, about eleven miles, and the rest on the next day.

There is a large country park here, giving visitors the opportunity to stroll around heath and grassland, as well as visit the recon-

Places to Visit in Breckland

Ancient House Museum
White Hart Street, Thetford.
Exhibits from local neolithic set-
tlements, housed in a fifteenth-
century timber framed building.

Thetford Priory
(English Heritage)
Remains of twelfth-century
priory.

Thetford Warren Lodge
Two miles north of Thetford on
the Brandon road.
Ruins of a fourteenth-century
hunting lodge, built for the prior
of Thetford's gamekeeper.

Grimes Graves
(English Heritage)
Weeting, 2 miles north of
Brandon on the B1106.
Stone Age flint mines. Descend
into one of the pits down a
number of ladders, where many
small galleries, or tunnels, can
be seen disappearing into the
gloom.

Weeting Castle
(English Heritage)
Not far from Grimes Graves —
the remains of a moated castle.

Kilverstone Wildlife Park
A mile north-east of Thetford, off
the A11.
50 acres of parkland housing a
collection of animals, with
emphasis on Latin American
species. There is also a pleasant
walk alongside the River Thet,
and some attractive gardens.

Euston Hall
4 miles south-east of Thetford on
the A1088.
Seventeenth-century hall, home
of the Duke and Duchess of
Grafton, containing a famous
collection of paintings.

**East Wretham Heath
Nature Reserve**
5 miles north-east of Thetford on
the A1075.
Norfolk Naturalists Trust reserve,
with nature trail across typical
Breckland heath and woodland:
examples of the curious meres,
small lakes whose water levels
seem to rise and fall mysteriously
but are, in fact, dependent upon
the water table in the surrounding
chalk.

Iceni Village and Museum
Cockley Cley, 4 miles south-west
of Swaffham.
Reconstruction of Iceni encampment on original site.

❉ structed Anglo-Saxon village. Like Santon Downham, West Stow
was buried in a sandstorm, and it was this which preserved the
Anglo-Saxon site well enough for twentieth-century archaeologists
to reconstruct it.

Euston. The present situation of the village of Euston dates back to the seventeenth century, when (as at Edensor, near Chatsworth in Derbyshire) the entire village was moved from its former site because it obscured the view from Euston Hall. The hall itself is set in a great park, its gardens laid out by William Kent and Capability Brown. It houses a fine collection of paintings, including works by Van Dyck, Lely and Stubbs. Only the church remains in its original position, built very much in the style of Sir Christopher Wren and with a beautiful panelled interior.

The Peddars Way. Further evidence of the importance of the Breckland region in bygone times is the number of ancient tracks which have been discovered. The Icknield Way leaves Breckland to the south-west, eventually ending up in the south of England. The Peddars Way is probably the best known ancient track. Although what exists today is by no means complete, the fifty miles or so which take the traveller from Knettishall Heath in the northern reaches of Suffolk, to Holme-next-the-Sea on the North Norfolk coast, follow the line of the original path except where the hand of modern development has obscured it.

The Peddars Way/Norfolk Coast Path is now a National Trail, officially opened by the Prince of Wales in 1986 and financed mainly by the Countryside Commission. The coast path from Holme to Cromer links up with the Weavers Way, running from Cromer to Great Yarmouth, providing one of the most varied long-distance walks in Britain. Anyone interested in this ancient monument, either for its historical and natural interest, or as a walker delighting in the varied beauty of the countryside through which it passes, may join the Peddars Way Association, whose address is in the Useful Information chapter. As well as providing its own route guide, the association also has a regularly updated accommodation list.

Those who do not wish to walk the entire length of the Peddars Way may manage short stretches of the path. The terrain is not arduous, and the peaceful forest tracks and green lanes, with their abundance of wildlife, make even the shortest stroll a pleasant experience.

The Peddars Way, popular with walkers

8

CONSTABLE COUNTRY

The River Stour forms the boundary between Suffolk and Essex, and it is this valley and the surrounding countryside which is associated with the artist John Constable. Many of the places immortalised in his paintings can still be seen, only superficially changed by the passage of time. Places such as Flatford Mill and Willy Lott's Cottage, Lavenham, Clare, Dedham and Long Melford all possess beautiful links with the past which must be seen to be appreciated. The peaceful Suffolk countryside in which he grew up has changed, but not beyond recognition. Despite the twentieth century there are still places where it is possible to leave the car and savour the tranquillity which Constable felt and captured so remarkably on canvas.

John Constable was born at East Bergholt in 1776. His father, Golding, a miller, owned mills at Dedham and Flatford and two windmills at East Bergholt. John went to school at Dedham and Lavenham, but showed little academic flair. The surrounding countryside however, inspired him to paint from an early age. Despite his stated wish to become a painter, his businesslike father made him work at milling when his education was over. With some encouragement from his mother, he went to London at the age of nineteen to study art. Four years later, he was admitted as a student at the Royal Academy.

At the age of twenty-eight he received a commission to paint *Christ Blessing Little Children*, an altarpiece for Brantham Church, one of his only two religious works (the other is in the church at Nayland). Constable had no love for that style of painting, but a commission was something a struggling artist could hardly afford to reject.

His real ambition was to paint the beautiful countryside in which he was brought up, in a manner frowned upon at the time by the Royal Academy.

He was similarly thwarted in love. He met Maria Bicknell, the grand-daughter of Dr Rhudde, the rector of East Bergholt, and in 1800 they decided to marry. Rhudde opposed the marriage, and it was not until Constable inherited his father's estate in 1816 that the couple were united, when the artist was 40 years old. Maria lived only another twelve years, but in that time Constable painted his best and most well-known works. The *Hay Wain*, shown at the Royal Academy in 1818, was poorly received. When the painting appeared in Paris, where impressionist painting had already taken off, he became an instant celebrity, and was awarded a gold medal by the King of France. It was not until 1829, a year after his wife's death, that Constable received recognition from the Royal Academy — by then a hollow gesture to him.

While many parts of the country have names associated with famous people or things, most smack of twentieth-century commercialism. Constable Country, however, became known thus during the artist's lifetime. He was travelling on a coach between London and Dedham, when he heard a fellow traveller (who didn't know him) enthusiastically describe the Vale of Dedham as 'Constable's Country'. The artist himself wrote: 'I love every stile and stump and lane…as long as I am able to hold a brush, I shall never cease to paint them.'

Manningtree. Constable's father owned two yards on the quay here. The river barges so often depicted in Constable's paintings used to journey between here and the mills at Flatford and Dedham, and further up the Stour. Possibly his *Boats at Anchor* was sketched here. Mistley Towers, a mile east of Manningtree on the B1352, are two towers which were designed by Robert Adam in 1776, while Mistley Environmental Centre has twenty acres of woods and grassland overlooking the River Stour. There are lakeside and woodland walks, and horses, goats, rabbits and geese can be seen.

Brantham. Just opposite Manningtree, on the other side of the head of the Stour Estuary, Brantham is unremarkable as a village except that its church has an altarpiece painted by Constable in 1804.

East Bergholt. Although Constable's birthplace no longer survives, the small cottage which served as his studio still stands, as part of the Post Office. The west tower of the church was never completed, although the top extremity has been capped with concrete to protect it against decay. According to legend, at the end of each day the Devil undid the work just done. A more likely explanation is that when Cardinal Wolsey, who was financing the building work, fell from grace, the funds and the building came to an end. As a result there is a rather curious wooden building in the churchyard housing the bells intended for the tower which was never finished. In the church-yard are the graves of Constable's parents, and that of Willy Lott.

At East Bergholt Lodge a woodland garden containing over 350 varieties of trees and shrubs and more than 140 different types of rose can be seen.

Flatford. It was East Bergholt and nearby Flatford which pro-vided the young artist with the inspiration for many of his fine paintings. Flatford Mill, built in 1733 and now a field study centre owned by the National Trust, featured in several of Constable's works, and Bridge Cottage near the mill is a restored thatched cottage housing an exhibition about the artist. From the car park there is a path down to the bridge over the Stour. Along the right bank can be seen the side of the mill, with its sluice gate and trees overhanging the river bank. The left-hand route leads round to the other side, with the quiet mill-pond and Willy Lott's Cottage beyond — a scene instantly recognisable as the setting for the famous *Hay Wain*. Willy Lott, the mill-hand, is reputed to have lived in this cottage for eighty-eight years.

Dedham. This small village, not far from East Bergholt, is where Constable went to school. He made the daily journey on foot, and the scenery along the way undoubtedly provided the inspiration for *The Cornfield*. Parts of the village are recognisable in several well-known paintings, including *Dedham Lock and Mill*, and the *Valley of the Stour*. It may be difficult, however, to find the exact viewpoint used for some of these pictures. Constable tended to indulge in a certain amount of artistic licence, moving features like a church to join the background in a totally different view.

The church has some interesting commemorative pews, one to the people of Dedham in Massachusetts, with whom there are close links, including the forbears of General Sherman, the American Civil War hero. Another recalls the first manned landing on the moon, with a quotation from Psalm 8.

The village contains a variety of medieval timber-framed houses and public houses, and some fine Georgian buildings, including the

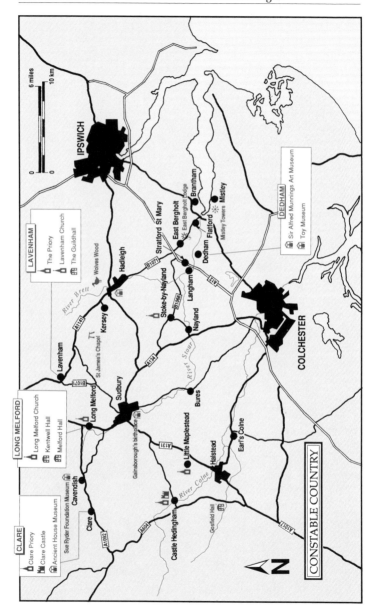

Willy Lott's Cottage, the scene of Constable's Hay Wain

Flatford Mill, another National Trust property and now a field centre

grammar school which the young artist attended. Sir Alfred Munnings, another famous artist, also made Dedham his home, and a collection of his work is on show to the public at Castle House. The Duchy barn, an interesting building in its own right, is the home of the CPRE Countryside Centre, a tourist information centre, and the Dedham Art and Craft Centre is a converted church which houses the Toy Museum.

Stratford St Mary. The church stands apart from the village, now separated by the A12. Some most unusual lettering picked out in the flint flushwork reminds people to say their prayers. Across the road, the village street leads past some attractive timbered houses and inns, which once provided a major coaching stop.

Langham. Maria Bicknell and John Constable used to meet at the church and rectory here. Not far away, between the church and the bridge to Stratford St Mary, is Gun Hill, where Constable painted *Dedham Vale*.

Stoke-by-Nayland. The church at Stoke-by-Nayland is another building which featured in more than one of Constable's landscapes, and it is not difficult to see why. The 120ft-high Perpendicular tower rises majestically above the surrounding trees and Tudor houses. There are some impressive decorations inside, as well as memorials to the Tendring family, whose subsequent connection with the Howard family produced two of Henry VIII's wives: Lady Catherine Howard and Anne Boleyn. Near the church are two fine timber-framed buildings: the Guildhall and the Maltings.

Nayland. The Church of St James at Nayland contains *Christ's Blessing of the Bread and Wine*, once criticised by someone who thought Constable's representation of Christ too closely resembled his own brother! The inn in the main street is reputed to be the last from which a navy press-gang operated. The village has several half-timbered cottages, and Fen Street, with its succession of footbridges over the mill-stream, has the charming flavour of Venice.

Bures. St Mary's Church contains the family monument to Sir William Waldegrave, and above it a tablet to the memory of Mary Constable, aunt of the painter. To the north-east of the village is St Stephen's Chapel, a small thatched building from the thirteenth century, containing relics of the de Vere family (the Earls of Oxford), brought from Colne Priory in Essex. The chapel is thought to be on the site of an earlier wooden chapel which was the scene of the coronation of St Edmund in 855.

Earls Colne. The medieval priory at Colne no longer exists, and an eighteenth-century red brick Gothic house now occupies the site. The village itself has many timber-framed, thatched and weather-boarded cottages and houses.

Halstead. The white weatherboarded mill is quite an eye-catching building, and was bought by the Courtaulds at the beginning of the last century. The church contains some monuments to the Bourchier family, one of whom fought at Crecy. The nearby village of **Gosfield** is worth a visit for its Tudor Hall and tree-fringed lake.

Little Maplestead. About three miles north of Halstead, this little village has a curious round church, a common sight in medieval times, but now there are only five left in the country (there is another in Cambridge). Modelled on the Holy Sepulchre in Jerusalem, it was built by the Knights Hospitallers of St John as a stopping-off point for pilgrims to the Holy Land.

Hadleigh. Standing on the River Brett, a tributary of the Stour, Hadleigh (a name derived from heath-covered place) was one of the more important of the old wool and cloth towns. The church is surrounded by many fascinating buildings, including the fifteenth-century half-timbered Guildhall with its two overhanging upper storeys.

The church itself, one of the largest in Suffolk, has an elegant lead spire. Inside, the 600-year-old Angelus Bell, one of the oldest in the country, is inscribed: *Ave Maria Gracia Plena Dominus Tecum*. Perhaps the man who made the bell had other things on his mind when it came to putting in the inscription, as he forgot to invert the words laterally in the mould, and they appear backwards on the finished article!

A carved bench-end in the church depicts a wolf holding a human head by the hair. Legend has it that after St Edmund was killed by a Danish arrow, his head was hacked off and thrown into a thicket. His followers arrived to find the head being guarded by a grey wolf. Guthrum, the Danish leader who was defeated by King Alfred and who subsequently embraced Christianity, was buried here.

A short walk of one-and-a-half miles can be taken, starting from the public library, then going down Duke Street and across the medieval Toppesfield Bridge. Turn right, following the riverside path to Bridge Street. Then right again, onto the High Street, with its marvellous collection of houses spanning more than six hundred years of vernacular architecture. Hadleigh is also headquarters of the

East Anglia Tourist Board, and visitors are sure to find a visit to the Tourist Information Centre at Toppesfield Hall worthwhile.

Two miles east of Hadleigh on the A1071 is **Wolves Wood**, a remnant of Anglo-Saxon forest with a rich variety of plants, animals and breeding birds. Walks through the wood are, however, restricted to the nature trails.

Kersey. With claims on the title of the most beautiful village in England, Kersey has a strong weaving background, evidenced by the typical weavers' cottages, some half-timbered, some colour washed plaster, which line the steep village street. The place is somewhat unusual in that it was built across a valley, rather than along it. A stream, which was undoubtedly put to good use in the village's textile days, crosses the bottom of the street in a ford. This colourful medieval village is overlooked by a fifteenth-century church containing some old painted panels from a rood screen, and hammer-beams supporting the nave roof.

Sudbury. This busy little market town nestling in a loop in the River Stour was the largest of the Suffolk wool towns, and kept its industry, as it was a port. It was also the birthplace, and home for many years, of the painter Thomas Gainsborough.

Fifty years before Constable's time, Gainsborough had an easier life. He married young, to a girl whose father provided a comfortable dowry. The young artist paid his bills by painting portraits of wealthy patrons, including the Cobbold brewing family. While Gainsborough loved to paint landscapes, it was the informality and grace of his portraits which won him far-reaching acclaim when he moved first to Bath and later to London. A statue of him by Bertram Mackennal ARA (who designed the head of George V on coins) stands outside St Peter's Church, on Market Hill.

The house where Gainsborough was born, formerly a sixteenth-century inn, is now preserved as a museum and exhibition gallery, and indeed, it is the only artist's birthplace open to the public in the country. Of the exhibits, there is the intriguing *Portrait of a Boy*. When it was first cleaned, part of a young girl appeared, prompting the conclusion that Gainsborough had originally painted a portrait of a boy and girl together, and that the painting was subsequently cut in half. Why it was cut, and the whereabouts of the Gainsborough Girl, remains a mystery.

The Georgian buildings around Market Hill are quite cheerful, although much of the rest of Sudbury has been taken in by its recent

A peaceful way to spend an afternoon, boating on the River Stour

expansion as part of the GLC overspill scheme.

Near the river, on Stour Street, are some half-timbered houses dating back to the time when Sudbury was one of the most important weaving towns. One firm still continues the long tradition of weaving silk, and was specially commissioned to weave the silk for Princess Anne's wedding dress.

Castle Hedingham. Seven miles south-west of Sudbury, Hedingham Castle can boast one of the best surviving examples of a Norman tower keep in Western Europe. Built in 1140, it was the home of the de Veres, the Earls of Oxford, for over 500 years. Its four floors and roof have been preserved, and there is much fine decorative stonework inside.

The writings of England's greatest playwright, William Shakespeare, have been variously attributed to others, and a serious contender is Edward de Vere, the seventeenth Earl of Oxford. The notion was put forward in 1918 by what some might have regarded as the aptly named J. Thomas Looney, a Gateshead schoolmaster. True, Edward was a poet, but his death in 1604 does predate such classics as King Lear, Macbeth, Antony and Cleopatra and The Tempest. Looney's answer to this is that Lear and Macbeth were misdated, and that the rest existed as unfinished manuscripts and were finished off by others after Edward's death. Nevertheless, the Oxford theory as to Shakespeare's true identity is taken seriously by many.

The village of Hedingham, over which the castle stands sentinel, lies in the valley below. Among the ancient streets and alleyways stands the church, which despite its sixteenth-century appearance outside, is really of the same vintage as the castle. It has a notable Norman wheel window over the high altar, and a double hammer-beam roof.

Nearby, the Colne Valley Railway recreates the heyday of steam with its collection of locomotives, rolling stock and an old lever-operated signal box. Apart from the attractions of steam rides, it even has the only railway carriage restaurant in the country to have acquired an Egon Ronay rating!

Three miles north-west of Castle Hedingham is the Toppesfield Museum of the Working Horse, with displays of farm implements, a forge and horse-drawn vehicles.

Lavenham. While there are many old towns and villages which prospered during the era of the wool industry, and whose thatched cottages and timber-framed houses are a beauty to behold, Lavenham has the most tourists. Constable went to school here, and used to visit the Taylors of Shilling Old Grange, where Jane Taylor wrote the children's nursery song *Twinkle, Twinkle, Little Star*.

Virtually every street in the town centre is lined with timber-framed houses, particularly fine being the Swan Inn and the Wool Hall behind it. Indeed, no less than three hundred of Lavenham's buildings are listed as being of architectural and historical interest. The Guildhall is a magnificent early sixteenth-century building in the market place, which houses the local museum, while Little Hall dates from the fifteenth century and is now home to the Suffolk Preservation Society.

Places to Visit in Constable Country

Wolves Wood, RSPB reserve 2 miles east of Hadleigh on A1071. Woodland nature trails.

The Stour Estuary
Mudflats and saltmarshes especially popular with bird watchers.

Kentwell Hall
Long Melford.
Moated Elizabethan red brick manor.

Melford Hall
(National Trust)
Long Melford.
Turreted Tudor mansion with eighteenth-century and Regency interiors.

Colne Valley Railway
Castle Hedingham station.
A re-creation of a typical Essex branch line of the Victorian era. Displays of steam and diesel locomotives and carriages.

Lavenham Guildhall
(National Trust)
Sixteenth-century timber-framed building now housing museum depicting local industries.

Toppesfield Museum of the Working Horse
The Wheatsheaf, Gainsford End, Toppesfield, 3 miles north-west of Castle Hedingham.
Displays of farm implements, forge, horse-drawn vehicles etc.

Railway track walks
Hadleigh to Bentley. 8 miles west of Ipswich. Pleasant grassland walk along a disused railway track.
Long Melford to Lavenham. North of Sudbury, similar walk through rich grassland with varied flora, about 4 miles.

The church, paid for by the local wool merchants and the de Vere family, is a splendid example of late Perpendicular architecture, a mass of clear windows giving it a bright interior. The priory is a timber-framed house which has at various times been home to Benedictine monks, medieval clothiers and an Elizabethan rector. In the gardens over a hundred different varieties of herbs can be seen.

The famous hostelry, the Swan Inn, was a popular meeting place for off-duty American airmen during World War II. Apart from its continuing welcome to customers, the Swan also houses a large collection of memorabilia, including a section of the bar counter scored with the signatures of many of its American clientele.

Long Melford. Long Melford really lives up to its name, stretching along the A134 Bury St Edmunds to Sudbury road. This pictur-

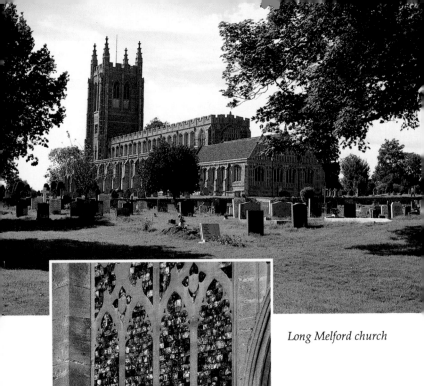

Long Melford church

Finely worked flint used as a decorative feature on Long Melford church

The Tudor summer house at Melford Hall

One of the many half-timbered buildings in Lavenham

esque town has a history going back to the Romans. Like many other Suffolk towns, Long Melford enjoyed a long period of prosperity through the wool trade. Melford Hall, now owned by the National Trust, stands at the edge of the green. Apparently, the hall, whose bricks were made from clay dug out of the green, was originally used by the abbots of Bury St Edmunds as a hunting lodge. The Reformation stopped this rather un-spiritual practice, and the place changed hands several times before being taken over in 1786 by the family whose descendants still live here.

Nearby, Kentwell Hall, approached from a mile-long tree-lined drive, is a moated Elizabethan mansion which was almost lost through neglect before it was acquired privately in 1971. Since then much refurbishment and renovation has taken place, including the creation of the award winning brick-paved Tudor Rose maze, set into the central courtyard.

The 150ft nave and chancel of Long Melford Church has over a hundred windows. Combined with the finely moulded arches and slender columns supporting the roof, the whole atmosphere is one of incredible lightness — the roof almost seems to float!

A six-mile walk starts from the northern end of the green, or near the magnificent church, where there is ample car parking. Follow the wall around to the A134 and turn left, past the entrance to Kentwell Hall. Turn right onto a concrete track signposted as a bridleway at the Garden Centre. In the distance, on your right, you can see Melford Hall, itself worth visiting if you have the time.

When the track turns right at Lodge Farm, continue straight on, following a footpath at the edge of a field. It descends gradually to a line of trees and a stream, Chad Brook. Follow the path along the headland of a vast field, with the stream to your right, towards Lineage Wood. An inviting track crosses the brook and disappears into the trees, but don't go over here! Keep to the left bank of the stream, past some impressive regimented rows of poplars. With the small village of Bridge Street well in sight, come to an old footbridge which crosses to the other side of the brook. Turn left onto the minor road and then cross over the A134, following the road into the village (signposted for Shimpling).

Just after turning onto the Shimpling road, and just before a line of houses, is a footpath signposted to the left. The path, which heads west for a clump of trees and Kiln Farm beyond, isn't clearly defined for some stretches. But with the trees ahead and Rowhedge Farm to the right, you can't go wrong. It can get rather muddy along here though, so boots can be an advantage if it is wet.

Past the wood the track becomes better defined. Turn left at Kiln Farm and carry straight on for the next mile, all the way to Kentwell Hall. Follow the track around to the front of the building and the final section of the walk, down the drive back to the green.

Cavendish. Four miles west of Long Melford on the A1092, Cavendish is a pretty village with a large green surrounded by thatched plaster cottages. The Sue Ryder Foundation has a home here, and its museum contains displays illustrating the work of the foundation.

Sir John Cavendish received some rough justice after his son treacherously stabbed Wat Tyler, leader of the 1381 rebellion, at Smithfield, after the king had given him amnesty. A mob descended on his home in Cavendish, out for revenge. He hid his valuables in the church belfry and fled. He was later caught and killed near Lakenheath.

Clare. The castle mound, with the remains of a keep still visible, is a sign that Clare once held a certain amount of strategic importance. The Iceni had a fort here in Iron Age times, and later a medieval castle was built here. The Icknield Way was the main route connecting East Anglia with the rest of the country, and Clare happened to be the nearest place to it on a navigable river which could be used to transport the vast quantities of stone needed to build the castle.

The castle mound was partially excavated in Victorian times to make way for a railway station, and during the digging a cross was unearthed. Made of gold, with a gold chain set with pearls, it bore the figure of Christ and was thought to contain a piece of the True Cross. It was presented to Queen Victoria.

Clare Priory, founded in 1248, was the first Augustinian friary in England. Several hundred years after the Dissolution, it became a priory again in 1953. Another place to visit is the Ancient House Museum, a fifteenth-century priest's house which has displays of local bygones.

9

COLCHESTER, THE NORTH ESSEX COAST AND INLAND

Colchester's importance throughout history lies in its geographical situation. Eight miles from the sea on the River Colne, the town was in an ideal trading position. A Celtic settlement was already established long before the Romans arrived. In about AD10, Cunobelin (immortalised as Shakespeare's Cymbeline), became king of south-east Britain, and built his capital, *Camulodunum*.

When the Romans invaded in AD43 the town was their major objective, and once taken became their first British colony in a short space of time. The Romans pillaged the surrounding countryside, and in AD60 the Britons rose against them. Prudently waiting until the main Roman force was elsewhere, Boudica and her tribe of Iceni sacked the town and massacred its inhabitants. They drove the enemy before them as far as London, and although she was later defeated and committed suicide, she will always be remembered as one of the first examples of the 'British Spirit', not afraid of taking on someone reputedly bigger and better.

The Romans subsequently reacted to this unfriendly display by fortifying the town with massive walls. In the wake of the Romans the town declined, although by the time of the Norman invasion it was considered important enough to build a castle there, on the site of the old Roman Temple to the Emperor Claudius. The fortunes of the town underwent many changes in the Middle Ages, and it was not until the Civil War that Colchester saw much action. In 1648 the Royalists held out against the Roundheads for three months before being beaten. In the streets there are still some signs of the siege. In

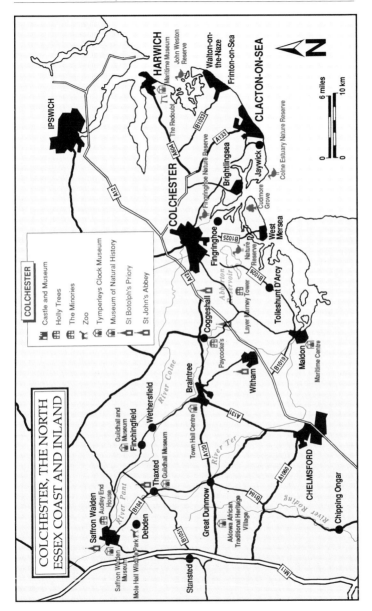

Napoleonic times it again became important as a garrison town, although a permanent military camp was not built until 1856.

Today, Colchester's main streets follow almost the same grid pattern left by the Romans, and their influence, with that of subsequent inhabitants, is everywhere to be seen. In late July or early August the Military Tattoo is held, a magnificent four-day event.

The Castle. As with the majority of remains from bygone ages, Colchester Castle is today but a shadow of its former self. The castle is now only the keep of what was once a huge fortress stretching from High Street to the north wall. Much of the foundations of the keep are the remains of the Emperor Claudius's Temple, and are still visible in places. The eleventh-century keep is the largest in Europe, despite a dismal attempt by a seventeenth-century ironmonger to become rich quickly by buying the castle with a view to demolishing it and selling the materials. The task proved too much for him: he succeeded only in removing the top two floors before bankruptcy ended his plans.

The museum inside the castle contains an outstanding collection of Roman relics, and prehistoric remains.

Holly Trees. Virtually next door to the castle is this Georgian house, built between 1718 and 1719. Worth visiting just for the house itself, Holly Trees also houses a museum of eighteenth- and nineteenth-century domestic life, and a collection of militaria. Almost opposite Holly Trees is the Minories, a late Georgian house containing an art gallery with some early work by John Constable and some personal relics.

Following East Hill across the river to East Street is the Siege House, an impressive fifteenth-century half-timbered house still bearing the pock-marks made by bullets in the siege of 1648.

St Botolph's Priory. Down Queen Street from the Minories, the remains of this Norman church stand outside the old Roman walls amidst modern carriageways, car parks and a railway station. In about 1100, the priory became the first in the country of the Augustinian Order. The siege during the Civil War took its toll, and now only the west front and part of the nave survive.

St John's Abbey. Originally a Benedictine monastery founded in the latter part of the eleventh century, all that remains now is the gatehouse, an addition built in the fifteenth century. The front is decorated with flint panels, with three large, empty statue niches around the archway. Like St Botolph's Priory, the building sustained heavy damage during the Civil War, and in the vault inside the gateway may be seen the track of a Cromwellian cannon-ball.

The Town Hall. A moot hall has existed on this site since the twelfth century, and although the present town hall was built more recently in 1902, the name 'Moot Hall' still survives in one room of the building. The Town Hall was built as the result of a competition among local architects, and the design which won, and was subsequently built, was by John Belcher. The Moot Hall is the scene of many concerts, as well as the famous 'Oyster Feast', held every year in October.

The Dutch Quarter. The line between the Town Hall and the castle forms the approximate southern boundary of an area known as the Dutch Quarter. Either of the Stockwell streets leads into it, as does Maidenburgh Street approached from the castle. Weaving is firmly 'interwoven' in the history of East Anglia, and the Flemish weavers who arrived in Colchester in the sixteenth century made this area their home. The Dutch Quarter is a pleasing collection of gabled and half-timbered houses.

The Roman Walls. Many of the old Roman walls are still standing, a tribute to the skill of their builders. The circuit of the walls is an interesting walk of only about one-and-a-half miles. What survives is not as it was in Roman times. After the siege of 1648 the facings and parapets were removed, so that in many places the original core of the wall may be seen. The best sections are along Balkerne Way, Park Folley and Priory Street, and particularly the impressive Balkerne Gate on the west side.

The Earthworks. Defences even older than the Roman walls are still visible. Pre-Roman Colchester was protected by a series of dykes and ramparts. Grimes Dyke, Triple Dyke and Bluebottle Grove are the main sections which can still be followed, and might have played a part in the defence of Colchester hundreds of years later. In 1940, some sections were incorporated into tank-traps, hastily built against Hitler's threatened invasion.

BEYOND COLCHESTER

Harwich. Still continuing its strong seafaring tradition, and Britain's second biggest passenger port, the town overlooks the estuaries of the Orwell and the Stour, and is adjoined by Parkeston and Dovercourt, together forming the Borough of Harwich. The port has a distinguished history. Christopher Jones, the master of the *May-*

The weathered walls of Colchester castle

flower, lived in Harwich, and a plaque can be found on his house in King's Head Street. There was, for a time, a Royal Naval dockyard here, and an interesting survivor can be found on Harwich Green. What looks like an enormous pigeon loft with gallows at one end is in fact a double treadwheel crane, built in 1667, and in use right up to World War I. When the old shipyard ceased in 1928, the crane was moved to its present site. To the south of the crane, just off the road towards Dovercourt, stands the Redoubt, one of the line of coastal defences built in 1808 against Napoleon's threatened invasion. The Redoubt now houses a small museum.

Samuel Pepys, the renowned diarist, was MP for the town during the time that it was the headquarters of the King's Navy. Historic houses abound in Harwich. Elizabeth I spent three days in a house in King's Head Street, and The Three Cups Hotel has played host to the country's two greatest seafarers, Drake and Nelson.

Pleasure cruises from Harwich have been operating for some

Ruins of St Botolph's Priory, Colchester

time — Charles II took the first. Apart from the ferries to Felixstowe and Ipswich, there are some pleasant cruises up the Orwell to Pin Mill and along the Stour Estuary towards Constable Country. Nearby Parkeston Quay is now the main terminal point for the port of Harwich, with regular sailings between here and Scandinavia, West Germany and the Netherlands. Over two million passengers pass through every year.

Dovercourt is a small resort in the hinterland of Harwich, and although it is now the residential portion of Harwich, it is in fact the older town, being mentioned in the *Domesday Book*. Just off Lower Marine Parade are two lighthouses standing on stilts. In the seventeenth century, coal shipments from Newcastle to London were so frequent that a large number of lights were set up at various points around the coast. Two were built at Harwich in 1665, one lit by a coal fire, the other candle-lit. These worked for over 150 years before being replaced by brick towers, which in turn were replaced by the current 'leading lights', also now obsolete. The large number of lighthouses is explained by the shifting sands around Landguard Point, south of Felixstowe. The channels into the ports of Harwich and Felixstowe are now marked by buoys.

The Tendring Peninsula Resorts are towns that need only short descriptions as they are places for residence rather than for visitors. **Walton-on-the-Naze** and neighbouring **Frinton** are quiet seaside resorts, set amidst some fine unspoiled countryside. Walton Heritage Centre is in a former lifeboat house containing rural and maritime history exhibits. The saltings inland of the Naze, to the north, provide some very pleasant walks and a few hours of peace and fresh air. **Holland-on-Sea**, **Clacton-on-Sea** and **Jaywick** sprawl along about five miles of coastline, making good use of the sandy beaches. The coast is sheltered from the north winds which blow across the Norfolk and Suffolk resorts, and so it is hardly surprising that the holiday camps and amusement arcades have sprung up in this area.

St Osyth. About four miles west of Clacton, St Osyth is a delightful and charming village with some attractive and fairly extensive historic ruins, including the thirteenth-century priory, and the flint-decorated fifteenth-century gatehouse. The village was originally called *Chiche*, after the creek on which it stood. Osytha, an Anglo-Saxon princess, was forced to marry Sigehere of Essex, despite having taken vows of virginity. She managed to flee on her wedding night, and founded a nunnery here. When the invading Danes could not incite her to give up her religion, they beheaded her, and a fountain is said to have sprung up on the spot where it fell. The village was renamed in her honour.

The priory was founded in 1118, and underwent many changes until it was handed over to Lord D'Arcy at the Dissolution, when it was transformed into a country house. It was sacked during the Civil War, and partly restored in the eighteenth century. The priory and deer park are open to visitors during the summer.

Brightlingsea. Situated between two creeks emptying into the River Colne, Brightlingsea is accessible only from the B1029 road from Thorrington. St Osyth, only three miles away but requiring an eight-mile journey by road, was once an important harbour, and has retained its fishing and boat-building atmosphere despite the expansion of the tourist industry over the last few years. Oyster fishing is still a thriving business here. A hotel in the High Street, called Jacob's Hall, is possibly one of the oldest surviving inhabited buildings in the country, dating back to 1250.

Mersea Island. Just across the water from Brightlingsea is Mersea Island, lying between the mouths of the Rivers Colne and Blackwater. Nine miles south of Colchester on the B1025 road, and reached by crossing the Pyefleet Channel over an ancient causeway called the Strood, Mersea Island and its main village West Mersea are peaceful places, even with the throngs of summer yachtsmen. Mersea Island Museum has exhibits on local and natural history, fishing equipment and bygones. Away from the village (more a small town), the wide mud-flats and small creeks provide a haven for a variety of seabirds and waders.

Tolleshunt D'Arcy. Roughly halfway between Colchester and Maldon on the B1026 road, Tolleshunt D'Arcy was the home of the D'Arcy family, who lived in the sixteenth-century hall surrounded by a square moat crossed by an Elizabethan brick and stone bridge.

Four miles north is **Layer Marney**, where the first and second Lords Marney had planned to build a large hall. Unfortunately they died without heirs, and the soaring gatehouse is all that had been erected when the building stopped.

The marshes along the Blackwater Estuary provide some good walking. A superb circular walk starts from Tollesbury, taking in Decoy Farm, Mill Creek, Tollesbury Wick Marshes, Shinglehead Point, and then back into Tollesbury. The route becomes apparent once you identify the names on the Ordnance Survey Landranger Sheet number 168.

Maldon. Situated in the calm upper reaches of the Blackwater estuary, this ancient town now has a thriving yachting community,

Maldon

and the Maritime Museum on the Hythe has displays of local maritime interest. The oldest part of the town is centred around High Street, where there are several houses dating from the fifteenth century. At the top of the hill stands All Saints Church, notable for its odd and unique triangular tower. Inside, two of the town's more colourful sons are commemorated. Thomas Cammock, who managed to have two wives and twenty-two children before he died in 1602, and Edward Bright, who died in 1750 weighing 43 stones. Maldon Museum is also on High Street, with a permanent display on local history and other changing exhibitions.

Maldon is home to a flourishing crystal sea-salt industry which started in medieval times, when salt was important for preserving fish and meat. The drying action of wind and sun on sea water flowing over the marshes and mudflats concentrates the water, and further treatment produces the characteristic flaky crystals of salt now very popular for cooking.

Coggeshall. The Paycocke family were rich merchants at the end of the fifteenth century. One of them built the splendid timber-framed house here, owned by the National Trust since 1924 and well worth a visit to see its intricate carvings and panelling. The close studding of the wooden uprights indicates it was built by a family who could afford the large quantity of good quality oak necessary. The infill, which originally would have been wattle and daub, was replaced with attractive red brick only at the beginning of this century. There are some excellent examples of sixteenth- and seventeenth-century oak furniture, and a special display of local crafts.

Also at Coggeshall is a restored twelfth-century barn, the earliest surviving timber-framed barn in Europe.

Braintree. Though not really a tourist town, it is interesting to note that Braintree originated from its position along the ancient route of pilgrimage from London to Bury St Edmunds and Walsingham, thus establishing a tradition of comfortable inns and hostels, some of which survive today. There are a couple of interesting museums in the town. The Braintree and Bocking Heritage Centre Museum in the Market Place has exhibits depicting the town's development through the ages, covering the wool and silk industries, engineering and early American history. The Working Silk Museum in South Street is England's last hand loom silk weaving mill. Its old textile machines are restored and in working order. Five miles north-west of the town is Saling Hall Garden, twelve acres of gardens and parkland including a walled garden dating back to 1698.

Great Dunmow. This little town has a history going back to Roman times, when it was an important staging point on Stane Street, the Roman Road running west from Colchester. Since medieval times it has been established as the traditional seat of the annual Flitch of Bacon Trials, in which a married couple had to convince the manorial court they had neither regretted nor offended their marriage for a year and a day. The couple who passed this test were awarded the Dunmow Flitch, a side of bacon. It was, however something of an ordeal, requiring couples to spend the duration of the proceedings kneeling on sharp stones, which perhaps explains why only eight couples succeeded in over 500 years. Today the 'trials' are still carried out, albeit in a more lighthearted and amusing annual ceremony.

Great Dunmow, not on the coast, was (perhaps surprisingly) the birthplace of Lionel Lukin, who designed and built the first lifeboat and tested it in the Doctor's Pond in the village in 1785 (a plaque commemorates the event). The boat employed safety principles not previously used, and it was claimed to be unsinkable even if upset by violent gales and filled with water.

Stansted Mountfichet. Just north of Bishop's Stortford and in the shadow of Stansted Airport, this small town traces its history back to Roman times. A castle was built here in the twelfth century, and a

reconstruction of it can be seen. The windmill here is the best-preserved tower mill in Essex, with most of the original machinery still intact.

Thaxted. Thaxted's past wealth came from the manufacture of cutlery, and later from the weaving trade. Like other East Anglian wool towns, its wealth is reflected for all to see in its fine church. It has two vaulted porches, one donated by Edward IV, the other by the Duke of Clarence. Down the narrow cobbled street from the church is the fifteenth-century timber-framed Guildhall, an unusual building with its arcaded ground floor, its overhanging upper floors topped by a twin gabled roof. The panelled room on the first floor was the meeting place of the town council, and the second floor was used as a schoolroom. It now houses a small museum.

Of the houses backing on to the rear of the Guildhall, one is called Dick Turpin's House and, although the famous highwayman was born in nearby Hempstead, this particular claim to fame may well be

Places of Interest in Essex

Colchester Zoo
Stanway Hall, 2 miles down B1022 road from Colchester.
Collection of primates, big cats and other animals.

Abberton Reservoir
Essex Birdwatching Society, 4 miles south of Colchester.
Largest reservoir in England, with public hide and picnic area. Famed for its varied bird life.

Ardleigh Reservoir
2 miles north-east of Colchester on the A137.
Large reservoir with birdwatching area.

Fingringhoe Wick
Essex Naturalists Trust nature reserve 4 miles south-east of Colchester.
Excellent nature trails and information centre, with facilities for disabled.

Bourne Mill (National Trust)
Sixteenth-century fishing lodge, later converted into a finishing mill for the cloth trade.

Layer Marney Tower
6 miles south-west of Colchester.
The highest Tudor gatetower in England.

St Osyth's Priory
10 miles south-east of Colchester just off the B1027.
Augustinian abbey with flint-panelled gatehouse.

Harwich Redoubt
Harwich.
Circular fort built in 1808 as part of the string of Martello towers and forts lining the East Coast as a defence against Napoleon.

Harwich Maritime Museum
Low Lighthouse, Harwich Green.
Displays of civilian and naval maritime activities.

Mersea Island Museum
West Mersea.
Displays of local and natural history as well as exhibits depicting local fishing industry.

Audley End House
(English Heritage)
Saffron Walden
Early seventeenth-century mansion, mostly demolished, and later remodelled by Vanbrugh.

Paycocke's (National Trust)
Coggeshall, 6 miles east of Braintree on A120.
Half-timbered merchant's house featuring a richly carved interior.

Spains Hall
Finchingfield, 8 miles north-west of Braintree on B1053.
Elizabethan manor house and gardens.

Finchingfield Guildhall and Museum
8 miles north-west of Braintree on B1053.
Fifteenth-century Guildhall displaying exhibits of local interest.

Thaxted Guildhall
7 miles south-east of Saffron Walden on B184.
Small local museum housed in fifteenth-century Guildhall.

a flight of fancy on the part of a past owner. Gustav Holst certainly lived in Thaxted at the time when he was composing the famous *Planets Suite*, in a thatched cottage in Monk Street. And Daisy, Countess of Warwick and one of Edward VII's mistresses, also lived here.

Debden. An attractive place amidst wooded countryside, Debden was an important fighter base during the Battle of Britain. The quiet little village overlooks the park which formed the estate of the Hall, an eighteenth-century country house demolished in 1936.

Saffron Walden. Another prosperous town in the Middle Ages, Saffron Walden takes its name from the saffron crocus, which it used to process to make dye. The dried stigmas were also used in cookery and herbalism. The Normans built a castle here, although only the keep remains today. The old part of the town, around the fifteenth-century church, has some very nice timber-framed houses, some with pargetting. The church itself is the largest parish church in Essex, another fine example of the Perpendicular style. The tomb of Thomas Lord Audley, Henry VIII's chancellor, is in the South Chapel. Also worth a visit are the Victorian gardens and maze at Bridge End, which boast a Dutch garden and pavilions.

Two miles west of the town is Audley End, a magnificent Jacobean mansion in impressive parkland beside the River Cam. Surprisingly, the present building is only a fraction of its former self. Three quarters of the original palace was demolished in the eighteenth century. Entering the park, which was landscaped by Capability Brown, the first view is of the imposing façade, with mullions and transoms crossing all the windows. Inside there are rooms full of paintings and exquisite furniture.

At Widdington, four miles south of Saffron Walden, is Prior's Hall Barn, a superb example of a medieval aisled barn.

Finchingfield. The residents of Finchingfield may have lost count of the number of times the classic view of the duck pond and village green, with tiled and thatched cottages gathered around, has appeared on calendars, chocolate boxes and jigsaw puzzles. Situated about eight miles south of Haverhill, it is without doubt a most attractive and picturesque village. It also boasts Spains Hall, an Elizabethan manor house. Its beautiful gardens include a 300-year-old Cedar of Lebanon tree.

Wethersfield. Two miles south-east of Finchingfield, this is a pleasant village — its squat church has a copper clad spire. Inside, a

Picturesque Finchingfield

list of former curates records the name of Patrick Branwell Bronte, father of the famous literary family, who started his ministry here before moving north.

Chipping Ongar. A market town whose name means just that ('chipping' is Old English for 'market'). The castle, of which only the mound survives, was probably built in Saxon times. St Martin's Church, an interesting building, has a rather curiously shaped font, and in the chancel wall a peep-hole facing the altar, behind which was a tiny cell for a hermit. David Livingstone, the famous missionary explorer, trained for his ministry here, and preached at the nonconformist chapel.

10
CAMBRIDGE

Cambridge naturally springs to mind as a great seat of learning, but the city's history goes back much further than the colleges, and was founded on principles more commercial than academic. Although the site of encampments of various military interests from the Romans onwards, its major importance was due to its position at the head of navigation on the River Cam, making it an ideal trading centre. When the college buildings did start to appear, it was this position on the Fenland waterways which allowed the extravagant use of building materials not natural to the region.

William the Conqueror built a castle here in 1068, as a forward position for his campaign against Hereward the Wake. Hereward nevertheless fought on for another three years from his base in the Fens before finally being overcome. Religious orders began to spring up, and it was probably as a result of these that the first colleges came about. In 1209, some scholars had to leave Oxford in rather a hurry after some trouble with the townsfolk. They came to Cambridge, and it was not long before a scholastic community was formed. By the mid-thirteenth century, this gathering of students and teachers was recognised as a university, despite the fact that they had no buildings of their own. In 1284 the first college was built next to a church called St Peter's, and was duly named Peterhouse by its founder, Hugh de Balsam, the Bishop of Ely.

The next two hundred years saw the addition of other colleges, and as they expanded, so did their powers. The university acquired the right to inspect weights and measures, in order that traders would not take advantage of the students. They even had their own courts, which could try offenders against members of the university.

Not surprisingly these powers, although rarely abused, led to unrest between the townsfolk and the university. (The townsfolk may not have relished the removal of a large number of buildings, including a church, to make way for King's College.) Similarly, the Backs, the peaceful gardens backing onto the river behind the colleges, were once common land on which the townsfolk grazed their sheep. The money which wealthy benefactors endowed on the various colleges was used tastefully, enhancing the city with a magnificent architectural heritage.

Many students who have passed through the university throughout the ages have helped shape events in history; Oliver Cromwell, Samuel Pepys, Isaac Newton, Charles Darwin, Milton, Tennyson, Wordsworth and Byron. Cromwell, a student at Sidney Sussex College, later became MP for Cambridge, and during the Civil War made the town his headquarters for the Eastern Association.

In the nineteenth century Cambridge expanded quite rapidly from a small town, and the arrival of the railway brought people, industry and housing, swallowing up some of the outlying villages. The centre of Cambridge, with its grand college buildings, narrow streets and alleyways, together with the peaceful open greens and the river, still retains a dignified charm which is unique among British towns and cities.

Cambridge has the highest concentration of buildings of interest of any town or city in East Anglia. At least two days are needed to see everything. The Tourist Information Centre in Wheeler Street organises very good guided tours of the city centre and the colleges. Two hours enables one to grasp some of the atmosphere and history of the place, but a thorough visit must be unhurried.

Cambridge is strangely akin to the Netherlands in one respect, that about ninety per cent of the population seems to travel on bicycles. Indeed, motorists seem to pay more regard to them here than elsewhere.

There are several places in Cambridge where cycles may be hired, but the city centre is small and an exploration on foot is preferable. The colleges are all open to the public, and it is possible to walk through the grounds and courtyards, and sometimes to enter the libraries and chapels. (There may be some restrictions at certain times of year, for example when exams are being held.) The following walks include all the main places of interest in the city centre. As they all start at the Market Place, and as the area covered is fairly

One of the many quiet courtyards in Cambridge

A lazy summer's afternoon punting on the River Cam, Cambridge

concentrated, it is possible to shorten the route, or combine it with the elements of another.

Starting off at the Market Place, go west along Market Street and turn left onto King's Parade, once the High Street of Cambridge. The left-hand side of the road with its shops, some dating back to the sixteenth century, are still intact. On the right, set back from the road, is the entrance gatehouse and magnificent screen of King's College. This part was built in the last century, designed to complement the style of the chapel which is considerably older. Continuing up King's Parade into Trumpington Street, turn right turn into Silver Street.

Queen's College. Just over the river on the right is Queens' College. Founded in 1448, this was one of the first colleges to be built in red brick when the rather expensive fashion of imported stone began to decline. The second court contains the President's Lodge, one of the few half-timbered Tudor college buildings. The curious wooden bridge across the river is the Mathematical Bridge, built on geometric principles, and originally held together without any fixing devices. In the last century, it was taken apart to discover the principles upon which it was built. Unfortunately those who dismantled it could not re-assemble it without the use of bolts.

St Catherine's College. Back up Silver Street and around the corner is St Catherine's College, its open court facing on to Trumpington Street. The chapel contains a memorial to Dr John Addenbrooke, who left £4,500 to found a hospital. Today's Addenbrookes Hospital is a vast complex standing on the southern outskirts of the city, renowned for its special skills in dealing with head injuries.

King's College. Retrace your steps to come to the impressive courtyard of King's College. The college was planned by Henry VI, although of his original layout only the chapel was built, and even that was not finished in his lifetime. The buildings around the courtyard were erected from 1724 to Victorian times, the last piece to appear being the screen and gatehouse, designed to complement the breathtaking Perpendicular style of the chapel. Inside the chapel the magnificent fan vaulting, and the carved screen and choir stalls are of particular interest. At the east end stands the altar, with Rubens' *Adoration of the Magi* behind it. Services are held daily except Mondays, during term time, when the famous choir of undergraduates and boys from King's School sings Evensong.

Clare College. Clare College is just behind King's, and although founded in medieval times by Elizabeth de Clare, the present buildings date from the seventeenth and eighteenth centuries. The college has a charming stone bridge over the river, built in 1640, the oldest surviving bridge in Cambridge.

Trinity Hall. Next door to Clare stands Trinity Hall, founded in 1350 by the Bishop of Norwich. Established to train priests, the college later began to specialise in law.

The Backs. The Backs of Cambridge are probably as well known as the colleges themselves. Immaculately kept lawns sweep down to the peaceful River Cam, where punters leisurely propel their flat-bottomed boats. It is now rare for a hapless punter to be seen clinging to his pole stuck in the mud on this stretch of river, as gravel has been spread along the river bed in the middle to stop poles sticking in.

Scholars' Piece, on the other side, was once common land. Bought by the colleges as each section became available, the gardens and paths were laid out to provide a quiet setting in which college members could relax and walk. The Backs can be reached from the rear entrance of King's College, further along the river at Clare Bridge, and by Garret Hostel Lane. Although the stretch of riverside bounded by these bridges is the part known as the Backs, the gardens and walks extend as far as St John's College.

Gonville and Caius College. On the opposite side of Trinity Lane to Trinity Hall is Gonville and Caius (pronounced 'Keys') College. The building of the two courts was separated by something like 200 years. The 'Gate of Honour' is the way out for the student who has successfully attained his or her degree. Opposite the open end of Caius Court is the Senate House, a classical-style building from which the newly conferred graduates make their way to the Gate of Honour. The ceremony in which students receive their degrees takes place at the end of June.

Trinity College. Trinity College, just up Trinity Street on the left, is Cambridge's largest college. Henry VIII founded it in 1546, bringing together a number of smaller institutions. The Great Court, probably the largest of its kind in the world, replaced the buildings which formed the original separate colleges. The fountain in the centre of the Great Court was built at the beginning of the seventeenth century by Italian craftsmen. After entering the Great Gate the chapel is on the right, containing Roubiliac's statue of Newton, along with commemorations of other famous members of the college. On the opposite side of the court to the Great Gate stands The Hall,

King's College from St Mary's church tower

Clare College

which contains Holbein's portrait of Henry VIII. The building was designed by Thomas Nevile, and through it is the courtyard which takes his name. Nevile's Court was finished in grand style by Sir Christopher Wren; at the far end is the library, which now houses a fine collection of statues and illuminated manuscripts. Trinity College has had many famous undergraduates, including members of the Royal Family. King Edward VII, then Prince of Wales, and his great-great-grandson, Prince Charles, both studied here.

The first tour finishes here, having followed the line of colleges to the west of King's Parade and Trinity Street. After coming out of Trinity, turn right to Market Street, on the left.

The second look at Cambridge concentrates on the area to the south of Market Street. The Market Square has a tradition going back to the early Middle Ages, although the present Square replaces houses destroyed by a fire in 1849. At the bottom of Peas Hill is Wheeler Street, where the Tourist Information Office is situated. The Saxon tower of St Benet's Church is the oldest building in the city, dating from about 1025.

Corpus Christi College. The church is linked by a sixteenth-century passage to the Old Court of Corpus Christi College, originally founded in 1352 by the merchant guilds of Corpus Christi and the Blessed Virgin Mary. This is the most ancient court in Cambridge, and unlike the buildings of other colleges, it has changed very little since it was built. Across the court is The Hall, which leads to the New Court, built about 1825 by William Wilkins, who also helped to design other college buildings. The west side of the New Court opens out on to Trumpington Street, just opposite St Catherine's, and on the left is St Botolph's, a fourteenth-century church which in medieval times stood just inside the city walls.

Pembroke College. A little further down Trumpington Street is Pembroke College, founded in 1347. It was here that Sir Christopher Wren first translated a design from the drawing board into stone. It was commissioned by Wren's uncle, the Bishop of Ely, who after spending eighteen years in prison decided that a building would be a fitting way to celebrate his release!

Along Trumpington Street particularly deep gutters line the road. They were installed in the seventeenth century in an attempt to improve the city's water supply.

Peterhouse. A little further along on the right is Peterhouse, distinguished as the first college in Cambridge. The original thirteenth-century buildings have been altered considerably. The arcade entrances on each side of the chapel lead into the courtyard, and the hall on the left features work from the William Morris studio.

Further down the road on the same side is the Fitzwilliam Museum, containing an outstanding collection of Greek, Roman and Egyptian antiquities. Apart from the ceramics and glassware, there

Places of Interest
In and Near Cambridge

American Military Cemetery
Madingley, 4 miles west of
Cambridge on the A1303
Graves and memorial to the
thousands of American service-
men who died operating from
Britain in World War II. Large
mural map of the war in Europe
displayed in the chapel.

Gog Magog Hills
4 miles south-east on the A1307
Iron Age earthworks, consisting
of circular ramparts and a ditch.
Later fortified by the Romans.

Pleasant walks through woods
and stretches of grassland.

Botanic Garden
Bateman Street
University botanic gardens used
for research, but open to the
public in summer.

Scott Polar Research Institute
Lensfield Road
Relics of Captain Scott's
expedition to the South Pole, and
exhibits from other trips.

is also a gallery of paintings by such artists as Constable, Cotman, Blake and Turner. From the entrance of the museum, a side street leads to Tennis Court Road, where Downing College is directly in front.

Downing College. Downing College differs from the style of the other colleges in that it is more open. Designed by William Wilkins in the early nineteenth century, the idea of the college came to fruition as early as 1749. The will of Sir George Downing provided for his estates to be used to found a new college, should certain relatives die childless. The surviving members of the family contested the will, and the legal wrangling lasted fifty years. After the building was started lack of funds delayed progress, and it was not until 1963 that the last building was completed, still in the same Greek style used by Wilkins 150 years earlier.

From Downing College, one can either emerge onto Regent Street, turning left to Emmanuel College a short distance up on the right, or go to the top of Tennis Court Road, and turn right onto Downing Street. On the right is the Museum of Geology and Archae- ology, its exhibits from all over the world dating from prehistoric to medieval times.

Emmanuel College. Emmanuel College, on St Andrew's Street,

Trinity Hall

The University Botanic Gardens, Cambridge

The tailplane of a B17 at the Imperial War Museum's site at Duxford Airfield

was originally the site of a Dominican Friary. After the Dissolution came a short period of disuse before Sir Walter Mildmay restored parts of the friary for use as a college. The chapel is another of Wren's works, this one showing Italian influences. One student at Emmanuel, John Harvard, emigrated to America, where the famous university in Massachusetts was named after him.

The return to the Market Place is along St Andrew's Street as far as Christ's College, and Petty Cury.

The last walk includes the area north of the Market Place. From Market Street or Petty Cury, a left turn into Sidney Street leads in a short distance, on the right, to Sidney Sussex College.

Sidney Sussex College. This is another college founded on the site of a friary, though few of the original buildings remain. Probably its most famous undergraduate was Oliver Cromwell, who later became MP for Cambridge.

Sidney Street opens out onto Bridge Street, and just up here on the right is the Round Church, built about 1130 in this unusual shape to commemorate the Holy Sepulchre in Jerusalem. The circular Norman nave, with its typical dog-tooth moulding arches, is capped with a conical roof, added in the nineteenth century to replace a fifteenth-century bell-tower.

St John's College. On the other side of the road, just down St John's Street, stretching back to the river and beyond, is St John's College, its early Tudor gateway richly decorated with the arms of its founder, Lady Margaret Beaufort. The gatehouse leads to the First Court, and beyond come the Second and Third, each younger than the previous. Joining this range of buildings with New Court, on the other side of the river, is the Bridge of Sighs. It borrows the idea of the covered bridge from one of the same name in Venice. Although the Cambridge version, built in 1831, has barred unglazed windows, the students passing through it were not necessarily looking their last upon the outside world as were the users of the original!

Magdalene College. Bridge Street becomes Magdalene Street over the river, and on the right is Magdalene College (pronounced Maudlin). Samuel Pepys studied here between 1650 and 1653, and on his death in 1703 his library came here, including the original manuscript volumes of his famous diaries. Just over the crossroads, on Castle Street, is the Folk Museum, which has displays of domestic and agricultural exhibits dating from medieval times. Kettle's Yard Art Gallery has a collection of twentieth-century paintings and sculptures on show.

Just off Castle Street on the right is the Castle Mound, in front of the Shire Hall. Nothing remains of the Norman castle now. After it fell into disuse, the stones were gradually sold off or 'borrowed' for other buildings, including several local colleges. The mound does, however, afford a good view of Cambridge.

Jesus College. Jesus College can be reached either by returning along Bridge Street and turning left into Jesus Lane, or by coming as far as Chesterton Lane (the crossroads just before Magdalene College) and taking the footbridge across the river onto Jesus Green. Jesus College grew from a twelfth-century convent, evidence of which can be clearly seen in the style of the chapel and cloisters. From Jesus Lane, a road behind Sidney Sussex College leads to a turn right on to King Street. The road follows round into Hobson Street, and at the end, on the left, is the entrance to Christ's College.

Christ's College. Founded by Henry VII's mother, Margaret Beaufort (as was St John's), the impressive gateway depicts her coat of arms, with a statue of her above. In the college gardens stands a mulberry tree under which Milton is said to have written *Lycidas*. The entrance is almost opposite the east end of Petty Cury, which leads back to the starting point.

Grantchester. This pretty little village lies just south of Cambridge, and has been a great favourite with undergraduates and tutors for generations. Rupert Brooke, who entered King's College in 1906, lived and wrote many of his famous poems in The Old Vicarage at Grantchester, a house almost as well known today as the home of best-selling novelist and former Tory party chairman Jeffrey Archer.

Duxford. As you approach Junction 10 on the M11, you cannot fail to notice the impressive array of aircraft parked outside a number of hangars. This is the Imperial War Museum's airfield, with exhibits which include one of the Concorde prototypes, B17 Flying Fortress, B52, Spitfire, Mustang, Vulcan, Victor, military vehicles and submarines. Duxford was an important base during the Battle of Britain, and it was from here that Douglas Bader's 'Big Wing' flew. The base also relived those hot summer weeks of 1940 when they used it for some of the scenes in the 1969 film *Battle of Britain*, which included actually blowing up one of the old hangars!

11
FENLAND

Today's Fenland is probably the most fertile arable land in the country, and yet it has not reached this state without some considerable effort over a long period of time. For hundreds of years the Fens existed as marshes, a wasteland of sedge and reeds. In the summer it was possible to graze sheep and cattle, and there were, of course, the proceeds from reed cutting, and some wildfowling. In the winter the rivers overflowed, flooding the peaty countryside to such an extent that no agriculture was possible.

The Romans recognised the problem and tried unsuccessfully to drain the land, as did later inhabitants, but it was not until the seventeenth century that sufficient technology existed to enable someone to tackle it. The Earl of Bedford owned about 20,000 acres of land near Whittlesey, and it was he, along with some others, who employed a Dutch engineer, Cornelius Vermuyden, to drain the land.

His first attempt was the Old Bedford River, a straight cut from Earith to Denver. This twenty-one mile stretch bypassed the Great Ouse, and allowed water to drain to the sea more quickly. Summer use of the land was improved, but it still tended to flood during the winter months. When the Civil War was over, Vermuyden returned to improve his original scheme by constructing another drainage cut called the New Bedford River. It was parallel to the first cut, never running more than one kilometre from the first. The strip of land between the two man-made rivers was called the Ouse Washes, as this was allowed to flood during the winter. Sluices at Earith and Denver controlled the flow of water in times of flood, directing it from the mainstream of the New Bedford River into the slightly

Denver Sluice and its board showing the tolls once levied for crossing the bridge

The Jenyns Arms
DENVER & HILGAY

GREAT OUSE RIVER BOARD
DENVER SLUICE BRIDGE

Tolls Authorised to be taken every time of
passing this bridge and Sluice   s.d.
For every   person passing on foot or, Easter Monday. 1.
For every   Horse. Mare, Gelding, Mule or Ass.   1.
For every   Ox, Cow, or Large Cattle.   1.
For every   Sheep, Lamb, Pig, or Calf.   1.
For every   Cycle. 3 or less number of wheels.   1.
For every   Cart or Carriage with two wheels,
including one horse. Mare, Gelding, Mule or Ass
if drawn by same.   6.
For every   Horse, Mare, Gelding Mule or Ass in addition   1.
For every   Waggon, Road Trolley, Van or Motor Cycle)
Implement, Thrashing or other Machinery
Vehicle or   arriage with four wheels if not laden) 1.0.
For the like if laden.   2.0.
For every Thrashing or Traction Engine or Steam
ro er whose full load weight does not exceed 5 tons 2.6.
N   Traction Engines or Steam rollers whose full
     ad weight exceed 5 tons are prohibited from
going over this Bridge and Sluice.

EXEMPTIONS

Members of the Board and Office   s, Servants and
workmen of the Board when engaged on the business
of the Board.
The Inhabitants on the west side of the sluice when
going or returning from divine Service on Sunday

THIS TOLL DISCONTINUED APRIL 1963

lower Old Bedford, from which it overflowed into the Washes. Modifications have been made since, but the basic drainage system remains.

Many other rivers received similar treatment, with straight drainage cuts like Forty Foot, Sixteen Foot and Middle Level Drains duplicating their courses. Natural drainage proved not to be enough. At the same time, water has to be pumped from the fields into the rivers, whose embankments are higher than the surrounding countryside. Windpumps were used in the old days, but modern diesel or electric pumps are now used, discharging water into tidal rivers when the tide is going out, then closing the sluices to stop it flooding back when the tide turns.

As the peaty land of the Fens slowly sinks in relation to the level of the sea, the pumps have to work harder. As the peat gradually dries out, it shrinks. A good example of this can be seen at Wicken Fen. Here, it is largely undrained, and higher than the surrounding land. Constant agriculture also depletes the soil, and eventually there will be nothing covering the underlying clay.

The winding rivers of the Fens, which the new cuts help to drain, are ideal for boating holidays. From the Great Ouse, one can reach Bedford, Huntingdon, Ely, Cambridge, and even venture east up tributaries into Breckland. Between Denver Sluice and Whittlesey lies a system of around seventy miles of waterways called the Middle Level. Based around the old course of the River Nene, it is reached by locks at either end, and offers some very peaceful cruising. To the west is the River Nene, which provides access to Peterborough and Northampton as well as being a link with the Grand Union Canal. As not all hire craft are licensed to travel the different systems, the exact route of the cruise must be stated at the time of booking.

King's Lynn. The ancient town of King's Lynn stands on the banks of the Great Ouse, and has for centuries been a prosperous trading port. In 1100 the first Bishop of Norwich, Herbert de Losinga, built the Church of St Margaret and the adjoining priory. Lynn was granted a Royal Charter some hundred years later, and became known as King's Lynn when Henry VIII confiscated all church property. The secret of Lynn's success was that, standing at the outfall of so many interconnected rivers, it was able to service the trading needs of towns in the East Midlands, Lincolnshire, Cambridgeshire and Norfolk. The splendid houses in the town testify to the wealth Lynn has enjoyed since medieval times. The arrival of the railways in the last century changed the town's circumstances to some extent, but today Lynn is not only a thriving port, but also a sizeable industrial centre.

Just south of the docks and the Fisher Fleet is the Tuesday Market Place, surrounded by some imposing buildings, including the nineteenth-century Corn Exchange and the seventeenth-century Dukes Head. The south-west corner of the Market Place leads to King Street, and not far down it is the Guildhall of St George, the largest and oldest example in England of a medieval merchant's house. In Shakespeare's time it was a theatre, and it is known that the bard himself appeared on stage here. After a long period of use as a warehouse, the Guildhall has reverted to use as a theatre, and is the focal point of the King's Lynn Festival.

Two hundred yards down King Street is the Custom House, built in the Palladian style in 1683. From here, King Street becomes Queen Street, and not far along it stands Clifton House. The house itself, largely rebuilt in the eighteenth century although the tower in the courtyard is Elizabethan, also has a fourteenth-century crypt with medieval tiled floors. At the far end of Queen Street is Thoresby College, opposite the Guildhall of the Holy Trinity. Built in 1421, this municipal building with its chequered face of flint and freestone proudly displays two royal coats of arms above its Elizabethan porch. Inside, the Regalia Room houses some astonishing items, including the gold and enamel 'King John's Cup', and 'King John's Sword', dating back to the times of the first charter awarded to the town in 1204 by King John.

Around the corner in St James' Street, is the Saturday Market Place, where a market has been held since the time of Bishop de Losinga. At the head of St James' Street is the park, containing The Walks, eighteenth-century avenues of lime and chestnut trees. Here stands the Red Mount Chapel, built in 1485 as a 'taster' for pilgrims on their way to the shrine at Walsingham.

Downham Market. Like King's Lynn, Downham Market lies along the border of Fenland, with Breckland not far distant to the east. Romantic links with the Civil War exist here too. The White Swan played host to a disguised Charles I, who was on his way to join the Scottish army at Newark. Another interesting inn is the seventeenth-century Crown.

Norfolk carr-stone is much in evidence in the buildings in the town, with some noteworthy Georgian houses and a fifteenth-century church with an unusual spire.

The Ouse Washes. Between Earith and Denver run the straight and parallel drainage cuts of the Old and New Bedford Rivers. The thin island bounded by these rivers is called the Ouse Washes, and is now one of the few places in Fenland which can really be called Fens. It is managed in almost the same way as the land would have been in medieval times, grazed in the summer, and generally flooded in the winter. (The Ouse Washes were intended to allow for winter flooding to ensure that the surrounding area remained properly drained.)

Apart from achieving the main task of draining the surrounding countryside, making it fit for year-round agriculture, the drainage

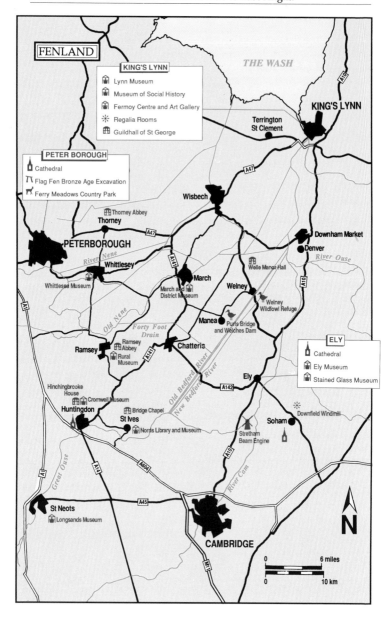

FENLAND

KING'S LYNN
- Lynn Museum
- Museum of Social History
- Fermoy Centre and Art Gallery
- Regalia Rooms
- Guildhall of St George

PETER BOROUGH
- Cathedral
- Flag Fen Bronze Age Excavation
- Ferry Meadows Country Park

THE WASH

KING'S LYNN

Terrington
St Clement

A47

Wisbech

Downham Market

Denver

River Ouse

Thorney Abbey

Thorney

PETERBOROUGH

River Nene

Whittlesey

Welle Manor Hall

Whittlesea Museum

March

Welney

March and
District Museum

Welney
Wildfowl Refuge

Old Nene

Forty Foot
Drain

Manea

Puris Bridge
and Welches Dam

Ramsey
Abbey
Rural
Museum

Ramsey

Chatteris

ELY
- Cathedral
- Ely Museum
- Stained Glass Museum

Hinchingbrooke
House

Cromwell Museum

Huntingdon

Bridge Chapel

St Ives

Norris Library and Museum

Ely

A142

Downfield Windmill

Soham

Stretham
Beam Engine

Great Ouse

A45

River Cam

St Neots

Longsands Museum

CAMBRIDGE

N

0 ——— 6 miles
0 ——— 10 km

Denver Windmill

system has turned the Ouse Washes into an important wildlife habitat. Of their 4,689 acres, over half is in the hands of various conservation bodies, notably the RSPB, the Cambridgeshire Wildlife Trust, and the Wildfowl Trust. The whole area was designated a Site of Special Scientific Interest in 1968, an indication of its national importance.

Black-tailed godwits, a species of bird once rarely seen in Britain, now breed here regularly along with snipe, mallard, coots, reed warblers and many others. In winter, flooding tends to vary in depth from several feet to a few inches, providing a wide range of habitat for a variety of waterfowl. The Ouse Washes are a particularly important habitat for the Bewick's swan, approximately half the British population come here — significant indeed as the total number of Bewick's swans in the world is something like 12,000, and about 1,000 of them winter on the Ouse Washes! The main places for observation can be found near Welney and Manea.

Ely. Before the draining of the Fens in the seventeenth century, Ely was literally an island of gault clay, surrounded by watery marshes. The name is derived from *Elig*, meaning 'island of eels', supposedly because St Dunstan took offence at the lack of celibacy amongst the monks there. As if eternal damnation were not enough, he turned them all into eels!

From every viewpoint in and around Ely, the cathedral dominates the skyline. The original abbey was founded in 673 by St Etheldreda, but like many other East Anglian monasteries, was sacked by the Danes in 870. A new monastery was built, and at the time of the Norman invasion, became the last stronghold of Anglo-Saxon resistance, under Hereward the Wake.

Romanticised by the novelist Charles Kingsley, Hereward's stand against the Normans was fuelled with a thirst for revenge after they had killed his brother whilst trying to dispossess his family at Bourne. Hereward, at the time an outlaw in Flanders, returned home and led the sacking of the Anglo-Saxon monastery at Peterborough. Afterwards, he took refuge on the Isle of Ely, making good use of the treacherous nature of the surrounding marshes. Despite several attempts to besiege the isle, Hereward continued to harry the Normans, and when eventually they did manage to break into Ely, Hereward was able to escape the bloodbath which followed. What became of him afterwards is unclear.

As a bishopric, Ely Cathedral survived the Dissolution, although

Cromwell, who lived in Ely for some time, caused it to be closed for seventeen years. Until the nineteenth century, and the Industrial Revolution which brought the railways into prominence, Ely was a significant port on the Great Ouse. Today it is a small and attractive market town presiding over an agricultural sea of rich black peat.

Almost inevitably the first visit in Ely will be the cathedral, a striking building begun in 1083, and not completed for 268 years. Had it not been for the untimely arrival of the Black Death, the nave and transepts would probably have been roofed in stone, but in fact, the building has been roofed in wood. The paintings on the ceiling were done in Victorian times. In the fourteenth century, the sacrist of the priory, Alan de Walsingham, designed the Lady Chapel and the octagonal central tower, replacing the former square one which had collapsed in 1322. This piece of architectural genius was accomplished in only twenty-six years, a considerable feat, and still a marvel to behold — four hundred tons of masonry, suspended without any apparent means of support.

From the Galilee porch at the west end, (so called because, as Galilee was the furthest place in the Holy Land from Bethlehem, so too is the west porch furthest from the altar) the whole length of the nave opens out to view — 537ft in all. Unlike Norwich Cathedral, there is no screen to interrupt the view of Norman columns and arches stretching away towards the fourteenth-century choir. A screen did exist — in fact it was the only Norman screen made of stone in England — but it was taken down in 1769 in an act of eighteenth-century 'restoration'.

Off the north-east corner of the north transept is the Lady Chapel. Its medieval stained-glass windows must have brought a blaze of colour inside this vaulted addition to the cathedral. Unfortunately, the windows and many of the carvings inside the chapel were destroyed by iconoclasts during the Reformation. However, examples of windows from the fourteenth century to the present day can be seen in specially lighted displays in the cathedral's Stained Glass Museum.

Around the cathedral stand a number of monastic buildings in 'The College', named thus rather than the more usual 'Close' found in other cathedral cities because of Kings' School, founded in the precincts by Alfred the Great after he defeated the Danes at Ethaldune. Across Palace Green from the west end stands the half-timbered Cromwell House in St Mary's Street. Cromwell lived in this

The Custom House, King's Lynn

house, now St Mary's vicarage, from 1636 to 1647. Back up St Mary's and across into High Street, there is a good view of the sixteenth-century Steeple Gate on the right, with the museum about a hundred yards further on.

Soham. The church at Soham is quite impressive. The town was once important as one of the first places to have a monastic community set up by St Felix, whose cathedral was at Dunwich. The Burgundian missionary met his death here, and the abbey was burned down later in a raid by the Danes.

Downfield Windmill can be found on Fordham Road. This brick tower mill was built in 1726 and is fully working when the wind is strong enough. Flour ground in the mill is for sale.

Lode. This place is significant mainly for its Augustinian priory,

Ely Cathedral

Anglesey Abbey. As with many other such buildings in East Anglia, the priory was given over to domestic use in the sixteenth century. Past owners include Thomas Hobson, several times mayor of nearby Cambridge, and owner of a livery stable and carrier's business. He kept 'forty good cattle', available for hire, although you had to make do with the beast Hobson chose for you, not necessarily the one you would have preferred, which gave rise to the immortal expression 'Hobson's choice'.

Anglesey Abbey was bequeathed to the National Trust in 1966 by the first Lord Fairhaven, and his nephew now lives here. The abbey is set in 100 acres of superb gardens, and across the lode, the nearby canal, is a fully restored watermill which can be seen grinding corn at weekends.

St Ives. When Ramsey Abbey was the most important place of the area, St Ives was a satellite owned by the abbey. It was the monastery which built the quaint fifteenth-century bridge over the River Ouse, with its tiny chapel in the centre — one of only three in England.

The town's name comes from St Ivo, a seventh-century Persian missionary whose remains were supposedly found here in the eleventh century when the monastery was founded. Oliver Cromwell was churchwarden at the All-Saints' Church, and a statue of him can be found in Market Hill. The Norris Museum on The Broadway has local collections ranging from prehistoric remains to bygones.

Huntingdon. Cromwell was born here in 1599, at Cromwell House in the main street. The grammar school which he and diarist Samuel Pepys attended is now the Cromwell Museum, and gives an insight into the Cromwell family and his side of the Great Rebellion (1640 to 1660). Cromwell lived here until 1631, when a quarrel with the town council inspired him to go and live in nearby St Ives.

Nearby Hinchinbrooke House, a thirteenth-century Benedictine nunnery now used as a school, also has associations with Cromwell and Pepys.

Four miles south-west of Huntingdon is Buckden Palace, the twelfth-century seat of the Bishops of Lincoln, parts of which have been restored. The gardens are also open to the public.

Ramsey. Now the local vegetable-growing capital, Ramsey was once important for its great Benedictine abbey. Part of it is now incorporated into the Abbey Grammar School, but the ruins of the fifteenth-century gatehouse are open to the public. The Rural Museum has examples of local and agricultural bygones.

Stilton. This is a small village south of Peterborough with a reputation from ages past for a cheese which it has never actually produced. The village was an important staging point on the Great North Road — now the A1 and thankfully diverted around the village. Leicestershire farmers took their produce to the seventeenth-century Bell Inn for delivery by coach to London, where the cheese became known as Stilton.

Peterborough. Once called *Gildenburgh* (or Golden Borough), Peterborough's riches were directly attributable to its monastery. Until the Dissolution the abbot exercised control over the area, and sheep farming provided a handsome income. The monastery then became the cathedral, a special dispensation on the part of Henry VIII. His first wife, Catherine of Aragon, was buried there, and he did not want the place to fall into disrepair.

Now Peterborough is a curious mixture of old and new, being the only cathedral city in the country also to be designated a new town. This new expansion has happened in the last thirty years as a result of the Greater London overspill scheme, and with incentives to attract businesses much of the old city has become overwhelmed by new developments.

The general layout of the city is attributed to Martin de Vecti, who as abbot from 1133 to 1155, rebuilt the town on the western side of the monastery, ensuring that its foundations lay in dry limestone rather than the oft-flooded marshlands to the east. Abbot Martin was responsible for laying out the market place and the wharf beside the river.

The cathedral is the focal point of the city, having risen from the monastery originally founded in 654 by Paeda, the king of Mercia. The present building is Norman, and is one of only three churches in Europe with an early painted wooden ceiling in its nave, and of those three, Peterborough's is by far the biggest. The eastern end of the cathedral, noted for its exquisite fan vaulting, was added in 1500. The Italian marble floor and the canopy over the high altar were added much more recently, in the 1890s.

Catherine of Aragon is buried in the north choir aisle, and Mary, Queen of Scots, lay in the south aisle for twenty-five years after her execution, before being reinterred in Westminster Abbey. The portrait of Old Scarlett, the gravedigger who buried both queens, can be seen on the west wall.

Up until the 1860s it would have been possible to hail a sedan chair outside the cathedral gate. Peterborough was one of the last cities in the country to operate a sedan chair service.

St John's Church is well known in local folklore for the story of Matthew Wyldbore, an old man who once lost his way out in the Fens when a heavy fog came down on him. Just as he thought he was going to spend an enforced night out in the open country, he heard the bells of St John's in the distance, and was guided back home by them. When he died, he left a legacy which paid for the bell-ringers to ring a peal of bells on the anniversary of that eventful night and 15 March is still known as Wyldbore's day.

Cathedral Square is dominated by the Guildhall, or Butter Cross. The present Guildhall is a seventeenth-century building. Previously, the Tudor Butter Cross was a simple shelter where the city weights and measures were kept, and local traders were allowed to sell their butter and eggs. The Royal Arms of Charles II, underneath the clock, were added at the behest of Lord Fitzwilliam, who contributed much towards the cost of restoration.

In Priestgate, at the junction with Cross Street, stands the museum, housing a unique collection of bone and straw marquetry work made by French prisoners of war during the Napoleonic Wars. Six miles south-west of the city on the A1 is a stone column surmounted by a French eagle. The monument stands as a memorial to 1,770 French soldiers who died at the Napoleonic prisoner of war camp at Norman Cross between 1796 and 1816. No trace of the camp remains other than the governor's house, now a private residence.

Just to the east of the city is Flag Fen, the only place in the country where you can see the timbers of a Bronze Age village. The site, discovered in 1982, was a man-made defensive island, built in the marshes from over a million timbers. The Fenland peat seems to have kept things in a 3,000 year time warp. Where most dry archaeological sites yield artefacts of bone, pottery and stone, here the peaty waters have 'pickled' everything. Marks in the timbers made by the axes which hewed them are still visible. Other remarkable finds include tools, and even grains of wheat, leaves, insects and barley pollen — all perfectly preserved.

Whittlesey. Five miles east of Peterborough on the A605, Whittlesey is one of the main towns producing the red clay bricks which make up so much of modern Britain, although the most commonly used type of brick takes its name from Fletton, just down the road

Peckover House, Wisbech

towards Peterborough. The industry is portrayed in the museum in the Town Hall in Market Street, with displays on local archaeology and agriculture.

The day after Plough Monday, the first Monday after the Twelve Days of Christmas, and thus the first day of hard work and the start of ploughing, was traditionally the time when the old custom of straw bear dancing took place. The day 'Straw Bear Tuesday' or 'Strawbower Day' originated in ceremonies recalling the pagan fertility rites often associated with the start of spring ploughing. Whittlesey was one of the last towns in England where this happened before it died out early this century. The custom was revived in the late 1970s and continues annually in a festival over the Friday and Saturday before Plough Monday. The straw bear, a man in a straw-covered costume, dances through the streets accompanied by groups of Morris dancers.

Whittlesey's most famous son was undoubtedly General Sir Harry Smith, who fought successful campaigns in the Napoleonic and Sikh wars and served as governor of Cape province in South Africa. Even his romantic life was adventurous. He rescued a young

Spanish lady at the Siege of Badajoz, who subsequently became his wife.

Not far away, in the woods near Holme, one of the iron columns which originally supported the Great Exhibition building stands with its top 12ft exposed. It was buried with the top flush to the surface in 1851, and its present state underlines the way the peat ground of Fenland is rapidly shrinking.

Thorney. This is a most un-Fen-like village, mainly because it is part of the Earl of Bedford's estate, and has been kept as a model estate village. Pretty houses and trees abound everywhere. A small abbey was founded at Thorney in 657, and although it was destroyed in the great Danish raid of 870, it was refounded by the Benedictines about a hundred years later, only to be sacked again during one of Hereward's scuffles with the Normans. Like so many others, the glorious buildings of Thorney Abbey suffered at the hands of Henry VIII's Dissolution, and all that stands now is the west end of the church and 117ft of the nave.

March. This thriving town, well established in Saxon times, takes its name from being on the boundary or 'march' between the East Angles and the Middle Angles. As with many other Fenland towns, it was built on an 'island' in the marshes, and it gained increasing prosperity through agriculture after the land was drained. The railway has also had a significant effect on the town's development, and a huge marshalling yard built in the 1930s was at the time reputed to be the biggest in the country.

The cast-iron memorial fountain to George V's coronation at the top of Broad Street should be seen. The extremely attractive church, dedicated to St Wendreda, has a sixteenth-century double hammer-beam roof decorated with a magnificent choir of 120 wide-winged angels, probably one of the best examples of its kind. The museum in High Street houses local agricultural exhibits.

Wisbech. Although ten miles from the sea on what is now an artificial River Nene, Wisbech maintains its long tradition as a sea port. A good trade also exists with Peterborough, twenty miles up-river. It is the wealth created by the years of shipping which has given Wisbech two of the most perfect Georgian streets in England — the Brinks. The North and South Brinks, sombre rows of mansions and warehouses, look out over each other on opposite sides of the river. The façade of the brewery, on the North Brink, has remained almost unchanged since it was built in 1790. Its present occupiers, Elgoods,

Places of Interest in Fenland

Buckden Palace
Huntingdon
Remains of old palace once
used as residence by the
bishops of Lincoln.

Peckover House
(National Trust) Wisbech
Merchant's house on the North
Brink of the River Nene. Rococo
interior, Victorian garden with
unusual trees.

Wildfowl Trust
Peakirk, 7 miles north of Peterborough on the B1443.
17 acres of water gardens
containing wildfowl, including
such exotic species as Chilean
flamingos, Coscoroba swans and
Andean geese.

Bridge Chapel
St Ives
Tiny chapel in the centre of a
fifteenth-century bridge.

Longthorpe Tower
(English Heritage)
near Peterborough
Early secular wall paintings
inside fourteenth-century tower.

Ramsey Abbey Gatehouse
(National Trust)
Ramsey
Ruins of fifteenth-century gate-
house.

Haddenham Farmland Museum
7 miles south-west of Ely

Collection of agricultural implements and local bygones.

March and District Museum
March
Displays on local life.

Norris Library and Museum
St Ives
Local collections

Wisbech and Fenland Museum
Museum Square, Wisbech
Displays on Fenland and natural
history.

Ferry Meadows
Nene Park, Peterborough. 2
miles west of city centre off A605.
500-acre country park with
grassland, woodland and lakes
for varied range of recreations.

Downfield Mill
5 miles south-east of Ely on
Fordham Road, Soham
Brick tower mill, built about 1726.
Can be seen in action, whole-
meal flour ground in the mill for
sale.

Denver Windmill
Denver
Six storey mill built around 1835.

Anglesey Abbey
(National Trust)
Lode, 6 miles north-east of
Cambridge off B1102
Thirteenth-century abbey, later
Tudor house, set in 100 acres of
gardens.

have been supplying local pubs with fine ales from here for over a hundred years. More recently, they have been credited with brewing the first low-alcohol bitter.

Octavia Hill was born in one of the houses on the South Brink in 1838. She worked with great energy in the field of housing reform, improving conditions for the poorer sectors of society, particularly in London. She was also one of the three founder members of the National Trust, and opposite, on the North Brink, is the National Trust-owned Peckover House, showing a handsome example of early eighteenth-century architecture and furnishings. The house was owned by Jonathan Peckover, a local banker, who merged his business with two others and went on to become one of the founder members of Barclays Bank in 1896.

The other person of note connected with Wisbech is commemorated in the splendid 68ft-high Gothic style memorial beside the old bridge. Thomas Clarkson dedicated his life to travelling the country, speaking in support of William Wilberforce's anti-slavery movement. Unveiled in 1881, the monument was designed by Sir Gilbert Scott, and contains bas-relief panels created by Josiah Wedgwood.

At **Tydd St Giles**, north-west of Wisbech on the nearby Cambridgeshire/Lincolnshire border, Nicholas Breakspear, the only Englishman to become pope, practised as a curate, and at Upwell, six miles to the south-east is Welle Manor Hall. This ecclesiastical medieval manor house has some of the oldest brickwork in the county. Norfolk Punch is also brewed here, an additional attraction for those who enjoy this delicious herbal drink, and a tasting is included in the tour of the house.

The rich dark peat of the Fens is not just used for food production. It is also an important flower growing area, and springtime visitors to Wisbech will be treated to a dazzling blaze of colour from the bulb fields surrounding the town.

USEFUL INFORMATION FOR VISITORS

The information has been obtained mainly from material produced by the East Anglia Tourist Board. Admission charges have been omitted, as they tend to be revised fairly frequently. Where available, telephone numbers have been included. It is also worth noting that although many places have opening times listed, these too can be subject to variation. If you are in any doubt, it pays to check first before taking a long trip.

Abbreviations
EH: English Heritage
ENT: Essex Naturalists' Trust
NCC: Nature Conservancy Council
NNT: Norfolk Naturalists' Trust
NT: National Trust
RSPB: Royal Society for the Protection of Birds
STNC: Suffolk Trust for Nature Conservation

Ancient Monuments and Historic Buildings

Norfolk
Baconsthorpe Castle (EH)
6 miles south-west of Cromer, off A148
Open: any reasonable time.

Binham Priory (EH)
Binham, 5 miles south-east of Wells, off B1388
Open: any reasonable time.

Blakeney Guildhall (EH)
Blakeney, 4 miles north-west of Holt
Open: dawn to dusk.

Burgh Castle (EH)
3 miles west of Great Yarmouth
Open: Easter-October, dawn to dusk.

Burnham Norton Friary
1 mile north of Burnham Market off A149
Open: all year, daily.

Caistor Roman Town (EH)
2 miles north of Great Yarmouth off A1064
Open: dawn to dusk.

Castle Acre Priory (EH)
4 miles north of Swaffham off A1065
Open: Easter-September, daily, 10am-6pm; October-Maundy Thursday, daily except Monday, 10am-4pm. Closed 24-26 December, 1 January.

Castle Rising (EH)
4 miles north-east of King's Lynn
off A149
Open: Easter-September, daily,
10am-6pm; October-Maundy
Thursday, daily except Monday,
10am-4pm. Closed 24-26 December, 1 January.

Cockley Cley Iceni Village
4 miles south-west of Swaffham
☎ (0760) 721339
Open: Easter-October, daily, 1.30-
5.30pm; mid July-mid September
daily 11.30am-5.30pm.

Creake Priory (EH)
3 miles south of Burnham Market
on B1355
Open: any reasonable time.

Grimes Graves (EH)
Weeting, 2 miles north of Brandon
off A1065
Open: Easter-September, daily,
10am-6pm; October-Maundy
Thursday, daily except Monday,
10am-4pm. Closed 24-26 December, 1 January.

New Buckenham Castle
New Buckenham, 16 miles south-
west of Norwich on B1113
☎ (0953) 860374
Open: all year, Monday-Friday,
8am-6pm, Saturday, 8.30am-1pm.

Norfolk Pillar
Great Yarmouth.
Open: July, August, daily except
Saturday, 2-6pm.

**North Elmham Saxon Cathedral
and Bishop's Castle** (EH)
5 miles north of Dereham on B1110
Open: any reasonable time.

Norwich Castle
see Norwich Castle Museum

Norwich Cathedral
Norwich
Open: May-September, Monday-
Sunday, 7.30am-7pm.

St Benet's Abbey
near Ludham, off A1062. Also
access by boat from River Bure
Open: no restrictions.

St John's Cathedral
Norwich
Open: all year, daily. Tower tours
May-September, Saturday 2.30-
4.30pm.

St Olaves Priory (EH)
6 miles south-west of Great
Yarmouth on A143
Open: all year.

St Peter Mancroft Church
Norwich
Open: all year, daily, 10am-4.30pm
or dusk.

**Shrine of Our Lady
of Walsingham**
Holt Road, Walsingham
☎ (032 872) 255
Open: all year, 6.30am to dusk.

Slipper Chapel
near Houghton St Giles, 2 miles
south-west of Little Walsingham
on B1105
Open: all year, daily, 9am-dusk.

Thetford Priory (EH)
Thetford
Open: Easter-September, daily,
10am-6pm.

Thetford Warren Lodge
Thetford
Open: view from outside any time.

Walsingham Abbey Grounds
Walsingham, near Fakenham
☎ (032 872) 259
Open: April, Wednesday; May-July
and September, Wednesday,
Saturday, Sunday; August,
Monday, Wednesday, Friday,
Saturday, Sunday, 2-5pm, or by
appointment.

Weeting Castle (EH)
Weeting, 2 miles north of Brandon
on B1106.
Open: any reasonable time.

Suffolk
Bungay Castle Ruins
Bungay
Open: all year, daily.

Bury St Edmunds Abbey (EH).
Remains of abbey including two
great gateways.

Clare Castle
Clare
Open: daily.
Earthworks and ruins.

Framlingham Castle (EH)
Framlingham
Open: Easter-September, daily,
10am-6pm; October-Maundy
Thursday, daily except Monday,
10am-4pm. Closed 24-26 December, 1 January.

Leiston Abbey (EH)
Leiston
Open: any reasonable time.

Orford Castle (EH)
Orford
Open: Easter-September, daily,
10am-6pm; October-Maundy
Thursday, daily except Monday,
10am-4pm. Closed 24-26 December, 1 January.

Q Tower
South Hill, Felixstowe
Open: May-September, Monday-
Saturday, 10.30am-5pm, Sunday,
10.30am-6pm.

St James's Chapel (EH)
Lindsey
Open: all year, dawn to dusk.

Sutton Hoo
near Woodbridge
☎ (03943) 7673
Open: April-mid September,
Saturday, Sunday, Bank Holiday
Monday, 2-4pm.

Theatre Royal (NT)
Westgate Street, Bury St Edmunds
☎ (0284) 755127
Open: daily excluding Sunday and
Bank Holidays, 10am-6pm. No
access while theatrical activity.

West Stow Anglo-Saxon Village
West Stow, 5 miles north-west of
Bury St Edmunds off A1101
☎ (028484) 718
Open: all year, daily, 10am-5pm.

Cambridgeshire
Bridge Chapel
St Ives
Open: on request of key from
Town Hall, Norris Library and
Museum, or B.R. Knight (Antiques), the Quay, during opening
hours.

Denny Abbey (EH)
Waterbeach, 5 miles north of
Cambridge off A10
Open: Easter-September, daily,
10am-6pm; October-Maundy
Thursday, Sunday only, 10am-
4pm.

Duxford Chapel (EH)
Duxford, 6 miles south of
Cambridge off A505
Open: all year, daily, dawn-dusk.

Ely Cathedral
Ely
Open: summer, daily, 7am-7pm;
winter, Monday-Saturday, 7.30am-
6.30pm.

Flag Fen Bronze Age Excavation
Peterborough. Open: Easter-
October, daily, 11am-4pm.

Isleham Priory (EH)
6 miles west of Mildenhall on
B1104. Open: any reasonable time.

King's College Chapel
Cambridge
Open: mid March-mid October,
Monday-Saturday, 11am-3.30pm.

Longthorpe Tower (EH)
Western outskirts of Peterborough
Open: Easter-September, daily,
10am-6pm; October-Maundy
Thursday, daily except Monday,
10am-4pm. Closed 24-26 December, 1 January.

Peterborough Cathedral
Peterborough
Open: January-April and October-
December, weekdays, 7am-6.15pm;
May-September, 7am-8pm. Sunday
all year, 8am-5pm.

Ramsey Abbey
Ramsey, 12 miles north of Huntingdon on B1040
Open: April-October, Sunday,
2-5pm.

Ramsey Abbey Gatehouse (NT)
Abbey School, Ramsey
Open: Easter-October, daily, 10am-
5pm, and other times by appointment.

Thorney Abbey Church
Thorney, 7 miles east of Peter-
borough on A47
Open: all year, daily.

Essex
Chelmsford Cathedral
☎ (0245) 263660
Open: all year, daily, 8am-5.30pm.

Coggeshall Barn (NT)
Coggeshall, 10 miles west of
Colchester on A120
Open: April-October, Tuesday,
Thursday, Sunday, Bank Holidays,
1-5pm.

Hadleigh Castle (EH)
Hadleigh, Leigh, near Southend
Open: any reasonable time.

Harwich Redoubt
Main Road, Harwich
Open: May-September, Monday-
Saturday, 9am-5pm, Sunday,
10am-5pm; October-April, Sunday,
10am-12noon and 2-5pm.

Hedingham Castle
Castle Hedingham
☎ (0787) 60261 or 60804
Open: Easter, May-October, daily,
10am-5pm.

Mistley Towers (EH)
Mistley, 1 mile east of Manningtree
on B1352
Open: any reasonable time. Key
available from 18 Stour View
Close.

Mountfichet Castle
Stansted, 3 miles north-east of
Bishop's Stortford
☎ (0279) 813237
Open: March-November, daily,
10am-5pm.

Prior's Hall Barn (EH)
Widdington, 4 miles south of
Saffron Walden
Open: Easter-September, week-
ends and Bank Holidays, 10am-
6pm.

St Botolph's Priory (EH)
Colchester
Open: any reasonable time.

Tilbury Fort (EH)
Tilbury
Open: Easter-September, daily,
10am-6pm; October-Maundy
Thursday, daily except Monday,
10am-4pm. Closed 24-26 December, 1 January.

Boating

CRUISER HIRE

Blackwater Yacht Charters Ltd
The Old Ship, Heybridge Basin,
Maldon
☎ (0621) 55789

Broads and Fens
Boat Enquiries Ltd
43 Botley Road, Oxford

☎ (0865) 727288
Cruisers, narrow boats and hotel
boats on Broads and Fens.

Blakes Holidays Ltd
Wroxham, Norwich, NR12 8DH
Instant bookings: 2/3 berth
cruisers, ☎ (0603) 782911; 4 berth
cruisers, ☎ (0603) 782913; 6/11
berth cruisers, ☎ (0603) 782915;
Yachts and houseboats, ☎ (0603)
782915; Free colour brochure,
☎ (0603) 782141 or 783226.

Broads Tours Ltd
☎ (0603) 782207

Bounty Boats Ltd
Riverside Estate, Brundall,
Norwich, NR13 5PW
☎ (0603) 712070

Harbour Cruisers
Riverside, Brundall, Norwich
☎ (0603) 483522

Horning Pleasurecraft Ltd
Ferry View Estate, Horning,
Norwich, NR12 8PT
☎ (0692) 630366

Hoseasons Holidays Ltd
Sunway House, Lowestoft, Suffolk,
NR32 3LT
Instant bookings:
Broads cruisers, ☎ (0502) 501515;
Fens cruisers, ☎ (0502) 501010;
Free colour brochure, ☎ (0502)
501501.

Moore & Co
☎ (0603) 783311

**Richardsons New Horizon
Boating Holidays**
The Staithe, Stalham, Norfolk
☎ (0692) 81522

Stalham Yacht Services Ltd
The Staithe, Stalham
☎ (069280) 288

Fens only
Two Tee's Boat Yard
70 Water Street, Chesterton,
Cambridge, CB4 1PA
2, 3 and 4 berth cruisers
☎ (0223) 65597

Westover Boat Company Ltd
PO Box 43, Hemingford Grey,
Huntingdon, PE18 9DD
☎ (0860) 516343

DAY BOAT HIRE

Norfolk
Acle
Anchor Craft, Acle Bridge
☎ (0493) 750500

Denver
Daymond Services, Frojo Fleet
Quay, Denver Sluice
☎ (0366) 383618

Great Yarmouth
Johnson's Yacht Station Ltd,
St. Olaves Bridge
☎ (049379) 218

Hickling
Whispering Reeds Boatyard
☎ (069261) 314

Horning
Ferry Boatyard Ltd
Ferry Road
☎ (0692) 630392

Norwich
Highcraft
Griffin Lane, Thorpe St Andrew,
Norwich
☎ (0603) 701701

Potter Heigham
Pennant Holidays
☎ (0692) 670711

Maycraft Ltd
River Bank
☎ (0692) 670241

Stalham
Stalham Yacht Services Ltd
The Staithe
☎ (069280) 288

Wroxham
Faircraft Loynes, The Bridge
☎ (0603) 782232

Broads Tours Ltd
☎ (0603) 782207

Moore & Co
☎ (0603) 783051

Suffolk
Lowestoft
Waveney River Tours Ltd
Mutford Lock, Bridge Road,
Oulton Broad
☎ (0502) 574903

Cambridgeshire
Cambridge
Scudamores Boatyards, Granta
Place
☎ (0223) 359750

Tyrrell's Marine Ltd
23-27 Bermuda Road, Cambridge,
CB4 3JX
☎ (0223) 352847/63080

Huntingdon
Huntingdon Marine & Leisure Ltd
Bridge Boatyard, Huntingdon,
PE18 9AS
☎ (0480) 53628

Purvis Marine Boatyard
Hartford Road
☎ (0480) 53628

Essex
Dedham
D.E. Smeeth
The Boatyard, Mill Lane
☎ (0206) 861748

REGULAR EXCURSIONS
INCLUDING GROUP HIRE

Norfolk
Norfolk Wherry Trust
63 Whitehall Road, Norwich
☎ (0603) 624642
Wherry *Albion* can be chartered for
groups up to 12.

Wherry Yacht Charter
Barton House, Hartwell Road, The
Avenue, Wroxham
☎ (0603) 782470. Groups up to 12
for Broads cruising on wherry
yachts *Olive* and *Norada*, and
pleasure wherry *Hathor*.

Brundall
Tom Phillips
111 Norwich Road, Wroxham,
NR12 8RY
☎ (0603) 783462 or (0860) 442237
Private skippered trips on the
Broads in 25ft power boat.

Burnham Overy Staithe
Bill's Ferry
William Scoles, The Old Rectory,
Great Snoring, Fakenham
☎ (0328) 820597
Trips to Scolt Head Bird Sanctuary.

Great Yarmouth
Norfolk Yacht Tours, Riverside,
Martham
☎ (0493) 653597

Accompanied sailing trips through
three Broads nature reserves.

Pennant Steamers Ltd
Broads Haven, Potter Heigham,
NR29 5JD
☎ (0692) 670711 or (0493) 850378.
MV *Golden Galleon* carries up to
200, two licensed bars.

Horning
Mississippi River Boats
Browns Hill, Irstead, NR12 8XU
☎ (0692) 630262
Double-decked Mississippi paddle
boat, carries up to 100. 1-2 hour
cruises on Broads, bar, meals by
arrangement.

Hunstanton
Searle's Hire Boats, Beach Road
☎ (04853) 2342
45 seater motor launch, 2 hour
cruises to see seals on Seal Island
in the Wash. Also half-hour coastal
cruises.

Norwich
Southern River Steamers, Elm Hill
☎ (0603) 501220
1, $1^1/_2$ and $3^1/_4$ hour Broadland
river cruises.

Stalham
Stalham Water Tours
28 St Nicholas Way, Potter
Heigham
☎ (0692) 670530
1-$2^1/_2$-hour Broads cruises. Depart
Richardson's Boatyard, Stalham.

Wroxham
Broads Tours Ltd
☎ (0603) 782207
Broadland tours in all-weather
motor launch.

The Home & Colonial Launch Co
The Riverside, King's Head Hotel,
Station Road
☎ (0692) 630106
Edwardian style river boats with
silent electric motors, ideal for
viewing wildlife.

Suffolk
Ipswich
P & Q Sailing Centre and Holiday
Charter, Deer Park Lodge,
Mannings Lane, Wolverstone
☎ (047384) 293
Two cruising yachts for parties of
up to five per yacht.

Lowestoft
Waveney River Tours Ltd
Mutford Lock, Bridge Road,
Oulton Broad
☎ (0502) 574903. Broads cruises on
Waveney Princess carrying up to
125 passengers, and *Enchantress*
carrying up to ninety-two.

Orford
Lady Florence
☎ (0394) 450210
50ft motor vessel cruising Rivers
Alde and Ore.

Snape
Snape Maltings
☎ (072888) 303/5
1 hour trip on the River Alde
aboard the *Lady Moyra*.

Waldringfield
Waldringfield Boat Yard
☎ (047336) 260
2 hour trips on the River Deben.

Essex
Bishop's Stortford
Adventuress Cruisers

April Cottage, South Mill Lock
☎ (0279) 508690. Excursions on the
River Stort.

Chelmsford
Chelmer & Blackwater Navigation
Ltd
Paper Mill Lock, Little Baddow
☎ (024541) 5520. Modern pleasure
barge carrying groups up to forty-
eight people.

Harwich
Orwell & Harwich Navigation Co.
Ltd, The Quay
☎ (0255) 502004
Afternoon and evening cruises on
MS *Brightlingsea* on Rivers Stour
and Orwell, and round Harwich
Harbour.

Maldon
Anglian Yacht Services
The Hythe
☎ (0621) 52290
Thames sailing barge *Reminder*
carrying groups up to twelve
people.

Country Code

Wherever you go in East Anglia's
countryside, follow the country
code:

Enjoy the countryside, and respect
its life and work.
Guard against all risk of fire.
Fasten all gates.
Keep your dogs under close
control.
Keep to public paths across
farmland.
Use gates and stiles to cross fences,
hedges and walls.

Leave livestock, crops and
machinery alone.
Take your litter home.
Help to keep all water clean.
Protect wildlife, plants and trees.
Take special care on country roads.
Make no unnecessary noise.

Country Parks

Norfolk
Fritton Lake
5 miles south-west of Great
Yarmouth on A143
Lake surrounded by wood and
grassland. Boating, fishing (in
season), putting green, picnic and
play areas. Shop, cafeteria.

Holt Lowes
1 mile south of Holt on B1149
Conifer wood and heathland,
nature trail. 98 acres of woodland,
and 113 acres heathland.

Mannington Gardens and Countryside
20 miles of waymarked footpaths
in picturesque countryside.

Sandringham
6 miles north of King's Lynn off
A149. 741 acres of wood and
heathland, nature trail.

Taswood Lakes
Mill Road, Flordon, Norwich
Five freshwater lakes set in
wooded grounds.

Suffolk
Brandon
1 mile south of Brandon on B1106
Open: May-October, 10am-9pm;
November-April, 11am-dusk.
Grounds of Brandon Park House,
set in Thetford forest. Forest walks,
picnic area, visitor centre.

Clare Castle
Clare, 7 miles north-west of
Sudbury on A1092
Open: daily
25 acres of grounds with gardens
at former railway station. Waterfowl, nature trail, butterfly garden.

Knettishall Heath
6 miles east of Thetford off A1066
Open: all year, daily until sunset.
350 acres of Breckland heath and
woodland. Picnic areas and toilets.
Peddars Way long distance path
starts at western end.

West Stow
5 miles north-west of Bury St
Edmunds off A1101
Open: all year, daily, 9am-1 hour
before sunset.
125 acres of grass and heathland,
lake and river. Also includes
reconstructed Anglo-Saxon village.

Cambridgeshire
Ferry Meadows
Nene Park, $2^1/_2$ miles west of
Peterborough off A605
☎ (0733) 234443
Sailing, windsurfing, fishing,
picnic areas, camping, model
railway. Visitor centre.

Grafham Water
6 miles south-west of Huntingdon
off B661
$2^1/_2$ sq mile reservoir with fishing
and sailing facilities. Public
footpaths, nature trails, bird hides
(one with disabled facilities).

Hinchingbrooke Country Park
☎ (0470) 51568
156 acres of woods, lakes and meadows. Watersports, walks, activities. Displays at Visitor Centre. Disabled facilities.

Wandlebury
4 miles south-east of Cambridge on A1307
Parkland with Iron Age hill-fort. Woodland walks, nature trail, picnic area.

Essex
Belhus Woods
1 mile north of Aveley
☎ (0708) 865628
158 acres of woodlands, lakes and open areas for walks and picnics. Fishing from 8am to dusk. Visitor centre.

Chalkney Wood
Earls Colne
☎ (0206) 383868
63 acres of ancient woodland.

Cudmore Grove
East Mersea, 6 miles south of Colchester
☎ (0206) 383868
35 acres of grassland and beach. Ranger service.

Danbury
4 miles east of Chelmsford off A414
Parkland with lakes and exotic trees and shrubs.

Epping Forest
5,928 acres of forest, mostly within Essex. Conservation centre at High Beach.

Fishers Green Countryside Area
Crooked Mile, Waltham Abbey
☎ (0992) 893345
Open: all year, daily.
Lake and riverside walks, nature study area and bird hides. Guided walks.

Garnetts Wood
Barnston, near Dunmow
☎ (0277) 216297
62 acres of ancient woodland.

Grove Woods
off A1015 between Eastwood and Rayleigh
☎ (0702) 546366
40 acres of recent woodland and old orchards.

Hadleigh Castle Country Park
5 miles west of Southend-on-Sea off A13
☎ (0702) 551027
450 acres of woodland, downland and marshes forming an important wildlife area.

Hatfield Forest (NT)
4 miles east of Bishop's Stortford
1,000 acres of pasture and woodland, with lake for fishing and boating. Nature reserve, nature trail.

Hockley Woods
3 miles north of Southend-on-Sea off B1013
☎ (0702) 546366
250 acres of coppiced woodland. Footpaths, horse trail, picnic and play area.

Langdon Hills
2 miles south-west of Basildon off A13
☎ (0268) 42066

Two parks, Westley Heights and One Tree Hill, comprising woodland, grassland and heaths overlooking the Thames estuary.

Lee Valley Regional Park
5 miles south-west of Harlow off B194
☎ (0992) 717711
Landscaped open parkland with sailing, angling, picnic and camping facilities.

Marsh Farm
South Woodham Ferrers, 7 miles south-east of Chelmsford on B1012
☎ (0245) 321552
320-acre country park with farm centre. Walks around the sea wall, farm tracks and nature trail. Visitor centre.

Mistley Environmental Centre
New Road, Mistley, 2 miles east of Manningtree
☎ (0206) 396483
Open: all year, daily, 10.30am-6pm.
20 acres of woods and grassland overlooking the River Stour. Horses, goats, rabbits and geese. Lakeside and woodland walks.

Thorndon
2 miles south of Brentwood off A128
☎ (0277) 211250
Mainly woodland with footpaths, fishing. Ranger service.

Wat Tyler Country Park
Pitsea, 1 mile south of Basildon Country park with emphasis on conservation and natural history. Other attractions include a

marina, craft workshops, national motorboat museum and rural life museum.

Weald
2 miles west of Brentwood
☎ (0277) 261343
420 acres of parkland containing woods and lakes. Fishing and horse riding by permit only. Visitor centre and ranger service.

Craft Shops and Galleries

Norfolk
Norfolk Naturalists' Trust Gift Shop
72 Cathedral Close, Norwich
☎ (0603) 625540

Norfolk Lavender
Caley Mill, Heacham, 3 miles south of Hunstanton on A149
☎ (0485) 70384
Open: Easter-October, daily, 10am-5pm; November-Christmas, Monday, Saturday, 10am-5pm; January to Easter, Monday-Friday, 10am-5pm.

Norwich Cathedral Shop
☎ (0603) 626290

The Mustard Shop
3 Bridewell Alley, Norwich
☎ (0603) 627889

Culpeper
19 Davey Place, Norwich
☎ (0603) 619153
Open: Monday-Saturday, 9.30am-5.30pm.

Langham Glass
The Long Barn, North Street,
Langham, 2 miles south-west of
Blakeney on B1388
☎ (032875) 511
Open: daily, 10.30am-5.15pm.

Alby Crafts
Alby, 4 miles north of Aylsham off
A140
☎ (0263) 761590
Open: Easter-Christmas, daily,
10am-5pm, except Monday.

Sheringham Pottery
30 Church Street, Sheringham
☎ (0263) 823552

Black Sheep
Ingworth, 2 miles north of
Aylsham off A140
☎ (0263) 733142/732006
Open: all year, daily except
Monday.

Wroxham Barns
Tunstead Road, Hoveton, near
Wroxham
☎ (06053) 3762
Open: all year, daily, 10am-6pm.

Caithness Crystal
Oldmedow Road, Hardwick
Industrial Estate, King's Lynn
☎ (0553) 765111
Open: all year, Monday-Friday,
9am-5.30pm.

.
Wansbeck Dolls' Houses
2 Chapel Yard, Holt
☎ (0263) 713933
Open: Monday-Saturday, 9am-
1pm, 2-5pm. Closed Thursday pm.

Dried Flower Centre
Cangate, Neatishead, 10 miles

north-east of Norwich off A1151
☎ (0603) 783588
Open: June-December, daily, 2-
4pm; January-May, Wednesday,
Saturday.

Suffolk
Easton Farm Park
Easton, Woodbridge
☎ (0728) 746475

Watson's Potteries
Wattisfield, 8 miles south-west of
Diss on A143
☎ (0359) 51239

Aspall Cyder House
Aspall Hall, Debenham, 7 miles
north-east of Stowmarket on B1077
☎ (0728) 860510
Open: weekdays, 9am-12.30pm,
1.30-3.30pm.

Craft at the Suffolk Barn
Fornham Road, Great Barton, 3
miles north-east of Bury St
Edmunds on A143
☎ (028487) 317
Open: mid March-Christmas,
Wednesday-Saturday, Bank
Holidays, 10am-6pm, Sunday,
12noon-6pm.

Snape Craft Centre
Snape Maltings, 1 mile south of
Snape on A1152
☎ (072888) 303/5
Open: daily, 10.30am-6.30pm.
Check winter opening times.

Nursey and Son Ltd
12 Upper Olland Street, Bungay
☎ (0986) 2821
Open: Monday-Friday, 9am-1pm,
2-5pm.

Aldringham Craft Market
Aldringham, near Leiston
☎ (0728) 830397
Open: Monday-Saturday, 10am-
5.30pm, Sunday, 10am-12noon, 2-
5.30pm.

Cambridgeshire
Eastern Counties Tannery Shop
London Road, Sawston, 5 miles
south of Cambridge off A1301
☎ (0223) 834757

Cambridge Brass Rubbing Centre
St Giles Church, Castle Street,
Cambridge
☎ (0223) 835055
Open: Tuesday-Saturday, 10am-
5pm; plus Monday, June-August.

Steeplegate Ltd
16-18 High Street, Ely
☎ (0353) 664731
Open: all year, daily except
Tuesday, 9am-5.30pm.

Essex
Six Apples Craft Centre
Shalford Road, Panfield, 2 miles
north-west of Braintree off B1053
☎ (0376) 44873
Open: Wednesday-Sunday, Bank
Holidays, 10am-6pm (January and
February, weekends only).

The Minories
74 High Street, Colchester
☎ (0206) 577067
Open: Tuesday-Saturday, 10.30am-
5pm, Sunday 2-6pm.

Cycling and Cycle Hire

East Anglia is ideal for cycling,
with no great hills and a wealth of
small lanes and back roads. Its is
possible to extend the scope of
cycling excursions by using trains.
The cycle can be taken into the
guard's van of most trains in East
Anglia if there is enough room, so
it pays to avoid travelling on
commuter trains.

The following establishments all
operate cycle hire. It may be best to
phone and reserve cycles in
advance during the peak holiday
period, and a phone call is always
wise, as some of the firms listed are
seasonal.

Norfolk
Bircham Mill Ltd
The Old Mill, Great Bircham
☎ (048523) 393

Broadland Cycles
High Street, Stalham
☎ (0692) 81055

Cycle Hire
St Peter's Road, Sheringham
☎ (0263) 822228

Dial House
The Harbour, Brancaster Staithe
☎ (0485) 210719

Dodgers
69 Trinity Street, Norwich
☎ (0603) 622499

Just Pedalling
Church Street, Coltishall, near
Norwich
☎ (0603) 737201

Lawfords Cycles
24 Northgate Street, Great
Yarmouth
☎ (0493) 842741

Magpie's Nest
112 Magpie Road, Norwich
☎ (0603) 617751

The New Inn
Roughton, near Cromer
☎ (0263) 761389

A.E. Wallis
38/40 High Street, Heacham
☎ (0485) 71683

Suffolk
The Bicycle Doctor
18 Bartholomew Street, Ipswich
☎ (0473) 59853

Seaside Hire Services
329 Whapload Road, Lowestoft
☎ (0502) 564759

E.J. Tooke
Blyth Road, Southwold
☎ (0502) 722204

Cambridgeshire
Armada Cycle
45a Suez Road, Cambridge
☎ (0223) 210421

S.M. Bishop
51 Station Road, Histon
☎ (002023) 2449

H. Drake
58 Hills Road, Cambridge
☎ (0223) 63468

Geoff's Bike Hire
65 Devonshire Road, Cambridge
☎ (0223) 65629

Pen Hayward & Son
Laundress Lane, Cambridge
☎ (0223) 352294

W.J. Ison
72 Chesterton Road, Cambridge
☎ (0223) 315845

University Cycle and Electrical
Shop
93 King Street, Cambridge
☎ (0223) 355517

Essex
Anglian Cycle Company Ltd
Unit 7, Peartree Business Centre,
Stanway, Colchester
☎ (0206) 563377

R & A Cycles
The Spinning Wheel, 16 Barfield
Road, West Mersea
☎ (0206) 38401

Fishing

The rivers of East Anglia provide
good fresh water fishing, and there
are many excellent spots around
the coast for sea fishing. The East
Anglia Tourist Board produces an
information sheet which is very
useful, and detailed information
and licences are available from the
National Rivers Authority, Aqua
House, London Road, Peterborough, PE2 8AG. ☎ (0733) 555667.

The National Rivers Authority
Anglian Region is split into three
areas, with main offices in Lincoln,
Huntingdon, and Ipswich, and
further district offices for each area.

Lincoln
(Northern Area Office)
Aqua House, Harvey Street,
Lincoln
☏ (0522) 513100

District Office:
Spalding ☏ (0775) 62123

Brampton
(Central Area Office)
Broomholme Lane, Brampton,
Huntingdon
☏ (0480) 414581

District Offices:
Ely: ☏ (0353) 666660
King's Lynn: ☏ (0553) 760607

Ipswich
(Eastern Area Office)
Cobham Road, Ipswich
☏ (0473) 727712

District Offices:
Norwich: ☏ (0603) 662800
Chelmsford: ☏ (0245) 478065

In addition, the following offices of
Anglian Water Services can
provide licences and local fishing
information:

Norwich: Yare House, 62/64
Thorpe Road, Norwich
☏ (0603) 615161

Colchester: 33 Sheepen Road,
Colchester
☏ (0206) 763344

Peterborough: North Street,
Oundle, Peterborough
☏ (0832) 73710

Cambridge: Chivers Way, Histon,
Cambridge
☏ (0223) 235235

Gardens Open to the Public

Norfolk

Alby Gardens
Cromer Road, Erpingham, 7 miles
south of Cromer on A140
Open: March-mid-December,
Tuesday-Sunday, 10am-5pm.

Bressingham Gardens
3 miles west of Diss on A1066
Open: Easter-September, Sunday,
Bank Holiday Monday; also
Thursday, June-mid September;
also Wednesday, August.

Congham Hall Herb
Lynn Road, Grimston, 5 miles east
of King's Lynn on B1153
☏ (0485) 600250
Open: April-September, Monday,
Wednesday, Sunday, 2-4pm.

Fairhaven Garden Trust
2 The Woodlands, Pilson Green,
South Walsham, 9 miles east of
Norwich off the B1140
☏ (060549) 449
Open: April, Sunday, Bank
Holidays; May-mid September,
Wednesday, Sunday, Bank
Holidays, 2-6pm.

Fritton Lake
5 miles south-west of Great
Yarmouth on the A143
Open: Easter-September, daily
10am-6pm.

Glavenside Gardens
Letheringset, 1 mile west of Holt
on A148
Open: all year, daily, 10am-sunset.

Gooderstone Water Gardens
Crow Hall Farm, 6 miles south-west of Swaffham
Open: Easter-October, Monday-Saturday, 10.30am-5pm, Sunday 1.30-6pm.

Holkham Park Gardens
2 miles west of Wells-next-the-Sea off A149
Open: all year, Monday-Saturday 10am-1pm, 2-5pm, Sunday 2-5pm.

How Hill Trust
How Hill, off A1062 near Ludham
Open: most days in summer.

Kelling Park Hotel and Aviaries
Weybourne Road, Holt
☎ (0263) 712235
Open: all year, daily, 10am-dusk.

Mannington Hall Gardens
Saxthorpe, 18 miles north of Norwich off B1149
Open: April-December, Sunday, 12noon-5pm or dusk if earlier; also June-August, Wednesday-Friday, 11am-6pm.

Norfolk Lavender
Caley Mill, Heacham, 2 miles south of Hunstanton on A149
☎ (0485) 70384
Open: all year, daily 10am-5.30pm.

The Pleasaunce
Overstrand, Cromer
☎ (0263) 78212
Open: June-October, Monday, Wednesday, Thursday, 2-5pm.

Pretty Corner Tea and Coffee Gardens
Sheringham

Open: Easter-October, daily 10am-5.30pm.

Rainthorpe Hall Gardens
Tasburgh, 8 miles south of Norwich off A140
☎ (0508) 470618
Open: May-September, Sunday and Bank Holidays, 2-5.30pm.

Sandringham Grounds
8 miles north of King's Lynn off A149
Open: Easter-September, Monday-Thursday, 11am-5pm, Sunday, 12noon-5pm.
House only closed mid-July to beginning August. House and grounds closed end July to beginning August.

Sheringham Park
Upper Sheringham, off A148
Open: all year, daily, sunrise-sunset.

Wellbank's Orchid World
Terrington St Clement, 5 miles west of King's Lynn on A17
☎ (0553) 827155
Open: all year, daily, 11am-5pm.

Willow Farm Flowers
Cangate, Neatishead, 9 miles north-east of Norwich off A1151
☎ (0603) 783588
Open: January-May, Wednesday, Saturday 2-4pm; June-December, daily, 2-4pm.

Wolterton Hall Gardens
near Erpingham, 5 miles north of Aylsham off A140
Open: June-August, Wednesday, 2-6pm.

Suffolk

Akenfield
1 Park Lane, Charsfield, 11 miles north-east of Ipswich off B1078
Open: June-September, daily, 10am-7pm.

Blakenham Woodland Garden
Little Blakenham, 4 miles north-west of Ipswich off the A45/B1113
Open: April-September, Wednesday, Thursday, Sunday, Bank Holidays, 1-5pm.

Clare Priory Gardens
Clare
Open: all year, daily except 1 and 2 January, 10am-6pm.

Craft at the Suffolk Barn
Fornham Road, Great Barton, Bury St Edmunds
Open: mid March-Christmas, Wednesday, Saturday and Bank Holidays, 10am-6pm, Sunday, 12noon-6pm.

East Bergholt Lodge
East Bergholt, 9 miles north-east of Colchester off A12
☎ (0206) 298278
Open: May-June, some Sundays, and by appointment.

Gifford's Hall
Hartest, off A134, near Bury St Edmunds. ☎ (0284) 830464
Open: Easter-October, daily 10am-6pm.

Helmingham Hall Gardens
8 miles north of Ipswich on B1077
☎ (047 339) 363
Open: May-September, Sunday, 2-6pm, also coach parties Sunday, Wednesday, by appointment.

Kentwell Hall
Long Melford
Open: April-September.

Letheringham Watermill Gardens
Letheringham, Woodbridge
Open: April-September, Sunday, Bank Holidays, 2-5.30pm.

The Priory
Water Street, Lavenham
☎ (0787) 247147
Open: Easter-October, daily, 10.30am-5.30pm.

Thompson & Morgan Seed Trials
Poplar Lane, London Road, Ipswich, $1^1/_2$ miles from A12/A45 interchange
Open: mid-July-September, daily 9am-4pm.

Cambridgeshire

Buckden Palace
Buckden, 4 miles south-west of Huntingdon off A1
Open: May-August, daily, 10am-6pm; September-April, daily, 10am-4pm.

Cambridge University Botanic Garden
1 Brookside, Cambridge
Open: all year (except 25-26 December), Monday-Saturday, 8am-4pm; February-April, October, 8am-5pm; May-September, Monday-Saturday, 8am-6pm, Sunday 2.30-6.30pm.

Crossing House
Meldreth Road, Shepreth, 8 miles south-west of Cambridge off A10
Open: all year, daily, any reasonable time.

Docwra's Manor
2 Heldreth Road, Shepreth, 8 miles
south-west of Cambridge off A10
☎ (0763) 60235/61473
Open: April-October, Wednesday,
Friday, 10am-5pm; first Sunday in
each month, 2-6pm; Bank Holidays, 10am-5pm.

Herb Garden
Nigel House, Wilburton, 5 miles
south-west of Ely on A1123
☎ (0353) 740824
Open: May-September, most days,
10am-7pm; closed Wednesday
during school terms.

Essex
Bridge End Gardens
Saffron Walden
Open: all year, daily, 9am-dusk.

The Fens
Old Mill Road, Langham, 4 miles
north of Colchester off A12
Open: April-September, Thursday,
Saturday, Sunday, 10am-5pm.

Hyde Hall Garden
Rettendon, 6 miles south-east of
Chelmsford off A130
Open: Easter-October, Wednesday,
Bank Holidays, 11am-6pm,
Sunday, 2-6pm.

Mark Hall Gardens
Muskham Road, off First Avenue,
Harlow
Open: all year, daily, 10am-5pm.

Olivers Orchard
Olivers Lane, off Gosbecks Road,
Colchester
Open: June-July, Monday-
Thursday, 9am-8pm, Friday-
Sunday, 9am-6pm; August,

Monday-Thursday, 9am-7pm,
Friday-Sunday, 9am-6pm;
September-October, daily, 9am-
6pm; November-Christmas,
Saturday, Sunday 9am-5pm.

St Osyth's Priory
3 miles west of Clacton on B1027
Open: May-September, daily 10am-
5pm.

Saling Hall Garden
Great Saling, 5 miles north-west of
Braintree off A120
Open: May-July, Wednesday,
2-5pm.

Spains Hall
Finchingfield, 9 miles north-west of
Braintree on B1053
Open: May-July, Sunday, 2-5pm.

Golf

Norfolk
Brancaster: Royal West Norfolk
Golf Club — 18 holes

Cromer: Links Country Park Golf
Club — 18 holes

Diss: Diss Golf Club — 9 holes

Downham Market: Ryston Park
Golf Club — 9 holes

East Dereham: Dereham Golf Club
— 9 holes

Fakenham: Fakenham Golf Club —
9 holes

Great Yarmouth: Gorleston Golf
Club — 18 holes

Hunstanton: Hunstanton Golf
Club — 18 holes

King's Lynn: King's Lynn Golf Club — 18 holes

Mundesley: Mundesley Golf Club — 9 holes

Norwich: Barnham Broom Hotel Golf and Country Club — 2 x 18 holes

Eaton Golf Club — 18 holes

Royal Norwich Golf Club — 18 holes

Sheringham: Sheringham Golf Club — 18 holes

Swaffham: Swaffham Golf Club — 9 holes

Thetford: Thetford Golf Club — 18 holes

Suffolk
Aldeburgh: Aldeburgh Golf Club — 18 & 9 holes

Beccles: Wood Valley Golf Club — 9 holes

Bungay: Bungay & Waveney Valley Golf Club — 18 holes

Bury St Edmunds: Bury St Edmunds Golf Club — 18 holes

Flempton Golf Club — 9 holes

Fornham Park Golf and Country Club — 18 holes

Royal Worlington Golf Club — 9 holes

Cretingham: Cretingham Golf Club — 9 holes

Felixstowe: Felixstowe Ferry Golf Club — 18 holes

Haverhill: Haverhill Golf Club — 9 holes

Ipswich: Ipswich Golf Club — 18 & 9 holes

Rushmere Golf Club — 18 holes

Lowestoft: Rookery Park Golf Club — 18 & 9 holes

Newmarket: Links Golf Club — 18 holes

Southwold: Southwold Golf Club — 9 holes

Stowmarket: Stowmarket Golf Club — 18 holes

Sudbury: Newton Green Golf Club — 9 holes

Thorpeness: Thorpeness Golf Club — 18 holes

Woodbridge: Woodbridge Golf Club — 18 & 9 holes

Cambridgeshire
Cambridge: Cambridgeshire Moat House Hotel Golf Club — 18 holes

Girton Golf Club — 18 holes

The Gog Magog Golf Club — 18 holes

Ely: Ely City Golf Club — 18 holes

Huntingdon: Ramsey Golf Club — 18 holes

Peterborough: Peterborough Milton Golf Club — 18 holes

Orton Meadows Golf Course — 18 holes

Thorpe Wood Golf Course — 18 holes

St Neots: St Neots Golf Club — 18 holes

Basildon: Basildon Golf Club —
18 holes

Braintree: Braintree Golf Club —
18 holes

Brentwood: Bentley Golf &
Country Club — 18 holes

Burnham-on-Crouch: Burnham-
on-Crouch Golf Club — 9 holes

Chelmsford: Three Rivers Golf
Club — 18 & 9 holes

Chigwell: Chigwell Golf Club —
18 holes

Clacton-on-Sea: Clacton-on-Sea
Golf Club — 18 holes

Colchester: Birch Grove Golf Club
— 9 holes

Stoke-by-Nayland Golf Club —
36 holes

Dovercourt: Harwich & Dovercourt Golf Club — 9 holes

Epping: Theydon Bois Golf Club —
18 holes

Frinton-on-Sea: Frinton Golf Club
— 18 & 9 holes

Harlow: Canon's Brook Golf Club
— 18 holes

Maldon: Bunsay Downs Golf Club
— 9 holes

Maldon Golf Club — 9 holes

The Quietwaters Club — 18 holes

The Warren Golf Club — 18 holes

Romford: Abridge Golf & Country
Club — 18 holes

Maylands Golf & Country Club —
18 holes

Saffron Walden: Saffron Walden
Golf Club — 18 holes

Southend-on-Sea: Thorpe Hall
Golf Club — 18 holes

Guided Town Tours

Registered 'Blue Badge' guides
endorsed by the East Anglia
Tourist Board operate guided
tours in several of the region's
towns and cities. Tours are booked
through the local Tourist Information Centres.

Norfolk
King's Lynn
May-September, Wednesday,
Saturday, 2pm.
Tours leave the Tourist Informa-
tion Centre at the Town Hall,
Saturday Market Place, and last
about $1^1/_2$ hours.

Norwich
May-September, Monday-
Saturday. Also Sundays June-
September. Tours leave the Tourist
Information Centre in Tombland,
and last about $1^1/_2$ hours. Also
specialised tours of Georgian
Norwich, Nelson Trail; details from
the Tourist Information Centre.

Suffolk
Bury St Edmunds
June-September, Tuesday, 2.30pm;
also July-August, Sunday, 10am.
Tours leave the Tourist Information Centre, Angel Hill, and last
about $1^1/_2$ hours.

Ipswich
May-September, Sunday, 2.30pm; Tuesday, 2.15pm. Tours take $1^1/_2$ hours, departing from the Tourist Information Centre.

Cambridgeshire
Cambridge
City Centre Tours, mid-June to mid-August, Wednesday, Friday, 7pm. Tours leave the Tourist Information Centre, Wheeler Street, and last about $1^1/_2$ hours. Specialised theme tours are also available throughout the year; details from the Tourist Office. Regular College Tours leave the Tourist Information Centre daily, up to five tours a day in the peak summer months.

Ely
Regular city tours operate during the summer months. Individuals wishing to join a tour should book at the Tourist Information Centre.

Essex
Colchester
Summer months. Tours leave the Tourist Information Centre, Town Hall, High Street, and last about $1^1/_2$ hours, finishing at Colchester Castle.

Saffron Walden
Guided walking tours, Thursday, Sunday, 2.30pm, leaving the Tourist Information Centre.

Historic Houses

Norfolk
Beeston Hall
Beeston St Lawrence, 3 miles north-east of Wroxham on A1151
Open: Easter-September, Friday, Sunday, Bank Holiday Monday plus Wednesday in August, 2-5.30pm.

Blickling Hall (NT)
2 miles north-west of Aylsham on B1354
Open: Easter-October, daily except Monday and Thursday, 1-5pm. Garden, shop and restaurant open same days as house and daily July-August. Garden hours 12noon-5pm.

Dragon Hall
King Street, Norwich
☎ (0603) 663922
Open: all year except 2 weeks over Christmas/New Year, Monday-Thursday, 10am-4pm.

Felbrigg Hall (NT)
2 miles south-west of Cromer on B1436
Open: Easter-October, daily except Tuesday and Friday, 1.30-5.30pm. Shop and restaurant 12noon-5.30pm, gardens from 11am.

Holkham Hall
2 miles west of Wells-next-the-Sea, off A149
Open: June-September, daily except Friday and Saturday, 11.30am-5pm.

Houghton Hall
halfway between King's Lynn and Fakenham, off A148
☎ (048 522) 569
Open: Easter-September, Thursday, Sunday and Bank Holidays, 1-5.30pm.

Mannington Hall
Saxthorpe, 6 miles north-west of
Aylsham, off B1149
☎ (026 387) 284
Open: by appointment only.

Oxburgh Hall (NT)
Oxborough, 8 miles south-west of
Swaffham
Open: April-October, daily except
Thursday and Friday, 1.30-5.30pm.

Sandringham House
8 miles north-east of King's Lynn,
off A149
Open: Easter-September, Monday-
Thursday, 11am-5pm, Sunday,
12noon-5pm.
House and grounds closed mid
July to beginning August.

Welle Manor Hall
Upwell, 6 miles south-east of
Wisbech on A1101
Open: all year, first Sunday in each
month, 3-5pm.

Suffolk
Christchurch Mansion
Ipswich
Open: all year, Monday-Saturday,
10am-5pm (dusk in winter).
Sunday, 2.30-4.30pm (dusk in
winter).

Euston Hall
4 miles south-east of Thetford on
A1088
Open: June-September, Thursday,
2.30-5.30pm.

Haughley Park
3 miles north-west of Stowmarket
off A45
Open: May-September, Tuesday,
3-6pm.

Ickworth (NT)
Horringer, 3 miles south-west of
Bury St Edmunds on A143
Open: April and October, Satur-
day, Sunday, Bank Holiday
Monday; May-September, daily,
1.30-5.30pm. Park open dawn to
dusk.

Kentwell Hall
Long Melford, 4 miles north of
Sudbury on A134
☎ (0787) 310207
Open: Easter-September, days and
times vary. Check for details.

Little Hall
Lavenham, 6 miles north-east of
Sudbury
☎ (0787) 247179
Open: Easter-October, Saturday,
Sunday, Bank Holidays, 2.30-6pm
or by appointment.

Melford Hall
Long Melford, 4 miles north of
Sudbury on A134
Open: May-September, Wednes-
day, Thursday, Saturday, Sunday,
Bank Holiday Monday, 2-6pm.

Otley Hall
Otley, 8 miles north-east of Ipswich
off B1079
☎ (047 339) 264
Open: Bank Holiday Sunday and
Monday only, 2-6pm. Groups at
other times by appointment.

The Priory
Water Street, Lavenham
☎ (0787) 247417
Open: Easter-October, daily,
10.30am-5.30pm.

Snape Maltings
2 miles south of Snape on A1152
☎ (072 885) 2935
Open: mid-July to mid-September,
selected weekday tours. View from
outside all year.

Somerleyton Hall
5 miles north-west of Lowestoft off
B1074
Open: Easter-May, Sunday,
Thursday, Bank Holidays; June-
September, Sunday-Thursday,
2-5.30pm.

Wingfield College
Wingfield, Eye, 7 miles east of Diss
off B1118
☎ (037 984) 505
Open: Easter-September, Saturday,
Sunday and Bank Holiday
Monday, 2-6pm.

Cambridgeshire
Anglesey Abbey (NT)
Lode, 6 miles north-east of
Cambridge off B1102
Open: house and gardens: April-
October, Wednesday, Sunday,
Bank Holiday Monday, 1.30-
3.30pm.

Buckden Palace
Buckden, Huntingdon
Open: May-September, Tuesday,
2-6pm.

Burghley House
Stamford
☎ (0780) 52451
Open: Easter-September, daily,
11am-5pm. Good Friday, 2-5pm.

Elton Hall
Elton, 8 miles south-west of
Peterborough on A605

Open: May-September, Sunday,
Bank Holiday Monday; also
Wednesday, June-September.

Hinchingbrooke House
Huntingdon, $^1/_2$ mile west of town
centre on A604
Open: Easter-August, Sunday,
Bank Holiday Monday, 2-5pm.

Island Hall
Godmanchester, near Huntingdon
Open: mid-June-mid-September,
Sunday, 2.30-5pm.

Kimbolton Castle
7 miles north-west of St Neots on
A45
Open: mid-July-August, spring and
August Bank Holidays, Sunday,
2-6pm.

Peckover House (NT)
Wisbech
Open: Easter-mid-October,
Saturday, Sunday, Monday, Bank
Holiday Monday, 2-5.30pm.

Wimpole Hall (NT)
10 miles south-west of Cambridge
off A603
Open: Easter-October, daily except
Monday and Friday, 1-5pm. Bank
Holiday Monday, 10am-5pm.

Essex
Audley End House (EH)
Saffron Walden
☎ (0799) 22342/22399
Open: Easter-September, daily,
1-6pm.

Gosfield Hall
Halstead
Open: May-September, Wednes-
day, Thursday, 2-4pm.

Layer Marney Tower
8 miles south-west of Colchester,
off B1022
Open: April-September, Thursday,
Sunday; also Tuesday in July and
August, 2-6pm; Bank Holidays
11am-6pm.

Paycocke's (NT)
Coggeshall, 6 miles east of
Braintree on A120
Open: Easter-September, Tuesday,
Thursday, Sunday, Bank Holiday
Monday, 2-5.30pm.

St Osyth's Priory
3 miles west of Clacton off B1027
Open: Easter, May-September,
daily, 10am-5pm.

Local Radio Stations

Local radio stations don't just give
a flavour of the area you happen to
be visiting, they also provide useful
information on traffic and road-
works, forthcoming events, and, of
course, local weather forecasts.

Norfolk
Radio Broadland (Norwich)
☎ (0603) 630621
Music, news and information,
including what's on, 24hrs a day.
Weather forecast on the hour.
Broadcasting to Norfolk and North
Suffolk.
260 metres MW (1152kHz)
102.4 FM stereo

BBC Radio Norfolk (Norwich)
☎ (0603) 617411
Music, news and local programmes. Holidaymakers'
information service including

emergency messages just after 8am,
1pm and 5pm news. Norfolk coast
camping and caravan site availability service during summer, Friday
6.45pm and Saturday just before
11am.
351 metres MW (855kHz)
95.1 FM stereo
344 metres MW (873kHz) West
Norfolk
104.4 FM stereo West Norfolk

Suffolk
Saxon Radio (Bury St Edmunds)
☎ (0284) 701511
Music, news, local programmes.
Daily diary broadcast throughout
the day.
240 metres MW (1251kHz)
96.4 FM stereo

Radio Orwell (Ipswich)
☎ (0473) 216971
Music, news, local events.
257 metres MW (1170kHz)
97.1 FM stereo

Cambridgeshire
Hereward Radio (Peterborough)
☎ (0733) 46225
Music, news, sport, general interest
items and travel information.
225 metres MW (1332kHz)
102.7 FM stereo

CN-FM (Cambridge)
☎ (0223) 235255
Music, news, general interest items
and travel information.
103.0 FM stereo

BBC Radio Cambridgeshire
(Cambridge)
☎ (0223) 315970
Music, news, sport, travel, local
interest programmes.

292 metres MW (1026kHz)
Cambridge
96.0 FM stereo Cambridge
207 metres MW (1449kHz)
Peterborough
95.7 FM stereo Peterborough

Essex

BBC Essex (Chelmsford)
☎ (0245) 262393
Music, news, sport.
392 metres MW (765kHz)
103.5 FM stereo
412 metres MW (729kHz) north-
east Essex
103.5 FM stereo north-east Essex
196 metres MW (1530kHz) south-
east Essex
95.3 FM stereo south-east Essex

Essex Radio (Southend-on-Sea)
☎ (0702) 333711
220 metres MW (1359kHz) North
Essex
102.6 FM stereo North Essex
210 metres MW (1431kHz) South
Essex
96.3 FM stereo South Essex

Mills

The following are those mills and
windpumps which may be visited.
Many others may be seen exter-
nally but are private.

Norfolk Windmills Trust, c/o
County Hall, Norwich.
☎ (0603) 611122, Ext 5124

Norfolk

Berney Arms Mill (EH)
near Reedham. Inaccessible by car.
Broads cruisers can moor at Berney
Arms, or footpaths from Halvergate or Wickhampton (approx 3
miles)
Open: Easter-September, daily
10am-6pm.

Billingford Windmill (NWT)
1 mile east of Scole on A143
Open: all year, apply for key at
Horseshoes public house, or by
appointment with NWT.

Bircham Mill
Great Bircham, 8 miles south-east
of Hunstanton on B1153
Open: Easter-April, Sunday,
Wednesday, Bank Holiday
Monday; May-September, daily
except Saturday, 10am-6pm.

Boardman's Mill (NWT)
How Hill, near Ludham
Open: all year, daily.

Cley Windmill
Cley-next-the-Sea, 4 miles north-
west of Holt off A149
☎ (0263) 740209
Open: Easter weekend, June-
September, daily, 2-5pm.

Denver Windmill (NWT)
Denver, just south of Downham
Market
☎ (0366) 3374
Open: all year, Monday-Saturday
by appointment.

Dereham Windmill
off A47, Cherry Lane, Norwich
Road, Dereham
☎ (0362) 695333
Open: April-September, every
weekend and Bank Holiday.

Horsey Windpump (NT)
Horsey Staithe, 3 miles north-west of Winterton on B1159
Open: Easter-August, daily, 11am-5pm.

Letheringsett Watermill
1 mile west of Holt off A148
Open: all year, Tuesday-Friday, 9am-1pm, 2-5pm; plus Saturday, Sunday, 9am-1pm in summer.

St Olaves Windpump (NWT)
St Olaves, 5 miles south-west of Great Yarmouth on A143
Open: all year, daily, 8.30am-6pm. Key held at Bridge Store, St Olaves.

Snettisham Watermill
Snettisham, 8 miles north of King's Lynn on A149
☎ (0485) 42180
Open: Bank Holidays, May-September, Saturday, Sunday, Thursday; also Wednesday, mid-July-mid-September, 10am-5.30pm.

Starston Windpump
Starston, 1 mile north-west of Harleston, off B1134
Open: all year, daily.

Stow Mill (NWT)
Paston, $1^1/_2$ miles south of Mundesley
☎ (0263) 720298
Open: all year, daily, 10am-dusk, or by appointment.

Stracey Arms Windpump (NWT)
just off A47 near Stracey Arms public house
Open: April-October, daily, 9am-8pm.

Sutton Windmill
Sutton, $1^1/_2$ miles south-east of Stalham off the A149
☎ (0692) 81195
Open: April-mid-May, Sunday-Wednesday, 1.30-5.30pm; mid-May-September, 10am-6pm.

Thurne Dyke Windpump (NWT)
Thurne, 3 miles north of Acle off B1152
Open: April-October, daily, 9am-5pm.

Wicklewood Mill (NWT)
3 miles west of Wymondham off the B1135
Open: all year, daily.

Suffolk
Bardwell Mill
8 miles north-east of Bury St Edmunds off A143
☎ (0359) 51331
Open: all year, Tuesday-Friday, 9am-5.30pm, Sunday, 2-5.30pm.

Buttrams Mill
Burkitt Road, Woodbridge
☎ (0473) 230000 ext 6519
Open: May-September, Saturday, Sunday, Bank Holiday Monday, 2-6pm. Other times by appointment.

Eastbridge Smock Drainage Windpump
The Museum of East Anglian Life, Stowmarket, 12 miles north-west of Ipswich on A1308
☎ (0449) 612229
Open: Easter-October, Monday-Saturday, 11am-5pm, Sunday, 12noon-5pm; June-August, Sunday, 12noon-6pm.

Herringfleet Marsh Mill
6 miles north-west of Lowestoft off B1074
Open: exterior accessible all year. Interior only on special days, advertised locally.

Letheringham Watermill
2 miles west of Wickham Market, off the B1078
Open: April-September, Sunday, Bank Holidays, 2-5.30pm.

Pakenham Watermill
Grimstone End, Pakenham, 5 miles north-east of Bury St Edmunds off A143
☎ (0359) 70570
Open: Easter, May-September, Wednesday, Saturday, Sunday, Bank Holidays, 2.30-5.30pm. Other times by appointment.

Saxtead Green Windmill (EH)
2 miles north-west of Framlingham on B1119
Open: April-September, Monday-Saturday, 9.30am-1pm, 2-6.30pm.

Thelnetham Windmill
Mill Road, Thelnetham, 7 miles west of Diss, off B1113
☎ (0473) 726996
Open: Easter-October, Sunday, Bank Holidays, 11am-7.30pm.

Thorpeness Windmill
Thorpeness, 2 miles north of Aldeburgh
Open: Easter, May, June, September, Saturday, Sunday, Bank Holiday Monday; July, August, Tuesday-Sunday, 2-5pm.

Woodbridge Tide Mill
Woodbridge

☎ (03943) 2548
Open: most days, May-October.

Cambridgeshire
Bourn Windmill
Caxton Road, Bourn, off A14
☎ (0223) 243830
Open: April-September, last Sunday in month, Bank Holidays, 2-5pm.

Downfield Windmill
Fordham Road, Soham, 5 miles south-east of Ely on A142
Open: all year, Sunday (except Christmas and New Year), Bank Holiday Monday, or by appointment, 11am-5pm.

Great Chishill Mill
Great Chishill, 12 miles south of Cambridge on B1039
Open: April-October, daily, 9am-5pm.

Great Gransden Post Mill
Caxton Road, Great Gransden, 10 miles west of Cambridge off B1046
Open: April-October, daily, 9am-5pm.

Hinxton Watermill
Mill Lane, Hinxton, 6 miles south of Cambridge on A1301
☎ (0223) 243830
Open: Sunday afternoons, 2.30-5.30pm, selected dates.

Houghton Mill (NT)
2 miles east of Huntingdon off A1123
Open: Easter-April, Saturday, Sunday, Bank Holiday Monday; May-September, daily except Thursday and Friday, 2-5.30pm.

Lode Water Mill (NT)
5 miles north-east of Cambridge off
B1102
Open: Easter-mid October,
Saturday, Sunday, Bank Holiday
Monday, 1.30-5.30pm.
Corn grinding on Bank Holiday
Monday and first Sunday in
month. See also Anglesey Abbey.

**Sacrewell Farm and Visitor
Centre**
Thornhaugh, 7 miles west of
Peterborough off A47
☎ (0780) 782222
Open: all year, daily.

Stevens Mill
Burwell, 4 miles north-west of
Newmarket off B1102
☎ (0223) 811233 during office
hours
Open: every other Sunday, by
appointment.

Essex
Aythorpe Roding Post Mill
5 miles south of Great Dunmow,
on B184
☎ (0245) 352232 Ext 293
Open: selected weekends and
National Mills Day.

Bourne Mill (NT)
Bourne Road, Colchester
☎ (0206) 572422
Open: Bank Holidays, July-August,
Saturday, Sunday, 2-5.30pm.

John Webb's Windmill
Thaxted, 10 miles north-east of
Bishop's Stortford
Open: May-September, Saturday,
Sunday, Bank Holidays, 2-6pm.

Mountnessing Windmill
2 miles north-east of Brentwood,
off A12
☎ (0277) 215777
Open: May-October, selected
weekends, and by appointment.

Rayleigh Windmill
The Mount, Rayleigh, 5 miles
north-west of Southend
☎ (0268) 775768
Open: April-October, Saturday,
10am-12.30pm or by appointment.

Stansted Mountfichet Windmill
Stansted, 2 miles north of Bishop's
Stortford on B1383
☎ (0279) 812096
Open: April-October, first Sunday
in every month, Bank Holidays,
every Sunday in August, 2-6pm.

Upminster Windmill
on A124, Upminster, Essex
☎ (04022) 22469
Open: April-September, 3rd
weekend every month, 2-5.30pm.

Museums

Norfolk
**Alby Lace Museum and Study
Centre**
Alby Craft Centre, 5 miles south of
Cromer on A140
☎ (0263) 768002
Open: mid-March-mid-December,
Tuesday-Friday, Sunday, 10am-
5pm.

Ancient House Museum
White Hart Street, Thetford
Open: all year, Monday-Saturday,
10am-5pm (closed Monday 1-2pm).

Also Sunday, June-September,
2-5pm.

Bishop Bonner's Cottage
East Dereham
Open: May-September, Tuesday-
Friday, 2.30-5pm, Saturday,
3-5.30pm.

Bridewell Museum
Bridewell Alley, Norwich
Open: all year, Monday-Saturday,
10am-5pm. Closed Sunday, Good
Friday, Christmas period, New
Year.

Broadland Conservation Centre
Ranworth, 4 miles north-west of
Acle
Open: April-October, Sunday-
Thursday, 10.30am-5.30pm,
Saturday, 2-5.30pm.

Broads Museum
Sutton, $1^1/_2$ miles south-east of
Stalham off A149
☎ (0692) 81195
Open: April-mid-May, Sunday-
Wednesday, 1.30-5.30pm; mid-
May-September, 10am-6pm.

Burston Strike School
Burston, 3 miles north-east of Diss
Open: all year, daily, 7am-dusk.

Bygones at Holkham
Holkham Park, 2 miles west of
Wells-next-the-sea on A149
Open: June-September, Sunday-
Thursday, 1.30-5pm; August,
11.30am-5pm.

Cockley Cley Iceni Village
3 miles south-west of Swaffham
☎ (0760) 721339
Open: Easter-October, daily, 1.30-
5.30pm; mid-July-mid-September,
daily, 11.30am-5.30pm.

Cockthorpe Hall Toy Museum
4 miles east of Wells-next-the-Sea,
off A149
Open: April-October, daily, 10am-
5.30pm; November-March,
Monday-Friday, 2-5pm, Saturday,
Sunday, 10am-5pm.

Cromer Museum
East Cottages, Tucker Street
Open: all year, Monday, 10am-
1pm, 2-5pm, Tuesday-Saturday,
10am-5pm, Sunday, 2-5pm.

Diss Museum
Market Place, Diss
Open: all year, Monday-Saturday,
9am-5pm, Sunday, 10am-6pm.

Dunham Museum
Little Dunham, 5 miles north-east
of Swaffham off A47
Open: April-September, daily,
10am-5.30pm; October-March,
11am-3pm, by appointment.

Elizabethan House Museum
South Quay, Great Yarmouth
Open: June-September, daily
(except Saturday); October-May,
Monday-Friday, 10am-1pm,
2-5.30pm.

Fleggburgh Bygone Village
Burgh St Margaret, 3 miles north-
east of Acle on A1064
Open: all year, daily, 10am-5pm
(dusk in winter).

The Forge Museum
North Creake, 7 miles north-west
of Fakenham on B1355
Open: June-September, daily,
12noon-5pm.

Glandford Shell Museum

3 miles north-west of Holt on
B1156
☎ (0263) 740081
Open: December-February,
Monday-Thursday, 9.30am-
12.30pm; March-November,
Monday-Thursday, 9.30am-
12.30pm, 2.30-4.30pm, Friday,
Saturday, 2.30-4.30pm.

Great Yarmouth Museum's Exhibition Galleries

Central Library
☎ (0493) 858900
Open: all year, Monday-Saturday,
9.30am-5.30pm.

Guildhall of St George (NT)

King's Street, King's Lynn
Open: all year, Monday-Friday,
10am-5pm, Saturday, 10am-4pm.

Holy Land Exhibition

North Pickenham, 3 miles south-
east of Swaffham
☎ (0760) 440427
Open: all year, daily, 9am-5pm.

John Jarrold Printing Museum

Whitefriars, Norwich
☎ (0603) 660211
Open: July-September, Tuesday,
10am-4pm. Other times by
appointment.

King's Lynn Centre for the Arts

King's Lynn
Open: all year, Monday-Friday,
9am-5pm, Saturday, 10am-
12.30pm. Closed Bank Holidays.

King's Lynn Museum

Old Market Street
Open: all year, Monday-Saturday,
10am-5pm. Closed public holidays.

Lifeboat Museum

Cromer
Open: May-September, daily, 9am-
12.30pm, 2-5pm (except in very bad
weather).

Maritime Museum for East Anglia

Marine Parade, Great Yarmouth
Open: June-September, daily
(except Saturday), 10am-5.30pm;
October-May, Monday-Friday,
10am-1pm, 2-5.30pm.

Museum of Gas and Local History

Fakenham
☎ (0328) 51696
Open: April-October, Thursday,
Sunday, 2-5pm, Bank Holidays,
10am-5pm.

Museum of Social History

27 King Street, King's Lynn
Open: all year, Tuesday-Saturday,
10am-5pm.

National Centre for Owl Conservation

Lothian Barn, Blickling Hall, 2
miles north-west of Aylsham on
B1354
Open: April-October, daily except
Monday and Thursday, 12noon-
5pm.

Norfolk Rural Life Museum

Gressenhall, 2 miles north-west of
East Dereham off B1110
☎ (0362) 860563
Open: Easter-October, Tuesday-
Saturday, 10am-5pm, Sunday, 2-
5.30pm, Bank Holiday Monday,
10am-5pm.

Norwich Castle Museum

Norwich
Open: all year, Monday-Saturday,

10am-5pm, Sunday, 2-5pm. Closed
Good Friday, Christmas period,
New Year.

Norwich School Art Gallery
St George Street, Norwich
☎ (0603) 610561
Open: Monday-Saturday, 10am-
5pm, when there is an exhibition.

Old Merchant's House (EH)
Row 111, South Quay, Great
Yarmouth
Open: Easter-September, daily,
10am-6pm. Guided tours only.

Regalia Rooms
Town Hall, King's Lynn
☎ (0533) 7663044
Open: Easter-October, Monday-
Saturday, 10am-4pm.

Royal Norfolk Regiment Museum
Shirehall Museum, Norwich
Open: Monday-Friday, 9am-
12noon, 2-4pm. Closed Bank
Holidays.
Opening summer 1990 following
move from Britannia Barracks.

Sainsbury Centre for Visual Arts
University of East Anglia, Norwich
☎ (0603) 56060
Open: all year, Tuesday-Sunday,
12noon-5pm.

St Peter Hungate Church Museum
Elm Hill, Norwich
Open: all year, Monday-Saturday,
10am-5pm. Closed Sunday, Good
Friday, Christmas period, New
Year.

Shirehall Museum
Walsingham, 5 miles south of
Wells-next-the-sea on B1105

Open: Easter-September, Monday,
10am-1pm, 2-5pm, Tuesday-
Saturday, 10am-5pm, Sunday,
2-5pm; October, weekends only,
11am-1pm, 2-4pm.

**Stranger's Hall Museum of
Domestic Life**
Norwich
Open: all year, Monday-Saturday,
10am-5pm. Closed Sunday, Good
Friday, Christmas period, New
Year.

Swaffham Museum
Town Hall, London Street,
Swaffham
Open: all year, Tuesday, Thursday,
12noon-4pm, Saturday and Bank
Holidays, 10am-4pm.

Toad Hole Cottage
How Hill, Ludham, 5 miles east of
Wroxham off A1062
Open: April-May and October,
Saturday and Sunday, 11am-5pm;
June-September, daily, 11am-6pm.

Tollhouse Museum
Tollhouse Street, Great Yarmouth
Open: June-September, daily
(except Saturday); October-May,
Monday-Friday, 10am-1pm, 2-
5.30pm.

Wolferton Station Museum
6 miles north-east of King's Lynn
off A149
☎ (0485) 40674

Wymondham Heritage Museum
Middleton Street, Wymondham
☎ (0953) 603000
Open: March-October, Thursday,
Friday, 2-5pm, Saturday, 10am-
12noon, 2-5pm.

Suffolk

Ancient House Museum
Clare, 7 miles north-west of
Sudbury on A1092
Open: Easter-September, Wednesday-Saturday, 2.30-4.30pm;
Sunday, 11am-12.30pm, 2.30-4.30pm or by appointment.

Beccles and District Museum
Newgate, Beccles
Open: April-October, Wednesday,
Saturday, Sunday, Bank Holidays,
2.30-5pm; November-March,
Sunday, 2.30-5pm, or by appointment. Closed Christmas Day and
New Year's Day.

Bungay Museum
Waveney District Council Offices,
Broad Street, Bungay
☎ (0986) 2548
Open: all year, Monday-Friday,
9am-1pm, 2-4pm.

Bury St Edmunds Art Gallery
Market Cross, Bury St Edmunds
Open: all year, Tuesday-Saturday
10.30am-4.30pm. Sunday by
appointment.

Bygones Museum
The Institute, Woolpit, 6 miles
north-west of Stowmarket on A45
Open: Easter-September, Saturday,
Sunday, 2-5pm.

Christchurch Mansion
Ipswich
Open: all year, Monday-Saturday,
10am-5pm or dusk, Sunday, 2.30-4.30pm or dusk.

Dunwich Museum
Dunwich, 4 miles south-west of
Southwold

Open: March-May, October,
Saturday and Sunday; June, July,
September, Tuesday,Thursday,
Saturday, Sunday; August, daily,
2-4.30pm.

**Dunwich Underwater Exploration
Exhibition**
Front Street, Orford
☎ (03945) 450678
Open: all year, daily, 11.30am-5.30pm.

Easton Farm Park
3 miles north-west of Wickham
Market off B1116
☎ (0728) 746475
Open: Easter-September, daily,
10.30am-6pm.

Gainsborough's House
Sudbury
Open: Easter-September, Tuesday-Saturday, 10am-5pm, Sunday,
Bank Holiday Monday, 2-5pm;
October-Easter, Tuesday-Saturday,
10am-4pm, Sunday, 2-4pm.

**Gershom Parkington Collection of
Clocks and Watches**
Angel Hill, Bury St Edmunds
Open: all year, Monday-Saturday,
10am-5pm, Sunday, 10am-5pm.

Halesworth and District Museum
The Almshouses, Steeple End,
Halesworth
Open: May-September, Wednesday, Sunday, Bank Holiday
Monday, 2-5pm.

Halesworth Art Gallery
Steeple End, Halesworth
Open: mid-May-mid-September,
Monday-Saturday, 11am-5pm,
Sunday, 3-6pm.

Ipswich Museum
Open: all year, except Bank
Holidays and 24-25 December,
Monday-Saturday, 10am-5pm.

Landguard Fort Museum
Ravelin Block, View Point Road,
Felixstowe
☎ (0394) 286403
Open: end April-October, Saturday
and Sunday.

Lanman Museum
Framlingham
☎ (0728) 723118
Open: Easter-September, daily
except Monday, Friday and
Sunday mornings, 10am-12.30pm,
2-4.30pm.

Lavenham Guildhall (NT)
☎ (0787) 247646
Open: Easter-October, daily, 11am-
1pm, 2-5.30pm.

Laxfield and District Museum
6 miles north of Framlingham
Open: June-September, Saturday,
Sunday, 2-5pm. Also Wednesday,
July and August.

**Lowestoft & East Suffolk Mari-
time Museum**
Whapload Road, Lowestoft
Open: May-September, daily,
10am-5pm.

Mechanical Music Museum
Cotton, 5 miles north of Stowmarket off B1113
Open: June-September, Sunday,
2.30-5.30pm.

Mildenhall and District Museum
6 King Street, Mildenhall
Open: all year, Wednesday,

Thursday, Saturday, Sunday, 2.30-
4.30pm, Friday, 11am-4.30pm.

Moot Hall
Aldeburgh
Open: Easter, Whitsun; June-
September, daily, 10.30am-1pm,
2.30-5pm.

Moyse's Hall Museum
Bury St Edmunds
Open: all year, Monday-Saturday,
10am-5pm.

The Museum of East Anglian Life
Stowmarket, 12 miles north-west of
Ipswich on A1308
☎ (0449) 612229
Open: Easter-October, Monday-
Saturday, 11am-5pm, Sunday,
12noon-5pm; June-August,
Sunday, 12noon-6pm.

**Museum of Grocery Shop
Bygones**
70 High Street, Wickham Market,
10 miles north-east of Ipswich off
A12
☎ (0728) 747207
Open: all year, Wednesday-
Saturday, 10am-12.30pm, 2.30-
4.30pm, or by appointment.

National Horse Racing Museum
High Street, Newmarket
☎ (0638) 667333
Open: Easter-November, Tuesday-
Saturday, Bank Holiday Monday
10am-5pm, Sunday, 2-5pm.

Q Tower
South Hill, Felixstowe
Open: May-September, daily,
10.30am-5pm, Sunday, 10.30am-
6pm.

Royal Naval Patrol Service Museum
Sparrows Nest, Lowestoft
Open: May-October, Sunday-Friday, 10am-12noon, 2-4.30pm.

Southwold Lifeboat Museum
16 Blyth Road, Southwold
☎ (0502) 722422
Open: June-September, daily, 2.30-4.30pm. Guided tours for school parties.

Southwold Museum
Southwold
Open: June-September, daily, 2.30-4.30pm.

Sue Ryder Foundation Museum
Cavendish, 5 miles north-west of Sudbury off A1092
Open: all year, Monday-Saturday, 10am-5.30pm, Sunday, 10am-11pm, 12.15-5.30pm.

Suffolk Regiment Museum
Gibraltar Barracks, Out Risbygate Street, Bury St Edmunds
☎ (0284) 752394
Open: all year, Monday-Friday, 10am-12noon, 2-4pm, subject to availability of curator.

Thorpeness Windmill
2 miles north of Aldeburgh
Open: Easter, May, June, September, Saturday, Sunday, Bank Holiday Monday; July and August, Tuesday-Sunday, 2-5pm.

Woodbridge Museum
Market Hill, Woodbridge
Open: Easter-October, Thursday-Saturday, Bank Holidays, 11am-4pm, Sunday, 2.30-4.30pm.

Cambridgeshire

Cambridge and County Folk Museum
2-3 Castle Street, Cambridge
Open: all year, Monday-Saturday, 10.30am-5pm, Sunday, 2.30-4.30pm.

Cambridge University Collection of Air Photographs
Free School Lane, Cambridge
Open: all year, Monday-Thursday, 9am-1pm, 2-5.30pm, Friday, 9am-1pm, 2-4pm. Closed Christmas and Easter weeks.

Cromwell Museum
Grammar School Walk, Huntingdon
Open: April-October, Tuesday-Friday, 11am-1pm, 2-5pm, Saturday and Sunday, 11am-1pm, 2-4pm; November-March, Tuesday-Friday, 2-5pm, Saturday, 11am-1pm, 2-4pm, Sunday, 2-4pm. Closed Bank Holidays (except Good Friday).

Ely Museum
Sacrist's Gate, High Street, Ely
Open: all year, Tuesday-Sunday, 10am-5pm.

Fitzwilliam Museum
Trumpington Street, Cambridge
Open: all year, Tuesday-Saturday (lower galleries), 10am-2pm, (upper galleries) 2-5pm, Sunday, (upper and lower galleries) 2.15-5pm. Closed Monday except Bank Holidays.

Haddenham Farmland Museum
6 miles south-west of Ely
☎ (0353) 740381
Open: first Sunday each month,

2-5pm; and May-October, Wednesday, 10am-5pm.

Kettle's Yard
Northampton Street, Cambridge
Open: house: daily, 2-4pm.
exhibition gallery: Tuesday-Saturday, 12.30-5.30pm, Sunday, 2-5.30pm. Closed Bank Holidays and Christmas to New Year.

Longsands Museum
Longsands Road, St Neots
☎ (0480) 72740
Open: every afternoon during school term.

March and District Museum
High Street, March
Open: all year, Wednesday, 10am-12noon, Saturday, 10am-12noon, 2-4pm.

Museum of Technology
Riverside, off Newmarket Road, Cambridge
Open: all year, first Sunday in every month, 2-5pm.

Norris Museum
The Broadway, St Ives
Open: May-September, Tuesday-Friday, 10am-1pm, 2-5pm, Saturday, 10am-12noon, 2-5pm, Sunday, 2-5pm; October-April, Tuesday-Friday, 10am-1pm, 2-4pm, Saturday, 10am-12noon. Closed Christmas, Bank Holidays.

Peterborough City Museum and Art Gallery
Priestgate, Peterborough
☎ (0733) 43329
Open: May-September, Tuesday-Saturday, 10am-5pm; October-April, Tuesday-Friday, 12noon-5pm, Saturday, 10am-5pm.

Rural Museum
Ramsey, 10 miles south-east of Peterborough on B1069
Open: April-September, Thursday, Sunday, 2-5pm.

Sacrewell Farm and Visitor Centre
Sacrewell, Thornhaugh, 8 miles west of Peterborough, off A47
☎ (0780) 782222
Open: all year, daily.

Scott Polar Research Institute
Lensfield Road, Cambridge
Open: all year, Monday-Saturday, 2.30-4pm. Closed some Bank Holidays.

Sedgwick Museum of Geology
Downing Street, Cambridge
Open: all year, Monday-Friday, 9am-1pm, 2-5pm, Saturday, 10am-1pm. Closed Christmas, Bank Holidays.

Stained Glass Museum
Ely Cathedral
☎ (0353) 665103
Open: April-October, Monday-Friday, 10.30am-4pm, Sunday, 12noon-3pm, Saturday, Bank Holidays, 10.30am-4.30pm.

University Museum of Archaeology and Anthropology
Downing Street, Cambridge
Open: all year, Monday-Friday, 2-4pm, Saturday, 10am-12.30pm. Closed Easter, Christmas-New Year.

University Museum of Classical Archaeology
Sidgwick Avenue, Cambridge

Open: all year, Monday-Friday,
9am-1pm, 2.15-5pm.

University Museum of Zoology
Downing Street, Cambridge
Open: all year, Monday-Friday,
2.15-4.45pm. Closed Easter,
Christmas and Bank Holidays.

Whipple Museum of the History of Science
Free School Lane, Cambridge
Open: all year, Monday-Friday,
2-4pm (except Bank Holidays and
possibly university vacations).

Whittlesea Museum
Town Hall, Market Street, Whittlesey, 5 miles east of Peterborough
on A605
Open: all year, Friday, Sunday,
2.30-4.30pm, Saturday, 10am-
12noon.

Wisbech and Fenland Museum
Museum Square, Wisbech
Open: all year, Tuesday-Saturday,
10am-5pm; October-March, 10am-
4pm.

Essex
Aklowa African Traditional Heritage Village
Brewers End, Takeley, 4 miles east
of Bishop's Stortford on A120
☎ (0279) 871062
Open: April-October, 10am-1pm,
1.30-4.30pm, by appointment only.

Barleylands Farm Museum
Wickford Road, Billericay
Open: April-September, Wednesday-Saturday, 11am-5pm, Sunday,
1pm-5.30pm; October-March,
Wednesday-Saturday, 11am-
4.30pm, Sunday, 1-5pm.

Beecroft Art Gallery
Station Road, Westcliff-on-sea
(Southend)
☎ (0702) 347148
Open: all year, Monday-Saturday,
9.30am-5.30pm. Closed Bank
Holidays.

Braintree and Bocking Heritage
Centre Museum
Market Place, Braintree
Open: all year, Monday-Saturday,
10am-5pm; Closed Bank Holidays.

Brewery Chapel Museum
Adams Court, Halstead
Open: April-October, Saturday,
Sunday, 2-4.30pm.

Bridge Cottage (NT)
Flatford, near East Bergholt off
B1029
Open: Easter-October, Wednesday-Sunday; June-August, daily, 11am-
5.30pm.

Burnham on Crouch Museum
9 miles south-east of Maldon.
Open: Easter-Christmas, Wednesday, Saturday, 11am-4pm, Sunday
and Bank Holidays, 2-4.30pm;
September, daily, 2-4.30pm.

Cater Museum
High Street, Billericay, 4 miles east
of Brentwood on A129
Open: all year, Monday, Wednesday, Thursday, 2-5pm, Tuesday,
Friday, Saturday, 12.30-5pm.

Chelmsford and Essex Museum
Oaklands Park, Moulsham Street,
Chelmsford
Open: all year, Monday-Saturday,
10am-5pm, Sunday, 2-5pm. Closed
Good Friday, Christmas Day, New
Year.

Colchester and Essex Museum
Colchester Castle
Open: April-September, Monday-Saturday, 10am-5pm, Sunday, 2.30-5pm; October-March, Monday-Friday, 10am-5pm, Saturday, 10am-4pm. Closed Good Friday, 25-27 December.

Dutch Cottage Museum
Long Road, Canvey Island
☎ (0268) 794005
Open: Spring Bank Holiday-September, Wednesday, Sunday, 2.30-5pm; Bank Holidays, 10am-1pm, 2.30-5pm.

Epping Forest District Museum
39-41 Sun Street, Waltham Abbey
☎ (0992) 716882
Open: all year, Friday-Monday, 2-5pm, Tuesday, 12noon-5pm.

Feering and Kelvedon Local History Museum
Branch Library, Kelvedon, 8 miles south-west of Colchester off A12
☎ (0376) 70307
Open: March-October, Monday, 2-4pm, Saturday, 9am-12.30pm; November-February, Saturday, 10am-12.30pm. Closed Bank Holidays.

Finchingfield Guildhall and Museum
8 miles north-west of Braintree on B1053
Open: April-September, Sunday, Bank Holidays, 2.30-5.30pm.

Fossil Hall, Museum of Palaeontology and Bookshop
Boars Tye Road, Witham
Open: all year, Monday, Tuesday, Thursday, Friday, Saturday, 10am-4pm.

Granary Bygones
Flatford
Open: April-October, daily, 11am-6pm.

Great Bardfield Cottage Museum
Dunmow Road, 7 miles north-east of Braintree on B1057
Open: Easter-September, Saturday, Sunday, Bank Holidays, 2-6pm.

Harlow Museum
Third Avenue, Harlow
Open: all year, Monday, Wednesday, Friday-Sunday 10am-5pm, Tuesday, Thursday 10am-9pm. Closed 11.20-1.30pm Saturday, Sunday.

The Hollytrees
High Street, Colchester
Open: all year, Monday-Saturday, 10am-1pm, 2-5pm (Saturday, October-March, closes at 4pm). Closed Good Friday, Christmas.

Maldon Maritime Centre
The Hythe, Maldon
Open: March-September, Saturday, Sunday, 11am-5pm; October-December, Saturday, Sunday, 11am-4pm.

Maldon Museum
71 High Street, Maldon
☎ (0621) 52493
Open: all year, Saturday 10am-12noon, 1-5.30pm, and most other times by appointment.

Maritime Museum
Low Lighthouse, The Green, Harwich
Open: Easter-October, Sunday, 2-5pm.

Mersea Island Museum
West Mersea, 6 miles south of
Colchester on B1025
☎ (0206) 383301
Open: May-September, daily,
2-5pm.

The Minories Art Gallery
74 High Street, Colchester
Open: all year except public
holidays, Tuesday-Saturday,
10.30am-5pm, Sunday, 2-6pm.

Museum of Natural History
All Saints Church, High Street,
Colchester
Open: all year, Monday-Saturday,
10am-1pm, 2-5pm (Saturday,
October-March, closes at 4pm).
Closed Good Friday, Christmas.

Museum of the Working Horse
The Wheatsheaf, Gainsford End,
Toppesfield, 6 miles south-east of
Haverhill off A604
Open: April-October, Saturday,
Sunday, Bank Holidays, 2-6pm.

National Motorboat Museum
Wat Tyler Country Park, Pitsea,
Basildon
Open: all year, daily, 10am-4pm.

Plotland Trail and Museum
Dunton, Basildon
Open: April-October, Sunday and
Bank Holidays, 2-5pm.

Prittlewell Priory Museum
Southend-on-Sea
Open: all year, Tuesday-Saturday,
10am-1pm, 2-5.30pm.

Queen Elizabeth's Hunting Lodge
Epping Forest, Ranger's Road,
Chingford

Open: all year, Wednesday-
Sunday, 2-6pm or dusk if earlier.

Rural Life Museum
Wat Tyler Country Park, Pitsea,
Basildon
Open: all year, daily, 10am-4pm.

Saffron Waldon Museum
Museum Street
Open: April-September, Monday-
Saturday, 11am-5pm, Sunday, 2.30-
5pm; October-March, Monday-
Saturday, 11am-4pm, Sunday,
Bank Holidays, 2.30-5pm.
Closed Good Friday, Christmas.

Sir Alfred Munnings Art Museum
Castle House, Dedham, 8 miles
south-west of Ipswich on B1029
☎ (0206) 322127
Open: May-September, Sunday,
Wednesday, Bank Holiday
Monday; also Thursday, Saturday
in August, 2-5pm.

Social History Museum
Holy Trinity Church, Trinity Street,
Colchester
Open: all year, Monday-Saturday,
10am-1pm, 2-5pm (Saturday,
October-March, closes at 4pm).
Closed Good Friday, Christmas.

Southchurch Hall
Southend-on-Sea
Open: all year, Tuesday-Saturday,
11am-1pm, 2-5.30pm.

**Southend-on-Sea
Central Museum**
Victoria Avenue, Southend-on-Sea.
Open: all year, Monday, 1-5pm,
Tuesday-Saturday, 10am-5pm.

Thaxted Guildhall
Town Street, Thaxted, 7 miles
south-east of Saffron Walden on
B184
Open: Easter-September, Saturday,
Sunday, Bank Holidays, 2-6pm.

Thurrock Local History Museum
Central Library, Grays
Open: all year, Monday-Saturday,
10am-8pm. Closed Sunday, Bank
Holidays.

Toy Museum
Dedham Art and Craft Centre,
High Street, Dedham
Open: January-March, Tuesday-
Sunday; April-December, daily,
10am-5pm.

Tymperleys Clock Museum
Tymperleys, Trinity Street,
Colchester
Open: April-October, Tuesday-
Saturday, Bank Holiday Monday,
10am-1pm, 2-5pm (closes 4pm
Saturdays in October).

Walton Heritage Centre
Walton-on-the-Naze
Open: July-August, daily, 2-5pm.

The Working Silk Museum
New Mills, South Street, Braintree
Open: (opening June 1990) all year,
Monday-Friday, 10am-5pm.

Nature Reserves

Norfolk
Blakeney Point (NT)
Access: by boat from Morston or
Blakeney, all year. No dogs
allowed May-July.

Breydon Water
Access: footpaths from Great
Yarmouth, Gorleston, and nearby
villages, all year.

Broadland Conservation Centre
(NNT)
Ranworth, 9 miles north-east of
Norwich off B1140
Open: April-October, Monday-
Thursday, 10.30am-5.30pm,
Saturday, 2-5.30pm, Sunday,
10.30am-5.30pm.

**Bure Marshes National Nature
Reserve** (NCC)
7 miles north-east of Norwich off
A1151 near Salhouse Broad
Open: early May to mid-September
(except weekends). Access to
nature trail by boat only (which
can be hired at Horning or
Wroxham).

Cley Marshes (NNT)
7 miles west of Sheringham off
A149. ☎ (0263) 740380
Access: permit only, obtainable
from the visitor centre.

Cley Visitor Centre (NNT)
7 miles west of Sheringham off
A149. Open: April-October,
Tuesday-Sunday, 10am-5pm.

Cockshoot Broad (NNT)
near Woodbastwick, off A1151
☎ (0603) 610734
Open: all times

East Wretham Heath (NNT)
5 miles north-east of Thetford on
A1075
☎ (095 382) 339
Open: all year, daily except
Tuesday, 10am-5pm.

Hickling Broad (NNT/NCC)
☎ (069 261) 276
Access: boats may pass through
public channels. Access ashore
restricted to permit holders. 2-hour
water trail departing 10am and
2pm from Pleasure Boat Inn,
operating May and September,
Tuesday-Thursday; June-August,
Monday-Friday.

Holkham (NCC)
near Wells-next-the-Sea
Access: all year, footpaths from
Holkham, Wells, Overy Staithe.

Holkham Hall Lake
☎ (0328) 710227
Access: organised groups, permit
only, from estate office.

Holme Bird Observatory (NOA)
Access: on foot along Thornham
sea wall and Holme beach road.
Permits available on the spot, all
year.
Open: daily 10.30am-4pm.

Holme Dunes (NNT)
☎ (048 525) 240
Access: by permit, all year, daily,
10am-5pm. Visitors should contact
warden at The Firs, 1 mile east of
entrance.

Horsey Mere (NT)
Access: restricted access by boat,
permit required off footpaths.
Apply National Trust office at
Blickling

Scolt Head Island (NCC)
Access: all year by boat from
Brancaster Staithe. No dogs April-
June.

Snettisham Pits (RSPB)
Near Dersingham
Access: on foot from Snettisham or
Dersingham, or along beach south
of public car park. Parties of ten or
more should contact the warden at
13 Beach Road, Snettisham

Strumpshaw Fen (RSPB)
☎ (0603) 715191
Open: all year, daily, 9am-9pm or
sunset when earlier.

**Surlingham and Rockland
Marshes** (RSPB)
opposite Surlingham Church, near
Norwich
Open: all year, daily.

Titchwell Marsh (RSPB)
off A149, near Brancaster
Access: all times, via sea-wall
footpath. Visitor centre open April-
October, weekends, some week
days.

Weeting Heath (NNT/NCC)
Open: April-August, permit only
from NNT warden on site.

Welney Wildfowl Refuge
(Wildfowl Trust)
13 miles south-east of Wisbech off
A1101
☎ (0353) 860711
Open: Unescorted visits: daily,
10am-5pm (except Christmas).

Wildlife Water Trail
How Hill, Ludham, off A1062
☎ (069262) 763
Open: April-May, October,
Saturday, Sunday, Bank Holidays,
11am-3pm; June-September,
Monday-Sunday, 11am-5pm.

Winterton Dunes (NCC)
8 miles north of Great Yarmouth
off B1159
Access: all year, no restriction.

Suffolk
Carlton Marshes
2 miles south-west of Lowestoft
Access: at all times by public
footpath.

Cavenham Heath (NCC)
8 miles north-west of Bury St
Edmunds off A1101
Access: all year. Access only to area
south of Tuddenham-Icklingham
track, parking at Temple Bridge.

Dunwich Heath (NT)
6 miles north of Leiston off B1125
Access: no restriction.

Havergate Island (RSPB)
off B1084, near Orford
Access: permit only, in advance
from: The Warden, 30 Mundays
Lane, Orford, Woodbridge, IP12
2LX

Minsmere (RSPB)
Near Dunwich
Open: all year, daily except
Tuesday, 9am-9pm or sunset when
earlier.
Access: free access to public hides
along the beach. Access onto
reserve restricted to permit
holders. Apply to: The Warden,
Minsmere Reserve, Westleton,
Saxmundham, Suffolk.

North Warren (RSPB)
$2^1/_2$ miles south of Leiston on
B1122
Access: all year, via public
footpaths.

Redgrave and Lopham Fen
6 miles west of Diss on B1113
☎ (037 988) 618. Access: all year.

**Walberswick and Westleton
Heaths** (NCC)
near Saxmundham. ☎ (0603) 620558
Access: by public footpaths, permit
only off paths.

Wolves Wood (RSPB)
2 miles east of Hadleigh on A1071
Access: all year, restricted to nature
trails.

Cambridgeshire
Fowlmere (RSPB)
8 miles south of Cambridge off
B1368. Access: at all times.

Purls Bridge and Welches Dam
(RSPB/CWT)
near Manea
Open: all year, public hides at both
locations; information centre at
Welches Dam.

Wicken Fen (NT)
8 miles south of Ely off A1123
Open: daily, dawn-dusk, permits
available from the warden on site.

Essex
Abberton Reservoir (EBWS)
4 miles south of Colchester off
B1026
Access: restricted to permit
holders, but picnic area and public
hide available all year.

Fingringhoe Nature Reserve
(ENT)
5 miles south-east of Colchester off
B1025
Open: all year, Tuesday-Sunday,
9am-5pm.

John Weston Reserve
Walton-on-the-Naze
Access: all year

Leigh National Nature Reserve
(NCC/ENT)
between Canvey Island and
Leigh-on-Sea
Access: all year.

Parndon Wood Nature Reserve
(Harlow District Council)
near Great Parndon off B181,
south-western outskirts of Harlow
☎ (0279) 30005
Open: all year, Sunday, 9am-1pm,
2-6pm; April-September, Tuesday,
7-9pm.

Roman River Valley Reserve
3 miles south of Colchester

Stour Wood and Copperas Bay
(RSPB)
4 miles west of Harwich off B1352
Access: at all times.

Riding

The following riding schools are all
approved by the Association of
British Riding Schools, or the
British Horse Society. Some offer
residential holiday courses, and
details of these can be found in the
Activity and Special Interest
Holidays booklet produced by the
East Anglia Tourist Board.

Norfolk
Albion Rides
Duck Row, Cawston, near Norwich
☎ (0603) 871725

Home Farm Riding Stables
Holme-next-the-Sea, near Hunstanton
☎ (0485) 25233

Reeves Hall
Hepworth, Diss
☎ (0359) 50217

Rose-Acre Riding Stables
Back Mundesley Road, Gimingham, near Mundesley
☎ (0263) 720671

Rosebrook Farm Equestrian Centre
South Lopham, Diss
☎ (0379) 88278

Runcton Hall Stud
Church Farm, North Runcton,
King's Lynn
☎ (0553) 840676

Salhouse Riding Centre
The Stables, The Street, Salhouse,
near Norwich
☎ (0603) 720921

Stanbrook Ridng Centre
Paddock Farm, Lower Road,
Holme Hale, near Swaffham
☎ (0760) 440510

Stiffkey Valley Stables
Old Wells Road, Great Walsingham
☎ (0328) 72377/72796

Strumpshaw Riding Centre
Buckenham Road, Strumpshaw,
near Norwich
☎ (0603) 712815

Waveney Valley Horse Holidays
Airstation Farm, Pulham St Mary,

Diss
☎ (0379) 741228

West Runton Riding Stables
West Runton, near Cromer
☎ (0263) 75339

Willow Farm Riding School
Ormesby St Margaret, Great
Yarmouth
☎ (0493) 730297

Suffolk
Blythwind Stud
Saint Helena Farm, Westleton,
Saxmundham
☎ (0502) 722768

The Laurels Stables
Horringer, Bury St Edmunds
☎ (0284) 88281/752835

Linkwood Riding Centre
Linkwood, Bradfield St George,
Bury St Edmunds
☎ (0284) 86390

Newton Hall Equitation Centre
Swilland, near Ipswich
☎ (047385) 616

Pakefield Riding School
Carlton Road, Lowestoft
☎ (0502) 572257

Poplar Park Equestrian Centre
Heath Road, Hollesley, Woodbridge
☎ (0394) 411023

Stoke-by-Clare Equitation Centre
Stoke-by-Clare, Sudbury
☎ (0787) 277266/278089

Tollgate Livery Centre
397 High Road, Walton, Felixstowe
☎ (0394) 285147

White Lodge Equitation Centre
White Lodge, Rendham Road,
Saxmundham
☎ (0728) 2338

Cambridgeshire
Fitzpatrick Riding Establishment
Fitz Farm, Offord Cluny, Huntingdon
☎ (0480) 810365

Miss E.A. Pickard
New Farm, Fox Road, Bourn,
Cambridge

Windmill Stables
Shepreth Road, Barrington,
Cambridge
☎ (0223) 871487

Essex
Aldborough Hall Equestrian Centre
Aldborough Hall, Aldborough
Hatch
☎ (081 590) 1433

Bambers Green Riding Centre
Takeley, near Bishop's Stortford
☎ (0279) 870320

Brook Farm Riding School
Stock Road, Stock, near Ingatestone
☎ (0277) 840425

Colne Valley Riding Centre
Brickhouse Farm, Colne Engaine,
near Colchester
☎ (07875) 2542

De Beauvoir Farm Riding Stables
Church Road, Ramsden Heath,
Billericay
☎ (0268) 710534/711302

Eastminster School of Riding Ltd
Upper Rainham Road, Hornchurch
☎ (04024) 47423/73980

Folkes Farm Riding and Livery Stables
Folkes Lane, Upminster
☎ (0277) 212002

Foxhound Riding School Ltd
Baker Street, Orsett
☎ (0375) 891367

Glebe Equestrian Centre
Mope Lane, Wickham Bishops, Witham
☎ (0621) 892375

Heron Stream Stud
Church Road, Rawreth, Wickford
☎ (03744) 3008

High Beech Riding School
Pack Saddle Farm, Pynest Green Lane, Waltham Abbey
☎ 081 508 8866

Hillingdon School of Riding Ltd
Churchgate Street, Harlow
☎ (0729) 35195

Lillyputs Riding and Livery Stables
272 Wingletye Lane, Hornchurch
☎ (04024) 53908

Longwood Equestrian Centre
Dry Street, Basildon
☎ (0268) 412184

Medway Riding Centre
Medway Farm, Southminster Road, Althorne, near Chelmsford
☎ (0621) 740419

New Hall School Riding Centre
New Hall School, Chelmsford
☎ (0245) 467588

Park Lane Riding and Livery Stables
Park Lane, Ramsden Heath, Billericay
☎ (0268) 710145

Rayne Riding Centre
Fairy Hall Lane, Rayne
☎ (0376) 22231

Woodredon Riding School
Woodredon Farm, Upshire, near Waltham Abbey
☎ (0992) 714312

Shows, Displays, and Other Events

Whether your interests are in boating, agricultural shows, historical pageants or air displays, there will undoubtedly be a large show on somewhere in East Anglia during the summer months. The events listed here simply scratch the surface, and it is best to consult your nearest Tourist Information Centre for details of forthcoming attractions.

May
Truckfest, East of England Showground, Peterborough
Hadleigh Agricultural Show, Hadleigh, Suffolk
Mildenhall Air Fete, RAF Mildenhall, Suffolk
Harwich Redoubt Fete, Harwich, Essex
South Suffolk Show, Ingham, Bury St Edmunds, Suffolk

June

Suffolk Show, Ipswich, Suffolk
Essex County Show, Great Leighs,
Chelmsford, Essex
Colchester Summer Show,
Colchester, Essex
Royal Norfolk Show, New
Costessey, Norwich, Norfolk
Aldeburgh Festival, Snape
Maltings (and other venues),
Suffolk
Dunmow Flitch Trials, Falberds
Ley, Great Dunmow, Essex
Stilton Cheese Rolling, Stilton,
Cambridgeshire

July

Tendring Hundred Show, Lawford
House Park, near Manningtree
North Norfolk and Norwich Horse
Show, Norwich
Norwich Union Carriage Driving
Trials, Sandringham
East of England Show, Peterbor-
ough, Cambridgeshire
Cambridge Folk Festival, Cherry
Hinton Hall, Cambridgeshire
Sandringham Flower Show,
Sandringham House, Norfolk

Tourist Information Centres

Norfolk
Cromer
Old Town Hall, Prince of Wales
Road
☎ (0263) 512497

Fakenham
Red Lion House, Market Place
☎ (0328) 51981

Great Yarmouth
Department of Publicity and
Entertainments, 1 South Quay,
Great Yarmouth
☎ (0493) 846345
Open: April-October

Marine Parade
☎ (0493) 842195

Hoveton
Broads Information, Station Road
☎ (0603) 782281

Hunstanton
The Green
☎ (04853) 2610

King's Lynn
The Old Gaol House, Saturday
Market Place
☎ (0553) 763044

Mundesley
2a Station Road
☎ (0263) 721070

Norwich
The Guildhall, Gaol Hill, NR2 1NF
☎ (0603) 666071

Ranworth
The Staithe, NR13 6HY
☎ (060 549) 453

Sheringham
Station Approach
☎ (0263) 824329

Thetford
Ancient House Museum, White
Hart Street
☎ (0842) 2599

Walsingham
Shirehall Museum, Common Place
☎ (0328) 820510

Wells-next-the-Sea
Wells Centre, Staithe Street
☎ (0328) 710885

Suffolk
Aldeburgh
The Cinema, High Street
☎ (072 885) 3637

Beccles
The Quay, Fen Lane
☎ (0502) 713196

Bury St Edmunds
6 Angel Hill
☎ (0284) 763233

Felixstowe
Felixstowe Leisure Centre, Sea
Front
☎ (0394) 28216/276770

Hadleigh
Toppesfield Hall IP7 5DN.
☎ (0473) 822922

Ipswich
Town Hall, Princes Street
☎ (0473) 258070

Lavenham
The Guildhall, Market Place
☎ (0787) 248207

Lowestoft
The Esplanade
☎ (0502) 565989

Santon Downham
Forestry Commission District
Office
☎ (0842) 810271

Southwold
Town Hall
☎ (0502) 722366

Stowmarket
Wilkes Way
☎ (0449) 676800

Sudbury
Public Library, Market Hill
☎ (0787) 881320/72092

Cambridgeshire
Cambridge
Wheeler Street
☎ (0223) 322640

Ely
The Library, Palace Green
☎ (0353) 662062

Huntingdon
The Library, Princes Street
☎ (0480) 425831/425801

Peterborough
Town Hall, Bridge Street
☎ (0733) 317336

Central Library, Broadway
☎ (0733) 48343

Wisbech
District Library, Ely Place
☎ (0945) 64009/583263

Essex
Braintree
Town Hall Centre, Market Square
☎ (0376) 550066/43140

Chelmsford
E Block, County Hall
☎ (0245) 283400

Clacton
23 Pier Avenue
☎ (0255) 423400

Colchester
1 Queen Street
☎ (0206) 46379

Dedham
Countryside Centre, Duchy Barn
☎ (0206) 323447

Great Dunmow
Council Offices, High Street
☎ (0371) 4533

Harwich
Parkeston Quay
☎ (0255) 506139

Maldon
Oakwood Arts Centre, White
Horse Lane
☎ (0621) 56503

Saffron Walden
Corn Exchange, Market Square
☎ (0799) 24282

Southend-on-Sea
Civic Centre, Victoria Avenue
☎ (0702) 355122
Information Bureau, High Street
Precinct
☎ (0702) 355120

Walton-on-the-Naze
Princess Esplanade, Walton-on-the-
Naze
☎ (0255) 675542

Travel

Bus and Coach Services
Norfolk
**Eastern Counties Omnibus
Company**
Great Yarmouth ☎ (0493) 842341

King's Lynn ☎ (0553) 772343
Norwich ☎ (0603) 760076

Suffolk
**Eastern Counties Omnibus
Company**
Bury St Edmunds ☎ (0284) 766171
Felixstowe ☎ (0394) 282747
Ipswich ☎ (0473) 253734
Lowestoft ☎ (0502) 565406

Cambridgeshire
Premier Travel Services Ltd
Cambridge
☎ (0223) 237262

Cambus
Cambridge
☎ (0223) 355554

United Counties Bus Co
Huntingdon
☎ (0480) 453159

Essex
Eastern National Ltd
Basildon ☎ (0268) 523431
Bishop's Stortford ☎ (0279) 652476
Braintree ☎ (0376) 21415
Brentwood ☎ (0277) 221204
Chelmsford ☎ (0245) 353104
Clacton-on-Sea ☎ (0255) 421151
Colchester ☎ (0206) 571451
Hadleigh ☎ (0702) 558421
Halstead ☎ Halstead 2487
Harwich ☎ (0255) 502866
Maldon ☎ (0621) 854731
Southend-on-Sea ☎ (0702) 430534

Rail Enquiries
Norfolk
Great Yarmouth
☎ (0603) 632055

King's Lynn
☎ (0553) 772021

Norwich
☎ (0603) 632055

Suffolk
Bury St Edmunds
☎ (0473) 690744

Ipswich
☎ (0473) 690744

Lowestoft
☎ (0603) 632055

Cambridgeshire
Cambridge
☎ (0223) 311999

Huntingdon
☎ (0480) 54468

Peterborough
☎ (0733) 68181

Essex
Chelmsford
☎ (0245) 252111

Clacton-on-Sea
☎ (0206) 564777

Colchester
☎ (0206) 564777

Harwich/Dovercourt
☎ (0206) 564777

Southend-on-Sea
☎ (0702) 611811

Ferry Companies
Sealink/British Rail
☎ 01 730 3440 or (0255) 243333
Harwich/Hook of Holland

DFDS Seaways
☎ 01 493 6696 or (0255) 240240

Harwich/Esbjerg
Harwich/Gothenburg
Harwich/Hamburg

P&O European Ferries
☎ (0394) 604100
Felixtowe/Zeebrugge

Norfolk Line
☎ (0493) 856133
Great Yarmouth/Scheveningen

Car Hire
Avis
Head Office: ☎ 01 848 8765
Cambridge: ☎ (0223) 212551
Colchester: ☎ (0206) 41133
Great Yarmouth: ☎ (0493) 851050
Norwich: ☎ (0603) 416719
Peterborough: ☎ (0733) 49489
Stansted: ☎ (0279) 870237
Thetford: ☎ (0842) 61002

Budget
Bury St Edmunds: ☎ (0284) 701345
Cambridge: ☎ (0223) 323838
Clacton-on-Sea: ☎ (0255) 222444
Ipswich: ☎ (0473) 216149

Godfrey Davis
Head Office: ☎ 01 950 4080
Cambridge: ☎ (0223) 248198
Colchester: ☎ (0206) 45676
Ipswich: ☎ (0473) 211067/8
Norwich: ☎ (0603) 400280
Southend: ☎ (0702) 351351

Hertz
Cambridge: ☎ (0223) 63443
Colchester: ☎ (0206) 866559
Harwich: ☎ (0255) 553111
Ipswich: ☎ (0473) 218506
Great Yarmouth: ☎ (0493) 857086
Norwich Airport: ☎ (0603) 404010
Peterborough: ☎ (0733) 73543

Willhire
Mildenhall: ☎ (0638) 712080
Bury St Edmunds: ☎ (0284) 62888
Cambridge: ☎ (0223) 68888
Chelmsford: ☎ (0245) 265853
Colchester: ☎ (0206) 867888
Chelmsford: ☎ (0245) 265853
Colchester: ☎ (0206) 867888
Ipswich: ☎ (0473) 213344
Norwich: ☎ (0603) 416411/660587
King's Lynn ☎ (0553) 766881
Great Yarmouth: ☎ (0493) 857130
Harwich: ☎ (0255) 504744
Southend-on-Sea ☎ (0702) 544441
Newmarket: ☎ (0638) 669209
Thetford: ☎ (0842) 61578

Transport and Machinery

Norfolk

Barton House Railway

Hartwell Road, Wroxham, 8 miles north-east of Norwich on A1151
Open: April-October, 3rd Sunday in each month, and Easter Monday, 2.30-5.30pm.

Bressingham Live Steam Museum and Gardens

3 miles west of Diss on A1066
Open: May-September, Sunday and Bank Holiday Monday; also Thursday from June-mid-September; also Wednesday in August 10am-5.30pm.

Broadland Tractor Museum

Ormesby St Michael, 7 miles north of Great Yarmouth on A149
Open: during summer season, daily, 10.30am-5pm.

Bure Valley Railway

Wroxham to Aylsham
Open: daily during the summer season.

Caister Castle Car Collection

West Caister, 3 miles north-west of Great Yarmouth, off A1064
Open: May-September, daily except Saturday, 10.30am-5pm.

City of Norwich Aviation Museum

Old Norwich Road, Horsham St Faith, off A140
☎ (0603) 32577
Open: Easter-October, Sunday, 10am-5pm; also June-August, 7pm-dusk; October-Easter, Sunday, 10am-1pm.

Forncett Industrial Steam Museum

Low Road, Forncett St Mary, Norwich
Open: May-October, Sunday 2-6pm. Steam days: July-September, 1st and 3rd Sunday in month.

Lotus Cars

Hethel, 7 miles south-west of Norwich off A11
☎ (0953) 608000
Open: all year except Christmas, Monday-Friday, tours and demonstrations 10.30am and 2pm. By appointment only.

Station 146

Seething Airfield Control Tower, Seething Airfield, Brooke, 9 miles south-east of Norwich, off B1332 or A146
☎ (0508) 50787
Open: May-October, 1st Sunday in month, 10am-5pm. Other times by appointment.

North Norfolk Railway
The Station, Sheringham
☎ (0263) 822045
Open: Easter-October, daily.
Steam trains from Sheringham to
Weybourne and Holt every
Sunday, and daily in August.

Strumpshaw Hall Steam Museum
8 miles east of Norwich off A47
☎ (0603) 714535
Open: May-September, daily
except Saturday, 2-5pm.

The Thursford Collection
Thursford, 6 miles north-east of
Fakenham, off A148
☎ (032 877) 477
Open: Easter-October, daily, 11am-
5pm.

**Wells & Walsingham Light
Railway**
Wells-next-the-Sea.
Open: April-September, daily. First
steaming from Wells is at 10am.

Wherry 'Albion', Ludham.
Norfolk Wherry Trust, 63
Whitehall Road, Norwich
☎ (0603) 624642
Open: all year by appointment.

Suffolk
East Anglia Transport Museum
Carlton Colville, 3 miles south-
west of Lowestoft on B1384
Open: May-September, Sunday,
Bank Holiday Monday, from 11am;
also Saturday from 2pm, June-
September; also Monday-Friday
from 2pm in August.

Long Shop
Main Street, Leiston
Open: Easter-September, daily,
10am-4pm.

**Norfolk and Suffolk Aviation
Museum**
Flixton, 4 miles south-west of
Bungay on B1062
☎ (050 845) 444
Open: April-May, September-
October, Sunday, Bank Holidays,
10am-5pm; June-August, 10am-
9pm; also July-August, Wednesday, 7-9pm, Thursday, 11am-5pm,
7-9pm. Other times by appointment.

**390th Bomb Group Memorial Air
Museum**
The Control Tower, Parham
Airfield, Framlingham, 3 miles
north of Wickham Market on B1116
Open: April-October, Sunday, 1-
6pm.

RAF Bentwaters
near Woodbridge
☎ (0394) 432945
Open: for pre-booked groups only.

Rake Factory
Little Welnetham, 4 miles south-
east of Bury St Edmunds on A134
Open: all year, Monday-Friday,
10am-4pm, Saturday, 9am-1pm.

Cambridgeshire
Fenland Aviation Museum
Bambers Garden Centre, Old Lynn
Road, West Walton, Wisbech
☎ (0945) 860814
Open: March-September, Saturday,
Sunday, 9am-5pm; other times by
arrangement.

Imperial War Museum Site
Duxford Airfield, 8 miles south of
Cambridge on A505, just off
Junction 10 of M11
☎ (0223) 833963

Open: mid-March to October,
daily, 10.30am-5.30pm; November-
March, 10.30am-3.45pm.

Nene Valley Railway
Stibbington, 7 miles west of
Peterborough on A47
☎ (0780) 782854. Talking timetable:
(0780) 782921
Open: Easter-October, Saturday,
Sunday; also June-August,
Tuesday-Thursday.
Steam trains running to Orton
Mere (Peterborough) and back.

Prickwillow Engine Museum
Main Street, Prickwillow, 4 miles
east of Ely on B1382
Open: April-September, daily,
dawn-dusk. Other times by
appointment.

Stretham Beam Engine
4 miles south of Ely on the A10
Open: all year, daily, 9am-6pm.

Essex
Audley End Miniature Railway
Audley End, near Saffron Walden
Open: April-October, Saturday,
Sunday, Bank Holiday Monday;
during school summer holiday,
daily, from 2pm.

Castle Point Transport Museum
The Old Bus Garage, Canvey
Island
☎ (0268) 684272
Open: April-September, last
Saturday in month, 11am-4pm.

Colne Valley Railway
Castle Hedingham Station, 4 miles
north-west of Halstead on A604
☎ (0787) 61174
Open: all year, daily, 11am-5pm.

Steam days most Sundays Easter-
October, plus Wednesday in school
summer holiday, Bank Holiday
weekends except Christmas.

East Anglian Railway Museum
Chappel Station, 6 miles west of
Colchester on A604
☎ (0206) 242524
Open: all year, Monday-Friday,
10am-5pm, Saturday, Sunday,
11am-5.30pm. Steam days April-
October, every other Sunday and
Bank Holidays.

Ford Motor Co Ltd
Eagle Way, Warley, Brentwood
☎ (081 526) 2570
Open: from March, Monday-
Friday, during business hours, by
appointment only. Tours at 9.30am
and 3.30pm.

Jaguar Motor Museum
Unit 3, Mill Lane, Maldon
Open: April-September, Wednes-
day, Sunday; October-December,
Saturday, Sunday, 10am-6.30pm.

Mark Hall Cycle Museum
Muskham Road, off First Avenue,
Harlow
Open: all year, daily, 10am-5pm.

US 8th Army Air Force

Today, the US 3rd Air Force
operates four major bases in
Suffolk and Cambridgeshire, along
with a number of other stand-by
bases. During World War II, the
numbers of American bases
throughout East Anglia were
considerable, although most have
since reverted to agricultural land

or other uses. Nevertheless, many former American airmen visit the region each year to seek out their old bases. The following list details each airfield with the groups based there during the war, and the current use of the land.

Norfolk

Attlebridge
8 miles north-west of Norwich
Then: 319th and 466th Bomb Group.
Now: Turkey farm.

Bodney
5 miles west of Watton
Then: 352nd Fighter Group.
Now: Control tower and some buildings remain.

Deopham Green
4 miles west of Wymondham
Then: 452nd Bomb Group.
Now: Agricultural land.

East Wretham
5 miles north-east of Thetford
Then: 359th Fighter Group.
Now: Army base.

Fersfield
4 miles north-west of Diss.
Then: 388th Bomb Group.
Now: Agricultural land.

Hardwick
4 miles north of Harleston
Then: 310th and 93rd Bomb Groups.
Now: Agricultural land. Some remaining buildings.

Hethel
4 miles east of Wymondham
Then: 320th and 389th Bomb Groups.
Now: Lotus sports car factory.

Horsham St Faith
4 miles north of Norwich
Then: 319th and 458th Bomb Groups, 56th Fighter Group.
Now: Norwich municipal airport.

North Pickenham
3 miles south-east of Swaffham
Then: 492nd and 491st Bomb Groups.
Now: Industrial area — Crane Fruehauf trailer factory.

Old Buckenham
3 miles south-east of Attleborough
Then: 453rd Bomb Group.
Now: Agricultural land.

Rackheath
5 miles north-east of Norwich
Then: 467th Bomb Group.
Now: Light industry, boat building.

Seething
5 miles north of Bungay
Then: 448th Bomb Group.
Now: Local flying club, agricultural land. Renovated control tower houses 448th Bomb Group honour roll and World War II memorabilia.

Shipdham
4 miles south-west of East Dereham
Then: 320th and 44th Bomb Groups.
Now: Arrow Air Services — air charter company.

Snetterton Heath
4 miles south-west of Attleborough
Then: 386th and 96th Bomb Groups.
Now: Snetterton motor racing circuit.

Thorpe Abbots

$4^1/_2$ miles east of Diss
Then: 100th Bomb Group.
Now: Agricultural land, memorial control tower.

Tibenham

6 miles north of Diss
Then: 445th Bomb Group.
Now: Local gliding club, agricultural land.

Watton

8 miles south-east of Swaffham
Then: 802nd Recon. Group and 25th Bomb Group.
Now: RAF station.

Wendling

4 miles west of East Dereham
Then: 392nd Bomb Group.
Now: Some buildings remaining, memorial obelisk.

Suffolk

Bungay

14 miles south-east of Norwich
Then: 310th and 446th Bomb Groups.
Now: Ross Poultry farm. Several buildings remaining. Memorial plaque in one.

Bury St Edmunds

3 miles south east of town at Rougham
Then: 47th, 322nd and 446th Bomb Groups.
Now: Farmers' co-operative and light industry.

Debach

4 miles north-west of Woodbridge
Then: 493rd Bomb Group.
Now: Agricultural land.

Eye

4 miles south-east of Diss
Then: 490th Bomb Group.
Now: Light industry and agricultural land. Memorial.

Framlingham

2 miles south-east of town at Parham. *Then*: 95th and 390th Bomb Groups. *Now*: Agricultural land. 390th Bomb Group Memorial Museum housed in control tower.

Great Ashfield

5 miles north-west of Stowmarket
Then: 385th Bomb Group.
Now: Agricultural land. Memorial in Great Ashfield churchyard.

Halesworth

10 miles south-west of Lowestoft
Then: 56th Fighter Group, later 489th Bomb Group, 5th Emergency Rescue Squadron and 496th Fighter Training Group. *Now*: Agricultural land, turkey farm.

Honington

6 miles south-east of Thetford
Then: 364th Fighter Group and Air Depot — 1st SAD.
Now: Operational RAF station.

Horham

7 miles south-east of Diss
Then: 47th, 323rd and 95th Bomb Groups. *Now*: Agricultural land, mushroom farm. Memorial in village.

Knettishall

5 miles east of Thetford
Then: 388th Bomb Group
Now: Agricultural land. Hangar and some buildings remain. Memorial.

Lavenham

6 miles north-east of Sudbury
Then: 487th Bomb Group.
Now: Control tower still standing.
Memorial in village.

Leiston

4 miles east of Saxmundham
Then: 357th and 358th Fighter
Groups.
Now: Agricultural land.

Martlesham Heath

2 miles south-west of Woodbridge
Then: (former Battle of Britain RAF
station) 356th Fighter Group
Now: New village and Post Office
research station. Memorial on
A1093.

Mendlesham

6 miles north-east of Stowmarket
Then: 34th Bomb Group.
Now: TV transmitter, light industry
and agricultural land. Memorial on
A140.

Metfield

4 miles south-east of Harleston
Then: 353rd Fighter Group and
491st Bomb Group.
Now: Agricultural land.

Rattlesden

5 miles west of Stowmarket
Then: 322nd and 447th Bomb
Groups.
Now: Agricultural land. Hangar
and control tower still standing.

Raydon

3 miles south of Hadleigh
Then: 357th, 358th and 353rd
Fighter Groups.
Now: Agricultural land. Hangar
and some buildings remain, used

as Government storage. Memorial
in village church.

Sudbury

Then: 486th Bomb Group.
Now: Agricultural land. Memorial
on Sudbury town hall.

Wattisham

5 miles south of Stowmarket
Then: 68th Observation Group,
479th Fighter Group and Air
Depot.
Now: Operational RAF station.

Cambridgeshire
Alconbury

5 miles north-west of Huntingdon
Then: 92nd, 93rd and 482nd Bomb
Groups.
Now: Operational NATO/USAF air
base.

Bassingbourn

2 miles north-west of Royston
Then: 91st (previously 17th) Bomb
Group.
Now: Army barracks. Memorial.

Bottisham

6 miles east of Cambridge
Then: 361st Fighter Group.
Now: Agricultural land. Control
tower and some buildings remain.

Duxford

8 miles south of Cambridge
Then: 78th and 350th Fighter
Groups.
Now: Imperial War Museum and
Aviation Museum. See Transport
and Machinery appendix for
further details.

Fowlmere

8 miles south of Cambridge

Then: 339th Fighter Group.
Now: Agricultural land. Hangar and a few buildings remain. Memorial.

Glatton

10 miles north-west of Huntingdon
Then: 457th Bomb Group.
Now: Agricultural land. Memorial in Conington churchyard.

Kimbolton

7 miles north-west of St Neots
Then: 17th, 91st and 379th Bomb Groups.
Now: Agricultural land.

Molesworth

10 miles west of Huntingdon
Then: 15th Bomb Squadron, 303rd Bomb Group. Post-war American air base until 1960.
Now: NATO base, former Cruise missile base.

Snailwell

3 miles north of Newmarket
Then: 350th Fighter Group.
Now: Agricultural land.

Steeple Morden

5 miles west of Royston
Then: 3rd Photographic Group and 355th Fighter Group.
Now: Agricultural land. Some buildings remain. Memorial.

Wittering

3 miles south-east of Stamford
Then: 55th Fighter Group (briefly).
Now: Operational RAF station.

Essex

Boreham

4 miles north-east of Chelmsford
Then: 394th Bomb Group.

Now: Test centre for Ford Motor Company.

Boxted

5 miles north of Colchester
Then: 386th Bomb Group, 56th and 354th Fighter Groups, 5th Emergency Rescue Squadron.
Now: Agricultural land, fruit farm.

Chipping Ongar

9 miles west of Chelmsford
Then: 387th Bomb Group.
Now: Agricultural land.

Debden

4 miles south-east of Saffron Walden
Then: 4th Fighter Group. *Now*: Army barracks. Memorial in camp.

Earls Colne

3 miles east of Halstead
Then: 94th and 323rd Bomb Groups. *Now*: Hangar and some buildings remain.

Gosfield

4 miles north-east of Braintree
Then: 365th Fighter Group, 397th and 410th Bomb Groups.
Now: Agricultural land.

Great Dunmow

9 miles east of Bishop's Stortford
Then: 386th Bomb Group.
Now: Agricultural land. Some scattered buildings remain. Memorial on A120.

Great Saling (Andrews Field), 4 miles north-west of Braintree
Then: 96th Bomb Group and 322nd Bomb Group Medium.
Now: Agricultural land. Some remaining buildings.

Great Sampford
6 miles east of Saffron Walden
Then: 4th Fighter Group (very
briefly).
Now: Agricultural land.

Little Walden
2 miles north of Saffron Walden
Then: 409th and 493rd Bomb
Groups, 56th and 361st Fighter
Groups.
Now: Agricultural land. Control
tower and some buildings remain.

Matching
5 miles south-east of Bishop's
Stortford
Then: 391st Bomb Group.
Now: Agricultural land.

Ridgewell
5 miles south-east of Haverhill
Then: 381st Bomb Group.
Now: Agricultural land. Two
hangars and some buildings
remain. Memorial.

Rivenhall
2 miles north-east of Witham
Then: 363rd Fighter Group and
397th Bomb Group.
Now: Agricultural land and
Marconi testing centre.

Stansted Mountfichet
3 miles north-east of Bishop's
Stortford
Then: 344th Bomb Group and Air
Depot.
Now: Civil airport — London's
third airport. Memorial plaque in
administration block.

Wethersfield
5 miles north-west of Braintree
Then: 416th Bomb Group.
Now: USAF stand-by base.

Wormingford
5 miles north-west of Colchester
Then: 55th and 362nd Fighter
Groups.
Now: Agricultural land.

Useful Addresses

Broads Authority
Thomas Harvey House, 18
Colegate, Norwich, NR3 1BQ
☎ (0603) 610734

Cambridgeshire Wildlife Trust
5 Fulbourn Manor, Fulbourn,
Cambridge, CB1 5BN
☎ (0223) 880788

**Camping Club of Great Britain
and Ireland**
11 Lower Grosvenor Place,
London, SW1W 0EY.
☎ 071 828 1012

Caravan Club
East Grinstead House, East
Grinstead, Sussex, RH19 1UA
☎ (0342) 326944

**Council for the Protection of
Rural England**
4 Hobart Place, London, SW1W
0HY
☎ (071 235) 9481

Cyclists Touring Club
69 Meadrow, Godalming, Surrey,
GU7 3HS
☎ (04868) 7217

East Anglia Tourist Board
Toppesfield Hall, Hadleigh,
Suffolk, IP7 5DN
☎ (0473) 822922

English Heritage
25 Savile Row, London, W1X 2BT
☎ (071 734) 6010

English Tourist Board/British Tourist Authority
Thames Tower, Blacks Road, Hammersmith, London, W6 9EL
Enquiries to BTA if writing from overseas.
☎ (081 846) 9000

Essex Birdwatching Society
11 Hearsall Avenue, Broomfield, Chelmsford, Essex, CM1 5DD

Essex Naturalists Trust
Fingringhoewick Nature Reserve, near Colchester
☎ (020628) 678/9

Forestry Commission
Santon Downham, Brandon, Suffolk
☎ (0842) 810271

Inland Waterways Association
114 Regents Park, London, NW1 8UQ
☎ (071 586) 2556

National Anglers' Council
5 Cowgate, Peterborough, PE1 1LR
☎ (0733) 54084

National Rivers Authority
Aqua House, London Road, Peterborough, PE2 8AG
☎ (0733) 555667

National Trust
36 Queen Anne's Gate, London, SW1H 9AS
☎ (071 222) 9251

National Trust
Eastern Regional Office, Blickling, Norwich, NR11 6NF
☎ (0263) 733471

Nature Conservancy Council
Northminster House, Peterborough, PE1 1UA
☎ (0733) 40345

Norfolk Naturalists' Trust
72 Cathedral Close, Norwich, NR1 4DF
☎ (0603) 625540

Norfolk Ornithologists' Association
Aslack Way, Holme-next-Sea, near Hunstanton
☎ (048525) 266

Peddars Way Association
6 Atthill Road, Norwich, NR2 4HW
☎ (0603) 23070

Ramblers' Association
1-5 Wandsworth Road, London, SW8 2LJ
☎ (071 582) 6878

Royal Society for the Protection of Birds
East Anglia Office, Aldwych House, Bethel Street, Norwich
☎ (0603) 615920

Suffolk Wildlife Trust
Park Cottage, Saxmundham, Suffolk, IP17 1PQ
☎ (0728) 3765

The Wildfowl Trust
Slimbridge, Gloucester
☎ (045 389) 333

Youth Hostels Association
Trevelyan House, St Albans,
Hertfordshire, AL1 2DY
☎ (0727) 55215

Walks
Area Rural Manager
Cambridgeshire County Council,
Shire Hall, Castle Hill, Cambridge
☎ (0223) 317404

Chelmsford Tourist Information Centre
County Hall, Market Road,
Chelmsford, Essex, CM1 1GG
☎ (0245) 283400

Department Planning and Property
Norfolk County Council, County
Hall, Martineau Lane, Norwich
☎ (0603) 222776

Ranger Service
Essex County Council County
Parks, Parks Office, Weald Country
Park, South Weald, Brentwood
☎ (0277) 216297

Suffolk County Council Planning Department
County Hall, Ipswich
☎ (0473) 230000, leaflet sales ext
6516

Zoos, Wildlife Parks, Rare Breeds and Farm Animals

Norfolk
Badley Moor Fish, Bird and Butterfly Centre
Badley Moor, East Dereham

Open: March-October, daily, 10am-5pm.

Banham Zoo and Monkey Sanctuary
The Grove, Banham, 6 miles north-west of Diss on B1113
☎ (095 387) 476
Open: all year, daily, 10am-6.30pm
or dusk if earlier.

Bure Valley Lakes Fisheries
Oulton, on B1354 between
Aylsham and Saxthorpe
☎ (0263) 87666
Open: all year, daily, 8am-dusk.

Cranes Watering Farm
Starston, 1 mile north of Harleston
on B1134
Open: all year, daily, Monday-Saturday, 10am-6pm, Sunday,
10am-12noon (all day during
summer).

Great Yarmouth Butterflies and Tropical Gardens
Marine Parade, Central Seafront,
Great Yarmouth
☎ (0493) 842202
Open: March-October, daily, 10am-dusk.

Hopton Butterfly and Bird World
Lowestoft Road, Hopton-on-Sea,
A12, near Lowestoft
☎ (0502) 731327
Open: March-December, daily,
9am-5.30pm.

Kelly's Birds and Aviaries
Weybourne Road, near Holt
☎ (0263) 711185
Open: all year, daily 10am-6pm or
dusk if earlier.

Kilverstone Wildlife Park
2 miles north-east of Thetford, off
A11
☎ (0842) 5369
Open: all year, 10am-6.30pm or
dusk.

Norfolk Shire Horse Centre
West Runton, 2 miles east of
Sheringham off A149
Open: Easter-October, Sunday-
Friday, 10am-5pm.

Norfolk Wildlife Park
Great Witchingham, 12 miles
north-west of Norwich off A1067
Open: all year, daily, 10.30am-6pm
or sunset.

Otter Trust
Earsham, 1 mile west of Bungay on
A143
Open: April-October, daily,
10.30am-6pm.

Park Farm
Snettisham, 4 miles south of
Hunstanton off A149
Open: April-September, daily
except Saturday.

Pensthorpe Waterfowl Park
Pensthorpe, 1 mile east of Faken-
ham on A1067
Open: Easter-October, daily, 10am-
5pm; November-mid December,
Saturday-Sunday.

**Pettits of Reedham Feathercraft
and Falabella Miniature Horse
Stud**
Camp Hill, 6 miles south of Acle on
B1140
Open: May-October, Monday-
Friday, 10am-6pm, Sunday,
1-5.30pm.

Redwings Horse Sanctuary
Frettenham, 6 miles north of
Norwich off B1150
Open: Easter-mid-December,
Sunday, 2-5pm.

Sea Life Centre
Southern Promenade, Hunstanton
☎ (04853) 33576. Open: all year,
daily in summer, 10am-8pm.

Thrigby Hall Wildlife Gardens
Filby, 5 miles north-west of Great
Yarmouth off A1064
☎ (049 377) 477. Open: all year,
daily, 10am-5pm or dusk.

Waveney Fish Farm
Park Road, Diss, on A1066
☎ (0379) 642697/652622
Open: water gardens: Easter-
October, daily. aquarium: all year.

Suffolk
Easton Farm Park
Easton, 3 miles north-west of
Wickham Market off B1116
☎ (0728) 746475
Open: Easter-September, daily,
10.30am-6pm.

**Mickfield Fish and Water Garden
Centre**
Debenham Road, Mickfield, on
A140, near Stowmarket
☎ (0449) 711336
Open: April-September, daily,
9.30am-5pm; October-March,
closed Tuesday and Thursday.

National Stud
Newmarket
Open: April-September, tours at
11.15am, 2.30pm weekdays,
11.15am Saturdays when racing in
Newmarket.

Norton Tropical Bird Gardens

7 miles east of Bury St Edmunds on A1088. Open: all year, daily, 11am-6pm or dusk in winter.

Suffolk Wildlife and Rare Breeds Park

Kessingland, 4 miles south of Lowestoft on A12
☎ (0502) 740291
Open: April-October, 10am-6pm.

Tropical Butterflies

Colethorpe Lane, Barrow, 6 miles west of Bury St Edmunds off A45
Open: mid March-October, daily, 10am-5pm.

Cambridgeshire

Brookcroft Bunnery

High Street, Croydon, 10 miles south-west of Cambridge off A14
☎ (0223) 207331
Open: April-October, Wednesday-Sunday, 10.30am-4pm; December-March, Saturday, Sunday.

Hamerton Wildlife Centre

8 miles north of Huntingdon, just off A1 and A604
☎ (08323) 362
Open: all year, daily, 10.30am-6pm.

Home Farm

Wimpole Hall, 8 miles south-west of Cambridge off A14/A603
☎ (0223) 207257
Open: Easter-October, daily except Monday and Friday, 10.30am-5pm; March, April, October, 11am-4pm.

Linton Zoo

Hadstock Road, Linton, 10 miles south-east of Cambridge on B1052
Open: all year except Christmas Day, 10am-6.30pm or dusk.

Stags Holt Farm Park

Stags Holt, off A141, March
☎ (0354) 52406
Open: Easter-September, daily except Monday, 10.30am-5pm.

Wildfowl Trust

Peakirk, 4 miles north of Peterborough on B1443.
Open: April-October, 9.30am-5.30pm; November-March, 9.30am-dusk.

Willers Mill Wild Animal Sanctuary and Fish Farm

Station Road, Shepreth, 7 miles south-west of Cambridge off A10
☎ (0763) 61832
Open: March-October, daily, 10.30am-6pm; November-February, Saturday, Sunday, 10.30am-dusk.

Wood Green Animal Shelter

Godmanchester
Open: all year, daily, 9am-3pm.

Essex

Ada Cole Memorial Stables

Broadlands, Broadley Common, 2 miles south-west of Harlow
Open: all year, daily, 2-5pm.

Basildon Zoo

London Road, Vange, Basildon
Open: all year, daily, 10am-6pm or dusk in winter.

Colchester Zoo

Maldon Road, Stanway, 3 miles west of Colchester off A12
☎ (0206) 330253
Open: all year, daily except Christmas Day, 9.30am-5pm or dusk.

Fullers Dairy Farm

Sible Hedingham, 3 miles north-west of Halstead on A604
Open: all year, Monday-Saturday, 9am-6pm, Sunday, 9.30am-12.30pm.

Hayes Hill Farm

Stubbins Hall Lane, Crooked Mile, Waltham Abbey
Open: all year, Monday-Friday, 10am-4.30pm, Saturday, Sunday, Bank Holiday Mondays, 10am-6pm.

Marsh Farm Country Park

South Woodham Ferrers, 5 miles north-east of Wickford off A130
☎ (0245) 321552
Open: mid-February-mid-November, daily, 10am-12.30pm, 1.30-4.30pm (1.30-5.30pm Saturday, Sunday, Bank Holiday Monday).

Mole Hall Wildlife Park

Widdington, 4 miles south of Saffron Walden off B1383
Open: all year, daily except Christmas Day, 10.30am-6pm or dusk.

INDEX